# The Older Gulathing Law



The Gulathing Law regulates relations between the social classes, the king and his officers, the clergy, and the peasantry. Parts of the law appear to be a social contract between two parties: on the one hand the people, on the other hand the church and the king.

This new edition, in modern English, contains many references to research that has been carried out since the appearance of previous editions in 1935 and 1981. In the Gulathing Law, differing interests are being balanced, and procedures described for solving conflicts. Personal rights are defined, and scales of fines and compensation are set up, graded according to the gravity of the insult, offence, and the social status of the persons involved. Large parts of the law text mirror the internal conditions in the farming community of Western Norway in the High Middle Ages: economic transactions, disputes, damage to life and property, and theft.

Accompanied by a translator's introduction and a commentary essay which place the Gulathing Law in a theological and church history perspective, this volume will be useful for both students and specialists of medieval Norwegian legal history and medieval Scandinavian law.

**Erik Simensen** has been Associate Professor of Scandinavian Studies (especially Norwegian) at the University of Oslo. He has worked on Old Norse dictionaries and has written articles on topics of Norwegian language history. He has translated charters from 1301–1310 (2002) and translated four Old Icelandic texts, including *Egils saga Skallagrímssonar* (2014).

**Torstein Jørgensen** is Professor emeritus from ViD Specialized University, Stavanger. He was co-founder and project leader of the national CoE, Centre for Medieval Studies, at the University of Bergen, and of the Nordic CoE, Nordic Centre of Medieval Studies. He has especially been working on relations between the papacy and the Norwegian church and society.

**Medieval Nordic Laws**
Series editors: Stefan Brink and Ditlev Tamm

*Medieval Nordic Laws,* edited by **Stefan Brink and Ditlev Tamm,** is part of the ***Routledge Medieval Translations*** series. These translations are the first translations into English of the earliest laws of Scandinavia, and are some of the earliest written sources for Scandinavia. These translated laws emanate from an international project of the same name and have never before been introduced to an international audience.

**Guta LAG and Guta Saga**
The law and history of the Gotlanders
*Christine Peel*

**The Danish Medieval Laws**
The laws of Scania, Zealand and Jutland
*Ditlev Tamm and Helle Vogt*

**The Liber legis Scaniae**
The Latin Text with Introduction, Translation and Commentaries
*Ditlev Tamm*

**The Borgarthing Law and the Eidsivathing Law**
The Laws of Eastern Norway
*Lisa Collinson, Torgeir Landro, and Bertil Nilsson*

**The Older Gulathing Law**
*Translated and edited by Erik Simensen with commentary essay by Torstein Jørgensen*

# The Older Gulathing Law

**Translated and edited by Erik Simensen with commentary essay by Torstein Jørgensen**

Routledge
Taylor & Francis Group
LONDON AND NEW YORK

First published 2021
by Routledge
2 Park Square, Milton Park, Abingdon, Oxon OX14 4RN

and by Routledge
52 Vanderbilt Avenue, New York, NY 10017

*Routledge is an imprint of the Taylor & Francis Group, an informa business*



*British Library Cataloguing-in-Publication Data*
A catalogue record for this book is available from the British Library

*Library of Congress Cataloging-in-Publication Data*
Names: Simensen, Erik, translator, editor. | Jørgensen, Torstein, 1951– writer of added commentary.
Title: The older Gulathing law / translated and edited Erik Simensen ; with commentary essay by Torstein Jørgensen.
Other titles: Gulaþingslög hin eldri. English.
Description: Milton Park, Abingdon, Oxon ; New York, NY : Routledge, 2021. | Series: Medieval Nordic laws | Includes bibliographical references and index.
Identifiers: LCCN 2020048083 | ISBN 9780367681500 (hardback) | ISBN 9781003134459 (ebook)
Subjects: LCSH: Law—Norway—History—Sources. | Law, Medieval—Sources. | Manuscripts, Old Norse. | Norway—History—13th century.
Classification: LCC KKN125 .G85 2021 | DDC 349.481—dc23
LC record available at https://lccn.loc.gov/2020048083

ISBN: 978-0-367-68150-0 (hbk)
ISBN: 978-0-367-68147-0 (pbk)
ISBN: 978-1-003-13445-9 (ebk)

Typeset in Times New Roman
by Apex CoVantage, LLC

# Contents

# Figures

# Maps

# A general introduction to the *Medieval Nordic Laws* translations

The oldest laws of the Nordic countries are written in the vernacular. The earliest manuscripts stem from the 13th centuries and are younger than the texts of the laws which for some of the laws date back into the 12th century. They are, of course, important in Nordic law and legal history, but they are equally significant for different branches of history, being the oldest written sources we have in the Nordic countries of the society at that time, dealing with the household and social, sometimes administrative and ecclesiastical and agrarian matters, and also for philology, being some of oldest written documents we have in the vernacular.

These laws for a long time were intensely studied by legal historians as the foundation of national law. During the last decade there has been a revival in the interest in these early laws in the Nordic countries, manifested in for example an influential conference series in early law at the Carlsberg Academy in Denmark, and an initiative of an interdisciplinary network project, called *Medieval Nordic Laws* (*MNL*), funded by The Leverhulme Trust and based at the University of Aberdeen, and also some other local initiatives. In order to open up the floodgates for also an international interest and research on these laws and to facilitate comparison, it was decided in the *MNL* project to translate the laws into English. Besides the obvious scoop of an international interest in the laws based on new translations, another gain with this initiative was the rethinking of the position of the laws in connection with the redaction of new introductions to the laws. The Nordic medieval laws were earlier subjected to thorough analysis from both legal and historical points of view and they have been translated into modern Nordic languages. This happened mainly in the 1930s and 40s but the laws have long played a central role in Nordic legal history. In the second part of the 19th century the Nordic laws were seen in German scholarship as important expressions of the so-called *Germanenrechte*, and intense learning was used in developing and describing a specific Nordic variant of such law. This approach was never fully accepted in the Nordic countries and a more critical study of the laws based on the idea that they reflected both older and newer layers of law started already in the 1920s, and has continued up to the 1980s in Scandinavia. Today's legal historians in the Nordic countries tend to see the laws in a European context and generally as new law written down as such. Most of the Nordic scholarship however was only published in Nordic languages. Research into the medieval legal world has continued in later years and a translation and introductions in English will thus also make the newest research accessible to an international public. Iceland holds a somewhat different position and has already seen two of the old law codes, the *Grágás* and the *Jónsbók*, given modern translations and introductions recently. The edition of the old Icelandic law has been an inspiration for the present project.

The work has been pursued on a national basis by local teams with occasional meetings to discuss the project. The original plan as to these new translations was to establish either as in Denmark a team of scholars working with the laws, or as Norway and Sweden individual experts already acquainted with the law in question to do the work. To assist these translators reference groups were assembled, with some of the most prominent scholars in the fields of law, legal history, Canon Law, history, and philology. A crucial question, when dealing with translations of this kind, is, of course, in each case to find a 'normative' text to base the translation on, chosen from the many (sometimes diverging) manuscripts which some laws can display. It has been up to each team or translator to make this decision. It would have been desirable but technically very complicated to bring also the original text. To make the volumes accessible to a broader readership, we have therefore decided not to have the Old Nordic texts included, which in most cases will be found online.

Stefan Brink
Professor of Scandinavian Studies
University of Aberdeen

Ditlev Tamm
Professor of Law
University of Copenhagen

# Foreword

This translation was undertaken under the auspices of the *Medieval Nordic Laws* (*MNL*), an international project which began at the University of Aberdeen in 2009 and was realized through cooperation between scholars from the universities of Aberdeen, Bergen, Copenhagen, Stockholm, Oslo and Trondheim and funded by the Leverhulme Trust.

The project has been led by the professors Stefan Brink (Aberdeen), Ditlev Tamm (Copenhagen), Torstein Jørgensen (Bergen/Stavanger), and Michel Gelting (Aberdeen/Copenhagen). Coordinator: Dr Lisa Collinson (Aberdeen).

Professor Torstein Jørgensen has discussed the contents of the Christian Law (Chs. 1–33) in a commentary essay (in footnotes referred to as TJ's comments).

The *Gulaþing* Law is an important source to Norwegian medieval history and has been extensively studied for a long time. Accordingly, this translation is heavily indebted to the works of other scholars, especially Knut Helle, Finn Hødnebø, Magnus Rindal, Knut Robberstad, and Jørn Øyrehagen Sunde. I thank Dr Christine I. Peel, who has corrected my English and improved numerous details in my manuscript. I also want to thank my son, Anders Simensen, for valuable assistance in preparing the manuscript for publication. For possible errors and infelicities I am solely responsible.

Oslo, October 2020
Erik Simensen

# Acknowledgements

The editor and the publishers would like to thank Det Norske Samlaget, Oslo, Skald, Leikanger, and Professor (em.) Ingvild Øye for their permission to reproduce maps. We also thank The National Archives of Norway and Magnus Rindal, editor of Den eldre Gulatingslova, for permission to reproduce the stemma on page 26 of his edition.

# Abbreviations and symbols

() are used to mark off words, phrases, or paragraphs inserted by the translator

\ / are put around words or phrases inserted (by the scribe(s)) between the lines in the MS

[marks the beginning of variants containing more than one word

AM The Arnamagnæan Manuscript Collection (*Den arnamagnæanske håndskriftsamling*), Copenhagen
Deichman The Deichman Library (*Deichmanske bibliotek*), Oslo
DonVar E donatione variorum, Codex Rantzovianus, in the Royal Library, Copenhagen
GuL The Older *Gulaþing* Law
Holm The Royal Library (*Kungliga biblioteket*), Stockholm
NKS The New Royal Collection (*Ny kongelig samling*) in the Royal Library (*Det kongelige bibliotek*), Copenhagen
NRA The National Archives of Norway (*Riksarkivet*), Oslo
ON Old Norse
UppsUB Uppsala University Library (*Uppsala universitetsbibliotek*), Uppsala
AM 78 4to, containing the so-called King Sverre's Christian Law
Deichman 11 8vo
Holm perg 31 4to
1B NRA 1 B
137 DonVar 137 4to
146 AM 146 4to
146 S slip of paper in 146
309 AM 309 fol.
315 e AM 315 e fol.
315 f AM 315 f fol.
474 NRA Charter Tønsberg 1550 (DN. vol. 22, no. 474)
713 UppsUB R 713
1633 NKS 1633 4to

For abbreviated titles of books and articles see Bibliography.

# Maps

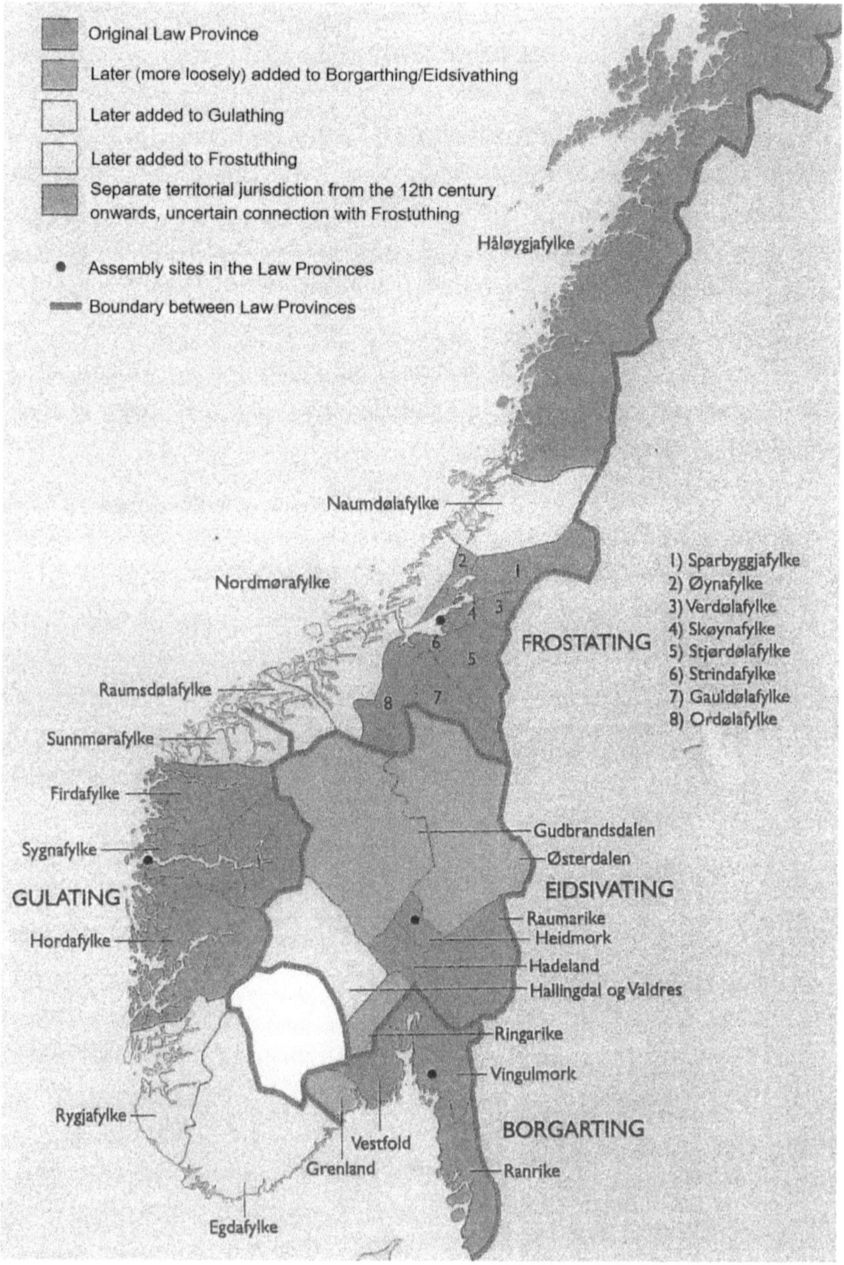


*Map 0.1* Law provinces of Norway

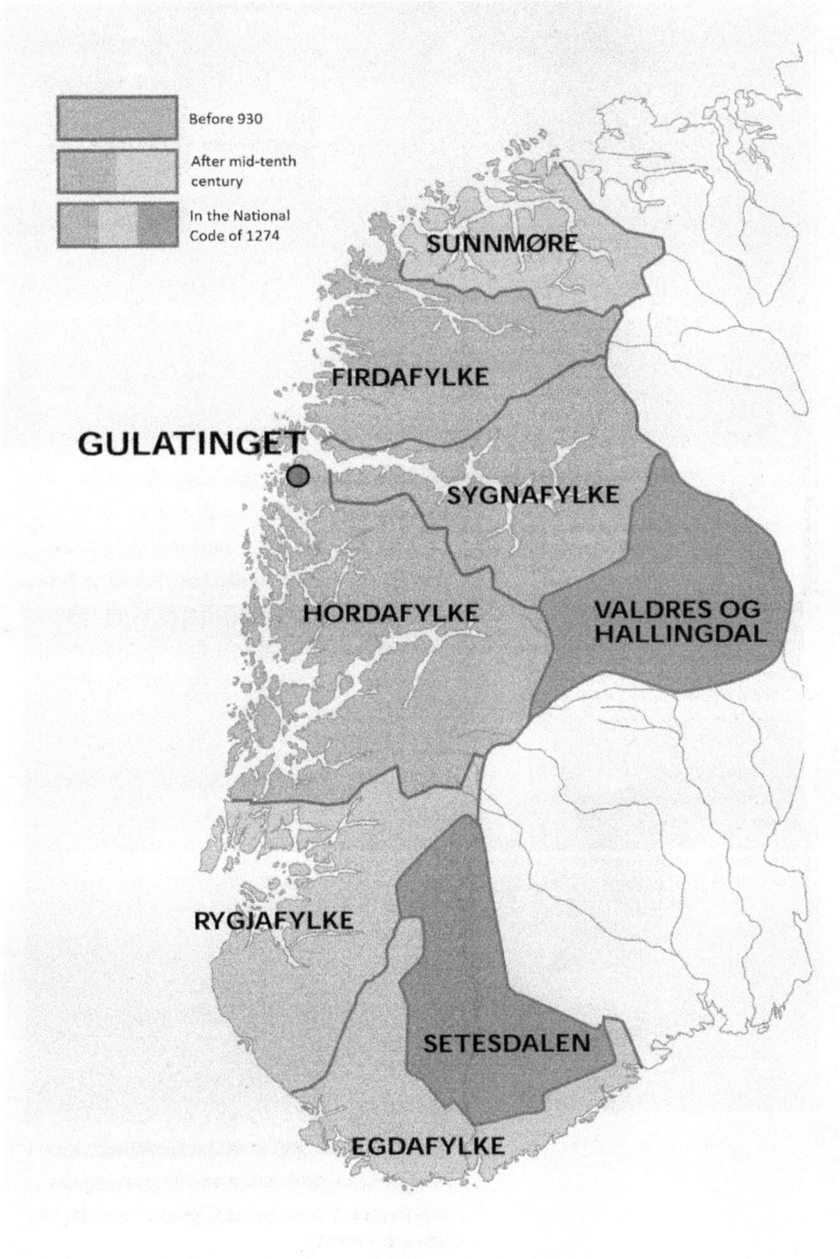


*Map 0.2* The law province of Gulaþing

# Part One

# Translator's introduction

# Translator's introduction

## 1 Norway in the 13th century

### *1.1 Population, livelihood, geography*

During the 13th century Norway was an agricultural society with an estimated population of approximately 300,000.[1] In general, each household lived on a self-sufficient farm, where the farmer was either the actual owner or (usually) a tenant (cf. Section 1.2). In Western, Southern, and Northern Norway most people lived in the coastal areas, along the fjords and in the fertile inland valleys, where fishing was almost as important as farming. Much of Eastern and Mid-Norway was covered by large forests, making farming more demanding. Here new farmland was cleared by the so-called slash-and-burn method. The forests provided ample grounds for hunting, whereas lakes and rivers were valued as fishing grounds. In the mountain areas shielings were built and grazing grounds utilized for summer pasture, giving rise to many disputes over rights and duties.

Villages were non-existent. Nevertheless there were rural communities called *heruð* (pl. of *herað*, cf. Section 1.5), in many cases centred on a church or a *þing* site. In some areas, especially in Southern and Western Norway, families lived in settlement clusters,[2] where farms were combined by having their houses, barns, and other buildings grouped together – often in one or more rows – in one yard. A famous example is the *Havråtunet* in Western Norway,[3] where eight farms have about sixty buildings in one yard. Towns were few and small, the most important ones being the capital, Bergen (approximately 7,000 inhabitants), and the religious centre, Nidaros (now Trondheim, approximately 3,000 inhabitants). Men living in towns were mainly craftsmen and merchants, subject to laws of their own, the so-called town laws.

1 In the decades around 1300. Estimates vary between 350,000 and 440,000. Moseng et al. 1999, 223.

2 In Norwegian: *klyngetun.*

3 On the island Osterøy, north of Bergen. See *Store norske leksikon* s.v. Osterøy.

### *1.2 Social structure*

In terms of social organization there was a strict hierarchy, with the king and the earl at the top, below them the bishops, then the landed men. These were rich and powerful farmers who had been endowed with land by the king, serving in return as his advisers and officers in the naval levy.

The rank and file, and the vast majority, were farmers and their families. The farmers were either free men (freeholders, householders, and tenants) or freedmen (ON *leysingjar*). The freeholder was a farmer who owned odal-land, which the householder did not, although he might be a landowner. Most farmers, however, were tenants. Due to their education and status, clerics originally belonged to the upper classes, but parish priests gradually became integrated into the peasant society (e.g. by marriage). In some respects there were differences with regard to gender: women were not allowed to engage in as big economic transactions as men did, and they inherited less than men, sons more than daughters.

At the bottom of the social pyramid were the slaves (thralls), who had no personal rights and were generally regarded as articles of trade. Nevertheless, during the High Middle Ages slavery was gradually and systematically reduced. At the end of the 13th century slaves had almost disappeared as a distinct social group.[4]

### *1.3 Economic structure*

Much land was owned by the king, acquired through inheritance, taxes, fines, and confiscations from adversaries. The biggest landowner, however, was the church, which had become rich through donations (often under wills), tithes, fines for violations of the Christian Law, and land-rent. It has been estimated that the church owned 40 percent of all landed property,[5] distributing it between local priests and churches, bishops, monasteries, etc.

The size and quality of farmlands were expressed in the land-rent, that is the rent paid by the tenant to his landlord. This was usually estimated at approximately one-sixth of the crop and was to be paid in natural products, mainly meal and butter, hides and fish; sometimes also in other goods, for example salt and iron. An important unit of measurement was the 'month's food' (*mánaðarmatr*), the amount of food which one man was supposed to need when serving one month in the naval levy. It was usually provided as butter (7.7 kg) and meal (24.7 kg). The counting by *mánaðarmatir* (pl.) was connected to the system of weights and measures through the ratio three *mánaðarmatir*: one *mǫrk*. In this way it was possible to formulate the land-rent, and hence the value of a farm, in two sets of terms. The value of these terms varied regionally. In Western Norway the average

4 Moseng et al. 1999, 91.
5 Ibid., 230.

size of a farm has been estimated at 4.5 *mánaðarmataból*,[6] about 10–12 decares or 2.5–3.0 acres. In Eastern and Mid-Norway the average size was 1.5 *markaból*, about 40–50 decares or 10–12.5 acres.

## *1.4 The church*

With the introduction of Christianity a large number of churches were built. As the law shows, the first churches were built of timber, hence the term 'stave churches'. Stone churches were built later, mainly from the beginning of the 12th century onwards.[7] The most prestigious churches were the cathedrals (the bishops' churches) and the royal chapels. On a lower level were the fifty–sixty primary churches, one for each *fylki*. In addition, each quarter and eighth of a *fylki*, in Eastern and Mid-Norway also each third (riding, *þriðjungr*), had its own church. These local churches gradually became regular parish churches. Some individuals (well-to-do farmers) built their own private churches (*hǿgendiskirkjur*), which eventually became integrated into the parochial system.

In the 13th century there were well over 1,000 churches in Norway; around 1300 the number had increased to about 1,200. It is very difficult, however, to estimate the average distance from a farm to the nearest parish church or assembly, because the topography and the settlement patterns varied greatly. The number of priests may have been one per 175–225 inhabitants (in 1970: one per 3,800).[8] This means that the priests lived fairly close to the people they served. They were often recruited from the farming society, to which they were connected by strong ties of loyalty. Nevertheless, due to their position they exercised extensive control – at least in theory – over people in their parishes, not only morally, but also over working life, by the rules prohibiting work on holy days, of which there were approximately 110 per year, Sundays included.[9]

The clerics enjoyed privileges: they were exempted from paying taxes and doing service in the naval levy. In addition to providing religious services they worked as diplomats and secretaries in the royal administration. Members of the higher clergy might also function as the king's advisers. As representatives of an international organization, however, they were bound by a double loyalty: on the one hand to the laws of the country, on the other hand to the church. This gave them an external base for their intellectual and political skills, which proved indispensable to the king in order to maintain and strengthen his authority. Thus their position should also be seen in an international context, more precisely: in connection with church history and Canon Law.[10]

6 Ibid. *Ból* means 'dwelling place, farm'.
7 Moseng et al. 1999, 253.
8 Ibid., 214.
9 Jón Viðar Sigurðsson 1999, 104.
10 These theological aspects are elucidated by Torstein Jørgensen in his commentary essay following the section on Christian Law.

## *1.5 Political structure*

Due to their material and intellectual resources the king and the church were the most powerful institutions in the country. The highest authority, however, was to be found in the legal thing assemblies, the *lǫgþing*, legislative assemblies whose status ranked above that of the king. There were four such regional assemblies, each the centre of a law province (also called *lǫgþing*): the *Borgarþing* (eastern coastal area), *Eiðsivaþing* (eastern interior), *Frostuþing* (also named *Frostaþing*) (centre and north), and *Gulaþing*, each with its own law. The *Gulaþing* originally comprised only the central parts of Western Norway, namely *Hǫrðafylki*, *Sygnafylki*, and *Firðafylki* (corresponding approximately to the regions Hordaland, Sogn, and Fjordane, respectively). In the latter half of the 10th century Sunnmøre, *Rygjafylki* (Rogaland), and *Egðafylki* (Agder) were added, and by 1274 – the year that saw the introduction of King Magnus the Law-Mender's Law of the Realm – the districts of Valdres, Hallingdal, and Setesdalen were also included in the *Gulaþing*.

The compound names mentioned (*Borgarþing*, etc.) primarily denoted (1) the site of the assembly, and (2) the assembly itself. Secondarily they might also denote the entire law province. When *lǫg* was added, giving forms like *Borgarþingslǫg*, etc., these names also had a dual meaning, on the one hand the law for the area in question, on the other hand the area for which the law was valid, that is the law province.[11]

The *þing* was a general assembly of free men on a fixed site where regular public meetings were formally held. The participants were united by being subject to a common law (*lǫg*), passed by the *þing* in question. The *þing* was primarily a judicial organ, but it also served as a forum for discussion of matters concerning common interests, such as questions of military defence, church matters, business transactions, possessions of land and odal, and relations to the king and his representatives. In addition to passing laws the legislative assembly also functioned as a court, as well as a court of appeal. An important function was to provide an area for solving conflicts of a more general nature, conflicts that could not be solved at the lower districts and local assemblies (quarter/riding *þing*, *heraðsþing*). It should be added that several conflicts were solved outside the assemblies, namely by the so-called *dómar*, specially appointed commissions consisting of six or twelve men trying to obtain agreement and reconcile the conflicting parties.[12]

In Western and Mid-Norway and parts of Eastern Norway the law provinces were subdivided into smaller areas called *fylki*, a unit corresponding roughly to the Anglo-Saxon shire. The *Gulaþing* consisted of six *fylki*. In Western Norway (except *Egðafylki* and Sunnmøre) these areas were further divided into quarters (*fjórðungar*) and eighths (*áttungar*), in Mid-Norway ridings (*þriðjungar*). An administrative/judicial unit on an intermediate level, below the *fylki*, was the

11 On the nature of the Norwegian assemblies and the issuing of laws see Sanmark 2004, 145.
12 Moseng et al. 1999, 39.

*sýsla*. The number of *sýslur* in Norway was approximately fifty. It is not clear how the division into *sýslur* was related to the other administrative units, but there seem normally to have been two *sýslur* per *fylki* in the *Gulaþing*, in some cases a few more.[13] The *sýsla* was governed by a sheriff (*sýslumaðr*). He was the king's highest representative in his district and had fiscal, judicial, and military authority. At a lower level the king's representatives were the *ármenn* (lit. 'messengers'). They were primarily managers of the king's estates, but over time they took on other duties as well, such as the authority to prosecute, and to collect fines to the king. The smallest administrative unit was the *herað*, corresponding roughly to the Anglo-Saxon hundred.[14]

## 2 The *Gulaþing*

### *2.1 The assembly*

According to Ari Þorgilsson's *Íslendingabók* (Chapter 2) an Icelander named Ulfljótr was the first man to bring a law to Iceland from Norway. This law was called *Ulfljótslǫg* and is said to have been modelled in part upon the *Gulaþing* Law of the time, with appropriate additions and omissions.[15] Ulfljótr came to Iceland at the time when the colonization was nearly completed (i.e. around 930). The concept of the *Gulaþing* is also known from *Egils saga Skallagrímssonar*. This means that it probably existed prior to 930. The kings' sagas inform us that King Håkon the Good (✝ c. 961) *setti Gulaþingslǫg* with the advice of Thorleif the Wise. The meaning of these words is not entirely clear, but they may be taken to imply that Håkon reorganized the *Gulaþing* in some ways, mainly by extending the area of the law province and changing its character from a general assembly for all free men (an *alþing*) into an assembly of a prescribed number of delegates – originally 375, later reduced to 246 – from the various smaller districts (*nefndarþing*).[16] The site of the assembly was somewhere in Gulen (hence the name *Gulaþing*) in the outer Sogn district. The exact location is not known, but it was probably Eivindvik.[17] During the reign of King Håkon Håkonsson the site was removed to Guløy, a peninsula c. 2.5 km SE of Gulen, and finally (c. 1300) to Bergen.

13 Andersen 1972, 646–7.

14 Helle 2001, 76–9; Sunde 2011a, 58.

15 It is uncertain whether the Ulfljótr episode can be taken as evidence for the existence of a complete and general *Gulaþing* Law before 930. See Jakob Benediktsson 1975; Helle 2001, 25; Riisøy 2019, 14. Ari's statement has been criticized and its importance revised by Sigurður Líndal (1969), who sees Ulfljótr's mission as an inquiry into what was accepted law in the *Gulaþing* on specific fundamental issues relevant to legal conflicts in Iceland. Bo Ruthström (2002, 345) has mentioned a number of factors supporting the conclusion that the Icelandic constitution should be seen as an Icelandic innovation rather than Norwegian import. It should be added that the historicity of the Ulfljótr episode is disputed, cf. the literature mentioned previously and Sundquist 2016, 150, 174–5, 389.

16 Helle 2001, 31–4, 66.

17 Ibid., 49–66.

## *2.2 The* Gulaþing *law*

### *2.2.1 The nature and content of the law*

In general, the *Gulaþing* Law may be seen as a large-scale attempt to impose a social organization on the West Norwegian farming community. As Knut Helle has pointed out,[18] parts of the law appear to be a social contract between two parties; on the one hand the people, on the other hand the church and the king. For each of these their mutual rights and duties are specified. Differing interests are being balanced, and procedures described for solving conflicts. Personal rights are defined, and scales of fines and compensation are set up, graded according to the gravity of the crime or insult/offence and the social status of the persons involved. The lawgivers want to secure a peaceful and stable society. This goal cannot be achieved without cooperation. Consequently, the law provides frames and organs for this, primarily the assemblies, where negotiations can be conducted in an orderly fashion. Negotiations are required, *inter alia* for the organization of defence and for the executive power of the king and his representatives. Large parts of the law text mirror the internal conditions in the farming community, economic transactions, disputes, marriage, slavery, farming, inheritance, social stratification, insults, damage to life and property, and theft. Most of the rules and provisions seem to have originated in the special needs of the farming community and the wish to restrain as much as possible the powers of the king and the church.

This law text[19] should more precisely be called The Older *Gulaþing* Law, since it must be distinguished from a younger *Gulaþing* Law, of which only the first section, the Christian Law, is preserved. The Older *Gulaþing* Law is the oldest record of Norwegian law. It remained the official law of Western Norway (and some adjacent areas, cf. earlier) until 1267, when it was replaced by the younger *Gulaþing* Law. The latter law was in force until it was replaced by King Magnus the Law-Mender's Law of the Realm in 1274. As a token of the importance of the *Gulaþing* Law it can be mentioned that 130 of its chapters have been incorporated, to a greater or lesser degree, into Magnus the Law-Mender's legislation.[20]

### *2.2.2 Origins and composition*

We do not know when the text was written, but there are reasons to believe that this was done during the reign of King Olav the Quiet (1066–93), or possibly earlier.[21] In all likelihood oral versions[22] of the pre-Christian parts may have existed

18 Ibid., 8.

19 In view of its composition (cf. later) it may more appropriately be described as a compilation. Sunde 2011b, 2014, 133 *et passim*.

20 Robberstad 1981, 404–5.

21 Knudsen 1960, 560; Eithun et al. 1994, 10–12; Helle 2001, 21–2.

22 It is not clear how these and the relationship between oral and written law in general are to be understood. See the discussion in Bagge 2010, 181–4, 195.

from the 10th century onwards (cf. earlier). The text has no well-formed composition, probably because it went through a series of revisions and extensions which did not result in re-editing on the part of the scribes (cf. later). Some provisions may even go back to pre-literary times,[23] but this is a disputed question.[24] The preserved law comprises 320 chapters according to the numbering introduced by Keyser and Munch in their edition 1846 (NGL I). This numbering has been kept in the edition of Eithun et al. (1994) as well as in translations. The facsimile edition of Hødnebø and Rindal (1995) distinguishes fourteen sections (319 chapters). The final preserved leaf ends with some lines from the old peace pledge, the *trygðamál* (in earlier editions numbered (Chapter) 320), here included as Section XV. Only six sections are expressly named *bǫlkr* in the text, namely Book I (Chapters 1–33, *hinn fyrsti bǫlkr bókar þessarar*), II (Chapters 34–50, *Kaupa bǫlkr*),[25] V (Chapters 72–102, *Landsleigubǫlkr*), VI (Chapters 103–130, *Erfðabǫlkr*), XI (Chapters 253–64, *Þjófabǫlkr*), and XIII (Chapters 295–315, *Útgerðarbǫlkr*). References to sections are given by Roman numerals, to chapters by Arabic numerals.

There are different chronological layers in the text. Scholars distinguish between an Olav text and a Magnus text, a feature which is especially conspicuous in the Christian Law (i.e. Chapters 1–33). It is generally assumed that the Christian Law was based on the provisions agreed between St Olav and his assistant Bishop Grimkjell.[26] These early Christian laws bear some resemblance to Anglo-Saxon church legislation and may have been influenced by corresponding English laws.[27, 28] The extent of this influence, however, is disputed. Some scholars[29] think that the scope of Anglo-Saxon influence has been exaggerated. Nevertheless, there are several parallels to Anglo-Saxon laws in the *Gulaþing* Law, as Torstein Jørgensen has pointed out (see his commentary essay). Still, it must be admitted that it is difficult to prove a causal connection between English and Norwegian legislation. During the reign of King Magnus Erlingsson (1161–84) the law was revised. For this reason the names of Olav and Magnus were inserted (with red letters) between or on the lines in the manuscripts to indicate which provisions were made by which king.[30] Similar distinctions can be found in Chapters 37 and 54. Different layers have also

23 Larson 1935, 26; Helle 2001, 13–15.

24 Vogt 2010, 61–2.

25 Some translators (Larson, Meissner) include Chapters 51–6 in this section. Taranger (1926, 205) also includes Chapters 57–71.

26 In the missionary period the church was dependent on the military power of the king for its expansion. For this reason it had no right to give laws on its own, but had to rely on the support of the kings. Sunde 2011a, 63.

27 Taranger 1890, 209–17; Helle 2001, 180–2.

28 It is also possible to see an Anglo-Saxon influence behind the organization of the naval levy. Cf. Riisøy 2014, 118, note 100.

29 Landro 2010, 227–9, 231; Bagge 2010, 195–6.

30 It is doubtful whether Olav in fact gave this law. It is attributed to him because this might provide the law with greater authority (see Rindal in Eithun et al. 1994, 9). There is now general consensus that the law was attributed to St Olav because the sagas and saints' lives created a myth that he was a great legislator. Vogt 2010, 37, 73, and 99.

been distinguished in other sections of the text, especially those dealing with wergild. Knudsen[31] and Hødnebø and Rindal[32] identified three systems of wergild: (1) Chapters 218–37 and 239, (2) Chapters 243–52, a simplified version of the former system, and (3) Chapters 316–19, which replaced the two foregoing systems. Strauch[33] distinguishes two systems: an older one (Chapters 218–37) and a younger one (Chapters 316–19).[34] Only this latter system is expressly characterized in the text as new. It was devised by the lawspeaker Bjarne Mårsson probably at some time during the first two decades of the 13th century.[35] Some other provisions have been stated twice, more or less differing in scope and detail: Chapters 4 and 5, 6 and 7, 238 and 240, 274 and 285, 276 and 287, 277 and 289. See also Iversen (2001, 87).

Over the years there has been a lively debate on the question of whether the *Gulaþing* Law should be considered an official code of law (i.e. a statute book, "Gesetzestext") or rather a private collection of law texts (i.e. a justice book, "Rechtsbuch"). The latter view was advocated by the legal historians Konrad Maurer and Ebbe Hertzberg on the grounds that the manuscripts of the *Gulaþing* Law differ in contents and composition and reflect rules from different stages in the development of Norwegian law. Yet both scholars believed that the oldest provisions were based on oral expositions of the law and reflected rules still in force in the 13th century. A proponent of the former view was the historian Absalon Taranger, who based his opinion on a comparison with Icelandic law. *Grágás* stated that new provisions (*nýmæli*)[36] should be valid for three summers only, which was the lawspeaker's term of office. If they were not recited anew every third summer at the general assembly and then at the local assemblies, they should be considered as abolished. Taranger's view was that Norwegian law had developed along similar lines. Whether new provisions introduced by the king should be accepted as binding law depended on older custom and usage. For this reason it was necessary to record older provisions in the law until custom decided what was to be accepted as current law. Thus the law might contain both old and new rules so long as the old rules were not quite outdated or irrelevant.[37] It is not unlikely that knowledge of the older rules might be of some help to the lawspeaker and the judges in their treatment of difficult questions and cases requiring more thorough investigation. The majority of later Norwegian scholars have followed Taranger,[38] although the opposing view still has its adherents (see Strauch 1999[39] and – less

31 Knudsen 1960, 563.
32 Hødnebø and Rindal 1995, 17.
33 Strauch 1999, 188.
34 Robberstad (1981, 370) assumed the existence of five such systems, one of them (Chapters 229–42) incomplete.
35 Helle 2001, 17–18.
36 Bagge (2010, 202) translates the word as "temporary resolutions".
37 Helle Vogt assumes (2010, 62) that "antiquated forms that were without meaning in practice might be preserved in order to provide a touch of antiquity and continuity".
38 Helle 2001, 15–17.
39 Strauch 1999, 188, 2011, 118.

categorically – 2016[40,41] and Jørn Øyrehagen Sunde[42]). Hødnebø[43] was inclined to reject both views as unfounded because he found no support for them in other Norwegian laws. He suggested that "the historical tendency" of the manuscripts might equally well be explained by the scribes' reluctance to delete or omit text found in the manuscripts they copied. The traditional views have also been dismissed by Bagge,[44] who, inferring from his discussion, *inter alia* of the legitimation of King Håkon's accession to the throne 1217, argues that

> the written versions of the regional laws can neither be regarded as authoritative law-books, promulgated by a competent legislator or legislative body, nor as purely "private" collections. They were one possible version of the law which could be superseded by others, oral or written, if they were thought to be better.

Some features of language and style show traces of oral transmission,[45] especially the use of *nú* (now) instead of *ef* (if) in casuistic paragraphs, the introductory formulation of cases to which the ensuing provisions and rules apply. Knudsen[46] and Helle[47] have also pointed out a number of other stylistic peculiarities, *inter alia* an extensive use of alliteration.[48] The language of the main manuscript can generally be described as North-Western Norwegian and the text seems to have been written in Bergen.[49]

### 2.2.3 *The manuscripts*

Larger or smaller parts of the *Gulaþing* Law are preserved in seventeen manuscripts, but only ten of these are relevant to textual criticism.[50] The relationship between them has been clarified by Magnus Rindal,[51] who has provided the following stemma (Figure 0.1) (dating of the manuscripts added).

40 Strauch 2016, 111–12.
41 Strauch seems to have modified his view (2013, 77), suggesting that the distinction seems to be less clear with regard to Norwegian laws, where the term 'Rechtsbuch' may be less appropriate.
42 In a radio interview July 5, 2016. See also Sunde 2019.
43 Hødnebø and Rindal 1995, 17.
44 Bagge 2010, 189.
45 Or at least oral presentation. Bagge 2010, 192.
46 Knudsen 1960, 564.
47 Helle 2001, 39–40.
48 A comprehensive list of examples is provided by Meissner (1935, xxxiv–xxxvii). It is disputed whether this stylistic feature reveals oral transmission. It may also be seen as a sign of literacy. Tamm 2002, 306.
49 Knudsen 1960, 564.
50 Eithun et al. 1994, 12–26.
51 In Eithun et al. 1994, 26.

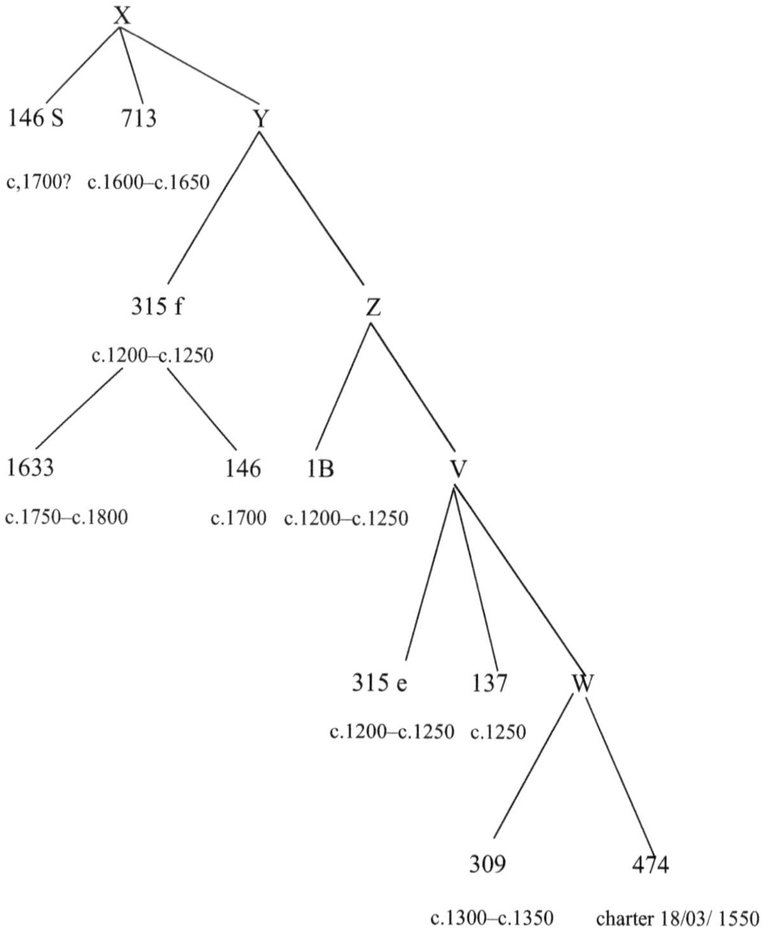


*Figure 0.1* Stemma

The main – and almost complete[52] – manuscript is the DonVar 137 4to, the so-called Codex Rantzovianus, named after its owner at the end of the 17th century, the Danish count Otto Rantzau. It is generally believed to have been written c. 1250. Newer research prefers a dating to c. 1260.[53]

Two important older fragments are the MSS AM 315 e (two leaves) and f (five leaves), both from c. 1200–50.

52 Three sheets seem to be missing. Larson 1935, 28; Eithun et al. 1994, 17; Hødnebø and Rindal 1995, 26–7.

53 Sunde 2019.

315 e contains parts of Chapters 71 and 87–90. 315 f contains parts of Chapters 9–12, 20–22, 152–53, and 156; transcripts of this MS. are NKS 1633 4to (eighty-eight leaves from the latter half of the 18th century) and AM 146 4to (a paper MS. with fifteen leaves from c. 1700).

1633 seems to have been written at a time when 315 f was more complete than it is now.

146 has fifteen leaves and contains text from the Chapters 28, 29, 31, 34, 43, 51, 57, 70, 74, 75, 81, 83, 91, 92, 97, 115, 122, 131, 150, 151, 156, 165, 166, 169, 172–75, 178, 179, 184, 188–93, 195–97, 205, 215, 223, 309, and 312. Important for text criticism is the fact that 146 contains text which seems to have been cut off from 137 after leaf 78, the first chapter of the section Concerning Personal Rights. An attached note (146 S) contains Árni Magnússon's excerpts from Chapters 179 and 180.

The fragment NRA 1 B, from c. 1200–1250, consists of rests of four leaves and contains parts of the Chapters 28, 30–32, 52, 53, 54, 55, 57, 82–86, and 287–89.

AM 309 fol., from c. 1300–1350, consists of one hundred leaves, where the leaves 93r–100v contain the Christian Law.

The Norwegian charter DN, vol. 22, no. 474, from Tønsberg 1550, contains a lawspeaker's summing up of a part of the Christian Law, probably part of Chapter 24.

UppsUB R 713, from c. 1600–1650, is an Icelandic MS. containing transcripts and excerpts from various laws, including two small parts of the Older *Gulaþing* Law, Chapters 179, 180, and 259.

Small parts of the *Gulaþing* Law are also preserved in the MSS. Deichman 11 8vo (from c. 1570) and Holm perg 31 4to (from c. 1600). Due to the limited extent of the extracts from the *Gulaþing* Law their positions in relation to the stemma are unclear, but Rindal (op. cit.) assumes that they would occupy positions higher up than 137. The so-called King Sverre's Christian Law (AM 78 4to) has parts of its content from the Christian Law of *Gulaþing*.[54] An example may be found in the latter's Chapter 28, where AM 78 4to contains text which is probably missing from other manuscripts.

### *2.2.4 Editions*

The *Gulaþing* Law has been edited by R. Keyser and P.A. Munch (in vol. I of *Norges gamle Love*, Christiania 1846, 1–118) and by B. Eithun, M. Rindal, and T. Ulset (*Den eldre Gulatingslova*, Norrøne tekster, nr. 6, Riksarkivet, Oslo 1994). The latter is a diplomatic edition. F. Hødnebø and M. Rindal have provided a facsimile edition of Codex Rantzovianus and fragments of some other medieval manuscripts (*Den eldre Gulatingsloven*, Corpus codicum Norvegicorum medii aevi, Quarto series, vol. IX, Selskapet til utgivelse av gamle norske håndskrifter, Oslo 1995).

54 Bøe 1964, 301; Robberstad 1981, 10.

### *2.2.5 Translations*

The *Gulaþing* Law has previously been translated into Danish by H. Paus (*Samling af Gamle Norske Love*, vol. I, Copenhagen 1751), into English by L. Larson (*The Earliest Norwegian Laws, Being the Gulathing Law and the Frostathing Law*, New York 1935), into German by R. Meissner (*Das Rechtsbuch des Gulathings*, Germanenrechte, Band 6, Norwegisches Recht, Weimar 1935), and into Norwegian (nynorsk) by K. Robberstad (*Gulatingslovi. Umsett av Knut Robberstad.* Norrøne bokverk 33, 4th ed. 1981 (1st ed. 1937)).

The present translation is based on the text of Eithun et al. 1994. Variants from other manuscripts than Codex Rantzovianus are included (between square brackets) where they represent significant differences as regards the contents of the law. See, for example, Chs. 28, 30, 53, 70, 122, 179, and 304. The numbering of chapters follows the edition in *Norges gamle Love*, vol. 1, which has set the standard for later editions and translations in this respect. The headings of the unnamed sections (see Section 2.2.2) are supplied by the translator. Explanatory notes of three kinds are added: (1) words and shorter phrases are inserted in parentheses into the running text in order to make the meaning more explicit; (2) footnotes refer to other chapters dealing with the same or related material and/or give explanations of details in the subject matter as well as references to relevant literature; (3) a glossary provides more extensive comments on a number of key concepts (references to corresponding pages in the text may be found in the Index). More detailed and supplementary information is provided by the works of Knut Helle (2001), Finn Hødnebø (1975), Magnus Rindal (1975, 1994), Knut Robberstad (1981), and Jørn Øyrehagen Sunde (2011a, 2019).

## Part Two

# The older *Gulaþing* law according to DonVar 137 4to

# I The book on Christian law

## 1 Here begins the *Gulaþing* law. The first book of this law says how we should observe our Christianity[1]

That is the beginning of our laws that we should bow to the east and pray to the holy Christ for good harvest and peace;[2] that we may retain our settled land and keep our liege lord[3] in health. Let him be a friend to us, and we to him. And let God be a friend to all.

## 2 Here are the new ordinances adopted in accordance with the guidance of King Magnus,[4] Archbishop Øystein,[5] Earl Erling,[6] and all the wisest men in Norway

The next thing is that he shall be King of Norway who is born in lawful wedlock as son of the King of Norway, unless he is dominated by ill will or insanity. But if these matters oust the oldest one from power, then that brother of his, having the same father, shall be king, the one whom the archbishop and the suffragan bishops[7] and those twelve wisest men whom the bishops appoint from each diocese, consider best fit. The laymen should make their decision after having sworn an oath that they will choose the one whom they think best fit before God. And even the bishops should be bound before God by this oath, although they do not swear, as much as the others who do swear, that they will conduct a fair discussion of this matter, just as the laymen who swear as far as God enables them to see what is proper.

1 On church law in general see Tamm 2002, 300–2; Bagge 2010, 195–202; Vogt 2010, 28–9, 43, 73.
2 This wording ties in with the heathen custom of sacrificing to the gods Njord and Frøy for fruitful harvest and peace.
3 ON *lánardróttinn*, lit. 'one who lends another person something', thus being his superior in this respect. Here it is used in a transferred sense, applied to the king as being master of the country.
4 Magnus Erlingsson, King of Norway 1161–84.
5 Øystein Erlendsson, archbishop of Nidaros 1161–88.
6 Erling Ormsson the Crooked (ON *skakki*), †1179, the father of Magnus Erlingsson.
7 The ordinary bishops, as opposed to the archbishop. They were not allowed to take oaths.

If the King of Norway has no lawfully begotten son left, then he is to be king who is the nearest heir according to the judgement of those who are appointed thereto, if he is deemed fit. And if he is not deemed fit, then he should be (king) whom those who are appointed thereto think best fit to observe the law of God as well as the law of the country. And if they disagree, then that party which outnumbers the others should have it their way, provided that they are joined by the archbishop and the other bishops, and confirm it with their oaths.

After the death of the king all the bishops, abbots, officers[8] of the King's retinue as well as all the men of the king's body-guard should go without further instructions north to (the shrine of) the Holy King Olav[9] for discussions with the archbishop. Each bishop should appoint twelve of the wisest men (in his diocese) to go with him, and they must all be on their way within the first month after the king's decease. There the crown of the deceased king should be presented (to the cathedral) for his soul,[10] and it shall hang there ever after to the honour of God and Holy King Olav according to the promise of King Magnus, the first king to be crowned in Norway.

But if anyone lets himself be chosen (king) in some other way he will have forfeited property and peace, and so will everyone who joins him in this respect, and be in the ban[11] of God, all holy men, the Pope, the archbishop, and all the suffragan bishops. If these men whom the bishops appoint to go with them, refuse to go, they are in excommunication[12] and will be fined forty *merkr* to the king, and they cannot be buried at a church in the event that they die in the meantime. Each man should undertake this journey at his own expense, but the king has to pay for those who held no royal property before. And if the archbishop is not in the country or is deceased, then all (other) men must (nevertheless) come to these deliberations as already ordered.

## 3 Both Olav[13] and Magnus determined this

The next thing is that we have ordered a meeting to be held every year here in Gulen, (with) as many delegates as we have agreed to. *Magnus:* That is sixty \ *Olav:* one hundred and two / from *Hǫrðafylki* and the same number from *Rygjafylki, Magnus:* fifty \ *Olav:* eighty / from *Firðafylki, Magnus:* but forty \ *Olav:*

8 They were: the landed men, the king's marshal, the standard-bearer, and the pages (*skutilsveinar*).

9 The sanctuary in Nidaros (now Trondheim).

10 This act of presentation was laid down in Magnus Erlingsson's letter of privileges to the church, as a token of perpetual subordination. The text of the letter has been translated and interpreted by Eirik Vandvik (†1953) in a book published after his death (†Vandvik 1962).

11 Referring to the *excommunicatio maior*, i.e. implying exclusion from the communion of believers and the rites, sacraments, and other services from the church, but not from membership in the church as such. Seierstad 1959, 79–82; Logan 1984, 536.

12 I.e. the *excommunicatio minor*, exclusion from the Eucharist and some other services from the church. Seierstad 1959, 79–82; Robberstad 1981, 306; Logan 1984, 536.

13 Olav Haraldsson, Holy Olav (995–1030), King of Norway 1016–28.

sixty-four / men from *Sygnafylki*,[14] *Magnus:* twenty \ *Olav:* twenty-seven / from *Egðafylki*, all delegates appointed as laid down in the laws,[15] but from Sunnmøre sixteen householders \ *Olav:* as many as want to (go). / [16] *Magnus:* Two landed men should stay behind in *Egðafylki*, two in *Rygjafylki*, one (landed man) in South Hordaland, one in *Firðafylki*, and one in Sunnmøre in order to protect peoples' homes from thieves and robbers.

But all *Magnus:* other *Both:* landed men within our law district should go to the general assembly from these six *fylki* unless they are prevented by the king's necessities or by their own. And those mass-priests \ *Olav:* all those from whom men buy services / that are appointed by the bishop, two from each *fylki*, and all the king's representatives, must come unless they are prevented by necessity. And they may be lawfully excused if the king visits the *fylki* and requires of his representative to make provisions for his (the king's) billeting in the neighbouring *fylki*.

Now the next thing is that there should come to this assembly as many delegates as are now enumerated, *Magnus:* on the Vigil of the Feast of St Peter (June 28th) \ *Olav:* Thursday after Easter / *Both:* while the sun is still up. If they do not come, they are liable to a fine, each man of those who are delegated to the *Gulaþing*, if he arrives later and after the oaths[17] have been sworn (in court).

If he arrives before, but still after our appointed day, he has to pay a fine of an *eyrir*. But if all men from a *fylki* fail (to arrive on time), then they will have to bring with them forty *merkr* (as a fine) the next spring; half of it goes to us in the same law district, the king is owed the other half. But if a quarter or an eighth of the men fails to come, then (there) should be subtracted from that amount according to their number. But if some men fail to do so, they must pay a fine of three *aurar*.

*Olav:* We should provide food and money for this from the six *fylki*, half a month's food to each man, unless his journey takes a longer time, and a *sáld* of malt and an *eyrir* of silver. Anyone who fails to contribute to this, hinders the journey for that delegate, and he is liable to pay a fine of three *aurar*.

*Magnus:* From the *Egðafylki*[18] one man has to go from each warship district, and the warship districts shall be equalized so that twenty men go (from each); and two months' food of butter and the same amount of meal should be provided, along with an *eyrir* of weighed silver or as much of counted silver as is coined

14 Now Sogn (except Gulen, which then belonged to *Hǫrðafylki*).

15 The delegates were at first probably chosen by local chieftains, later by the king's representatives (landed men, sheriffs, and *ármenn*). Nedkvitne 2011, 93.

16 The number of delegates was reduced during the time of Magnus Erlingsson, probably because fewer men were needed, and because the session of the general assembly was longer, which led to an increased need for food to the delegates.

17 Each delegate had to swear that he would judge as he thought was right before God and his own conscience, making no difference between friend and enemy in this respect.

18 According to the list in Chapter 315 the *Egðafylki* was supposed to provide sixteen warships, each with twenty-five thwarts.

from an *eyrir*, and a *sáld* of malt. Those are obliged to go (to the general assembly) whom the landed men appoint thereto, or the king's representatives or the sheriffs. This contribution should be paid in proportion to (one's) wealth. But three pounds[19] of butter shall be part of this contribution.

From *Rygjafylki*[20] 15 men (should go) from each quarter, and for each man one and half a month's food of butter and the same amount of meal should be provided, a weighed *eyrir* and a *sáld* of malt.

The same number from *Hǫrðafylki*,[21] and each man should be provided with one month's food, an *eyrir* of silver and a *sáld* of malt. From Sogn ten men from each quarter, and each man should be provided with one month's food of both kinds, a weighed *eyrir* and a *sáld* of malt. But thirteen men from each quarter of *Firðafylki*,[22] and each man should be provided with one month's food of both kinds, a weighed *eyrir* and a *sáld* of malt.

From Sunnmøre[23] each of the sixteen men (should be provided with) two months' food of both kinds, a weighed *eyrir* and a *sáld* of malt. Anyone who fails to contribute to this hinders the journey for that delegate and will be fined three *aurar*.

*Olav:* Whenever delegates in Gulen become liable to pay a fine, then that money must be paid there. The whole body of *Gulaþing* delegates owns that money. It is well if he (who is guilty) pays himself, or his friends; but if he is unwilling, then the king's representative or landed man must pay, each in his district, and take the doubled amount at (the man's) home.

## 4 Olav prescribed, but Magnus abolished this[24]

The next thing is that every year we should give one slave his freedom[25] here in Gulen. We have distributed this duty among the *fylki* so that each in its year should give freedom to one man. That man should be given his freedom on the first Sunday of the *Gulaþing* session. And all we delegates to the *Gulaþing* should (together) provide money for this, six *aurar*.[26]

19 Here c. 15 kg.
20 According to the list in Chapter 315 the *Rygjafylki* was supposed to provide twenty-four warships, each with twenty-five thwarts. The ship-levies are listed in Robberstad 1981, 319.
21 The ship-levies are listed in Robberstad 1981, 319–20.
22 According to Chapter 315 the *Firðafylki* was supposed to provide twenty warships, each with twenty-five thwarts. The ship-levies are listed in Robberstad 1981, 320.
23 According to Chapter 315 Sunnmøre was supposed to provide sixteen warships, each with twenty-five thwarts. The ship-levies are listed in Robberstad 1981, 321.
24 On this and the following chapter see Iversen 1997, 191–5.
25 King Athelstan in England instructed his bailiffs to give one slave his freedom every year. It is possible that the instructions given in Chs. 4 and 5 are influenced by English law. See also TJ's comment to paragraph 5.
26 The price of a slave varied from one *mǫrk* to one and a half *merkr*. Six *aurar* were equivalent to half the price; the slave himself was supposed to pay the other half.

If the man is not given his freedom on that Sunday, then those who are held liable to set the man free will be fined twelve *aurar* to the bishop,[27] and they must buy a slave and give him his freedom even if it is (done) later.

## 5 And this likewise

Now the next thing is that we should give freedom to a slave in each *fylki* of the *Gulaþing* law district. We have distributed this among the quarters. But those men whose duty it is to give the man his freedom must have given him this before Christmas Eve. If they have not, they will be fined twelve *aurar* to the bishop and they have to buy a slave and give him his freedom, even if it is (done) later.

## 6 Both Olav and Magnus

The next thing is that we have promised an ale feast, people call it a joint drinking, (that is) ale brewed from one *mælir* (of malt) for each husband and another *mælir* for his wife. At least three householders should join, unless someone lives so far away in the isles or high up on the mountain side that he cannot bring his ale to other men. In that case he alone has to brew as much ale as *Magnus:* each of them \ *Olav:* all three. / But he who has a farm supporting fewer than six cows, or a field smaller than that which is sowed with six *sáld* of seed-corn,[28] should give the ale feast only if he wants to. *Both:* That ale must be given by All Saints' Day at the latest. That ale should be blessed with thanks to Christ and the Virgin Mary for good harvest and peace. And if anyone does not brew by that time, he has to pay a fine of three *aurar* to the bishop and (still) give that ale feast even if it is later. But if anyone does not brew and is identified and convicted of sitting like this for twelve months such that he does not take part in ale feasts, then he must pay a fine of three *merkr* to the bishop.

## 7 Both Olav and Magnus

We have promised to make yet another ale feast, the husband and his wife sharing equally, and bless it on Christmas Eve[29] with thanks to Christ and the Virgin Mary for good harvest and peace.

27 The entire Christian Law seems to presuppose only one bishop in the *Gulaþing* law province at the time when our text was completed (cf. esp. Chs. 5, 9, and 15). Sunnmøre belonged to the diocese of Nidaros (until 1622). Around 1125 the diocese of Stavanger was established, including the districts of Rogaland, Agder, Eidfjord (in Hardanger), Hallingdal, and Valdres. The Magnus text, which is younger, also mentions only one bishop, but this carries less weight, since the mentioning of a bishop was part of the usual wording (cf., e.g. Chs. 3, 8, and 32).

28 When sown with six *sáld* the field may have had the size of c. 7.5 decares, about 1.8 acres.

29 The custom of brewing ale at Christmas time is mentioned in the saga about Håkon the Good. In some districts of Norway this custom has survived down to our time.

If that is not done, a fine of three *merkr* must be paid to the bishop. But if someone sits like this for three winters, that he does not give this ale nor pays the fines which we have stipulated for the sake of our Christianity, and he is convicted of this, then he will have forfeited every penny of his property; the king has one half of it and the bishop the other half. But he should be allowed to go to confession and do penance[30] and (then) stay in Norway. If he is not willing to (do this), then he must leave our king's realm.[31]

## 8 \ Magnus / alone decreed this

We have made an agreement with our bishop that he must provide us with his service, and we must reward it by paying full tithe,[32] both of all harvest and stock, and of all rightful catch of fish and game. If it (the tithe) is to be divided such that the bishop takes one fourth of it, the poor one fourth, the church one fourth, and the priest one fourth.

The bishop must come to each *fylki* each year, unless he is prevented by necessity, and provide people with such service as is proper. But that is a valid excuse, if the bishop is ill, or the king orders him to undertake a journey, or the archbishop sends for him to ordain another bishop, or other pressing necessities occur.

If a man sits like this for twelve months when he does not pay his tithe, then he owes three *merkr* to the bishop. And if he sits like this for two twelve-month periods when he does not pay his tithe, then he owes six *merkr* to the bishop. If he sits like this for three winters when he does not pay his tithe, then he has forfeited every penny of his property, in land as well as in movable property; the king is owed half of it, and the bishop the other half.

## 9 Olav alone decreed this[33]

We have made an agreement with our bishop that he must provide us with his service.[34] And we have to pay him for it, an *ertog* for every forty persons within

30 Confession and penance are parts of the *sacramentum poenitentiae*, based on the Bible (Mt. 16:19; 18:18; Jn. 20:23, etc.). The sinner was supposed to tell the priest about his sins, repent of them, do penance, and then receive absolution. Doing penance might imply fasting, saying prayers, or undertaking a pilgrimage. Acts of penance might be substituted by payment of indulgence money (*indulgentia*). If damage had been done, it had to be compensated. In serious cases only the bishop or the pope could grant absolution. From 1215 onwards (4th Lateran Council) every adult person was obliged to go to confession and communion at least once a year.

31 This renders the term *landeign konungs*, which is also used in Chs. 20, 22–25, and 28–30. On these occasions *eign* is used for the king's landholdings, rather than in the later sense of private property. Tore Iversen sees this term as a parallel to the term *dominium regis* and suggests that these sections should be dated to the beginning of the 12th century. Iversen 2001, 92–4; Sanmark 2004, 138, 229.

32 The tithe was introduced during the first half or around the middle of the 12th century, in Western Norway perhaps in the 1160s. Even the king had to pay tithe of his land, according to canonical law.

33 The procedure described in this chapter shows that Ch. 9 dates from a time when the bishop had no jurisdiction over ordinary people. Cf. also Chs. 19 and 33.

34 Which, amongst other things, was to perform confirmation of children.

our law province.[35] The bishop should earn that money in this way, that he should come to each *fylki* once every year and give people such service as is his duty.

If the bishop comes to a *fylki* or to a quarter, then he or his representative should summon an assembly and fix a date for the bishop to receive the payment; then it is well if people pay him. But if they refuse to pay him (what is due), and all men in the levy district refuse (to pay), then they are liable to a fine of three *aurar*. In that case the bishop or his representative should claim payment[36] from them in the assembly.

If fewer men refuse, then the bishop's representative must go home to (each of) them, taking with him those two neighbours who live next to him; then it is well if they accept to follow him. If they are not willing, then he must order them (to follow), in that case they will be fined three *aurar* to the king's representative. But he himself (the representative) should get (other) witnesses and go home to the other (person) and claim payment to the bishop and that fine which is stipulated, an *eyrir* for each *penningr*; then it is well if he pays. But if he is not willing, then he (the representative) should summon him to appear before the assembly, to be charged with robbery, in that case he is liable to a fine of twelve *aurar*[37] to the king's representative.

Our bishop and his representative and all priests shall bring all their lawsuits in the way that I have now told.

## 10 Both decreed this about churches

The next thing is that we shall maintain all those churches and observe those decrees about Christianity which Holy Olav and Bishop Grimkjell[38] laid down at the Moster assembly,[39] and all those churches that were built later. In each *fylki* there is one church which we call the primary church, which all men in the *fylki* are obliged to maintain. If that church collapses and the corner posts[40] come down, then we have to bring timber to the site within twelve months. If that is

35 These words show that the chapter was written at a time when there was only one bishop in the *Gulaþing* law province. During the reign of Olav the Quiet (1067–93) episcopal sees were established in each of the three big law provinces (i.e. Selja for the *Gulaþing*, Nidaros for the *Frostuþing*, and Oslo for Eastern Norway). But each of the bishops probably served in his diocese before episcopal sees came into being.

36 See Ch. 35.

37 Twelve *aurar* was the usual fine for robbery.

38 The missionary bishop came from England with Olav Haraldsson 1014 or 1015, last mentioned 1046.

39 The assembly which met at Moster in the district of Sunnhordland in the early 1020s, possibly 1022 (a corollary of J. R. Hagland's dating of the runic stone in Kuli, NW Norway; see Knirk 2017, 94).

40 The word shows that stave churches are meant. But this does not preclude the existence of stone churches. The first stone churches in Norway were presumably built at the end of the 11th century. Nevertheless, wooden churches continued to be the norm for several centuries after the introduction of Christianity. Robberstad 1981, 326; Sanmark 2004, 104.

not brought forward, all men in the *fylki* are jointly liable to a fine of fifteen *merkr*; half of which goes to the king, the other half to the bishop. If fewer men fail to do this (bring timber), a quarter or an eighth of the people, then the fine should be reduced in proportion to how many they are. If individual men fail (to perform this duty), they are liable to a fine of three *aurar* for each piece of timber that is needed, and provide timber, even if it is later. But an *eyrir* for each meal (for the working men). And an *eyrir* for each nail that is wanting. Now the church is built.

## 11 And both ordered this

Now all men in the *fylki* should build a fence around the church. Then the bishop or his representative should summon the men to this and appoint a day before which the fence shall be completed. Then it is well if that is the case.

But if it is not completed, and the church remains without a fence for twelve months, then all men in the *fylki* will have to pay for that three *merkr* to the bishop. If some men fail (to do this), they will have to pay a fine of three *aurar* to the bishop for each piece of timber that is needed and provide the timber, \ even if it is later /, and build a fence.

Now the church is built and there is a fence around it, then all men in the *fylki* should buy consecration from the bishop, and offer three nights' billeting for him with thirty men.[41]

## 12 And likewise about the building of churches

Now about all other churches which we are obliged to maintain: quarter churches and eighth churches, parish churches and private chapels. We shall maintain all those churches and not leave the site vacant.

If the church collapses and the corner posts fall down, then the men who own the church should bring timber to the site within twelve months. If that is not brought forward, then those who own the church must pay a fine of three *merkr* to the bishop and provide (the timber) and build the church, even if it is (done) later. If some men fail to do this, they will have to pay three *aurar* to the bishop for each piece of timber that is needed and provide the timber, even though it is later, and rebuild the church and not leave the site vacant.

If some individual men build a church, whether he is a landed man or a householder, or anyone who builds a church, he should maintain it and never leave the site vacant. If the church collapses and the corner posts fall down, then he has to bring timber to the site within twelve months; if that is not brought forward he must pay a fine of three *merkr* to the bishop and provide the timber and in addition build the church. If he does not and lets the site lie vacant for another twelve months, then he must once more pay a fine of three *merkr* for it to the bishop.

41 Cf. Chs. 14 and 33.

But if he lets the site lie vacant for three winters, then he has forfeited the land on which the church was built; then the land belongs to the king, and he may gain it as his property if he has the church (re)built within the first twelve months. If he does not, the householder must take his land back and build a church on it. If the householder has not done so within twelve months, then the king owns the land and it will never later return into the possession of the householder.

## 13 Concerning church fence

Now those men who have to maintain the church should build a fence around it, and have it completed within twelve months. If it is not completed within twelve months, a fine of twelve *aurar* must be paid to the bishop. If (only) some men fail to do so, they are liable to pay three *aurar* for each piece of timber that is needed and provide the timber, even if it is (done) later. Now all the churches are built and there are fences around them.

## 14 Concerning consecration of a church[42]

Now consecration shall be bought from the bishop. Whenever the site is consecrated, but not the church, consecration should be bought from the bishop for twelve *aurar*. But if neither the site nor the church is consecrated, consecration has to be bought from the bishop for three *merkr*; three nights' billeting for fifteen men (should also be granted to the bishop). Now all churches are built and consecration paid for them.

## 15 Concerning supervision of churches

Now the next thing is that our bishop shall govern the churches as Holy Olav promised Bishop Grimkjell at the Moster assembly and we agreed to later.[43] Our bishop must now appoint to all churches such priests[44] as are capable of giving proper services[45] to people.

We should provide them with such maintenance[46] as Holy Olav and Bishop Grimkjell laid down at the Moster assembly. But for parish churches (the arrangement will be) such as the householders and the priest appointed by the bishop

42 Adam of Bremen (c. 1075) mentions that Norwegians had to pay fees for baptism, confirmation, consecration of churches, ordination, sick call, and funeral, all of which he thinks should have been given free of charge. He thinks the reasons are the bishops' and priests' desire for money, and that people have neither the knowledge of nor the willingness to pay tithe. The regulation in Ch. 14 then seems to be older than Ch. 8.

43 The references to Holy Olav and Bishop Grimkjell may perhaps not be taken literally. It seems to have been a custom in Scandinavian as well as in other European laws to trace rules and provisions back to a glorious king in the past, a more or less mythical lawgiver. Landro 2010, 189–91.

44 On the appointment of priests see Landro 2010, 211–12.

45 I.e. the seven daily hours, *horæ canonicæ*, and other religious services.

46 The priest and his parishioners seem to be bound to each other by a set of mutual obligations.

agree to, that they (the priests) should stay twelve months where the bishop has placed them and give proper services to people.

Now he acquires a house and land[47] and friends, then the bishop must not remove him from his parish, because we do not want our churches to become objects of bargaining.[48]

If he proclaims fast-days or holy days wrongly once in twelve months, then he is liable to a fine of three *merkr* to the bishop. And if this happens again he must once more pay a fine of three *merkr* to the bishop. Then the bishop has the right to remove him from his parish and appoint another who knows how to give proper services to people.

Whenever they proclaim wrongly or disobey such order from the bishop as concerns our Christianity, then they are liable to pay for that to the bishop; for we have abolished punishing them by beating, because we enter into marriage relations with them or let them teach our sons. Our priests should enjoy the same personal rights[49] as any one of us enjoys with respect to any one else in this country.

## 16 Concerning the observation of Sundays

Now the next thing is that every seventh day is holy, and we call that day Sunday. The preceding Saturday is to be holy from nones onward, when a third of the day remains, and Monday night until cockcrow; so that one is not allowed to work, neither catch fish nor hunt birds, and not work in the field or in the meadow, other than that (kind of work) which is exempted: If men row their course on the sea, having their fishing-line on the outside, or carry load having been laid up on a work day. If they come home on a holy day to a harbourless coast, they have to drop their load on the shore and secure their ship; or people go by land and drive a horse with pack that is bound on a work day.

He who is identified and convicted of working on a Sunday is liable to a fine of six *aurar* for it and go to confession and do penance. If a man's foreign slave works without his master's consent, then he should have him flogged or pay a fine of three *aurar* to the bishop.

## 17 Concerning mass-days[50]

These are the days which Saint Olav and Bishop Grimkjell[51] laid down at the Moster assembly, thereby declaring a preceding fast and holiness from the preceding nones, they are to be observed just as Sundays.

47 Probably land given to keep the church in good repair and provide maintenance for the priest.

48 A church council at Westminster 1102 decided that churches and prebends should not be bought or sold.

49 Legal protection against assault and battery. Skre 1995, 209.

50 Landro 2010, 190–1, 229.

51 A comparison with other church laws reveals that Ch. 17 seems to date from Olav's Christian Law (with the exception of the Earlier Feast of St Olav, July 29th), whereas Ch. 18 seems to be younger, and probably Magnus text.

Now the Feast of St John the Baptist is the first (June 24th), the Feast of SS Peter and Paul the second (June 29th), the third the Feast of the Saints of Selja (July 8th), the fourth the Feast of St James (July 25th), the fifth the Earlier Feast of St Olav (July 29th), the sixth the Feast of St Lawrence (August 10th), the seventh the Feast of the Assumption of the Blessed Virgin Mary (August 15th), the eighth the Feast of St Bartholomew (August 24th), the ninth the Feast of St Matthew (Sept. 21st), the tenth Michaelmas (Sept. 29th), the eleventh the Feast of the Two Apostles (Oct. 28th), the twelfth All Saints' Day (Nov. 1st), the thirteenth the Feast of St Andrew (Nov. 30th), the fourteenth the Feast of St Thomas (Dec. 21st).

Now those days have been enumerated before which there is fast and holiness from the preceding nones, and for which fines must be paid as for Sundays if someone is working on those days.

## 18 More about mass-days

Now there are other holy days before which there is no nones-holiness or fast, but on which work is just as sacrilegious as if it were done on a Sunday. If people work on these days, they will have to pay a fine of three *aurar* to the bishop. But if a man's slave works without his master's consent, then a fine of one and a half *aurar* must be paid.

Now these days shall be enumerated. It begins with Christmas first, four days, but the fifth is the eighth day of Christmas, the sixth is the thirteenth day (Feast of the Epiphany, Jan. 6th); they are all equally holy. But on the days in between one is allowed to save one's live stock, if need be. Next to Christmas there is the Feast of St Brictiva (Jan. 11th), then the Feast of St Paul (Jan. 25th), then Candlemas (Feb. 2nd), then the Feast of St Matthias (Feb. 24th), then the Feast of the Annunciation (March 25th).

Now come four days when it is not allowed to open the earth[52] and bury the dead. Now the first is Maundy Thursday after nones, the second Good Friday, all the day, the third Easter Eve before nones, the fourth Easter Day, all the day. If someone buries a body (on any of these days), he is liable to a fine of three *aurar* to the bishop.

There are two days in the Easter week,[53] Monday and Tuesday, on which one is not allowed to work, unless it is to care for one's livestock if needed; but all Wednesday is holy.

Then there is the Feast of SS Philip and James (May 1st), then the Invention of the Cross (May 3rd).

Rogation Days[54] should be observed so far as it is allowed to work until midday the first three days, but all Thursday is as holy as Easter Day.

52 I.e. to dig a grave for burial.

53 The easter week began Easter Day.

54 The three days before Ascension Day.

Now is the Feast of St Hallvard (May 15th), then the Feast of St Botulf (June 17th), then St Swithun's Day (July 2nd), then the Feast of St Canute (July 10th), then the later Feast of St Olav (August 3rd), then the Feast of the Nativity of Our Lady (Sept. 8th), then the Feast of the Exaltation of the Cross (Sept. 14th), then Martinmas (Nov. 11th), then the Feast of St Clement (Nov. 23rd), then the Feast of St Nicholas (Dec. 6th). These days we must keep holy in our law district.

## 19 Olav alone ordered this

Now the priests should carve (and send forth) crosses[55] before holy days, each in the district where he gives the divine services, whether this is in the *fylkis* church, quarter church or eighth church.

Crosses must be carved (and sent forth) so as to come to all places in the priest's district. Crosses must come to all houses from which there is smoke. Every man should carry the cross to the next, except where several men live in the same yard, then each in his turn should carry it from the yard.

Crosses must be carried to the winter dwellings and not up to the mountains. Each householder is responsible for one house, in that the cross does not stop there, though he may own more (houses).

But if he does not send the cross forward, he is liable to a fine of three *aurar* to the priest who carved the cross. If the man denies and says that the cross did not come to his house, but his neighbour contradicts him and asserts that he (the neighbour) carried it to him, then he (the person accused) must confirm with an oath that the cross did not come to him. And he who was obliged to take an oath should pay a fine (if he refuses to take an oath); then it is well if he pays the cross fine.[56]

But if he refuses, then the priest must go home to him with two of his neighbours and claim the cross fine and summon him to appear before the assembly (being charged) for robbery,[57] then he is liable to a fine of twelve *aurar*.

## 20 Both Olav and Magnus

Now the next thing is that every seventh day we shall abstain from eating meat, we call that (day) Friday. Whoever is identified and convicted of having eaten meat on Friday[58] has to pay a fine of three *aurar* to the bishop, unless he eats without his knowledge (of the ban) and someone comes into his house and asks him why he is eating meat on Friday. Then, if he has bites of it in his mouth he should spit them out and say that "I ate this without knowing, and I do not know what day it is", then he will not be fined. But he should go to confession and do penance. If he swallows

55 Message sticks formed as small crosses, dispatched to inform people about holy days and fast-days.

56 I.e. the fine of three *aurar* mentioned earlier in the same chapter.

57 This is legal procedure according to the rules in Chs. 35 and 36.

58 This is the only type of *abstinentia* mentioned in the GuL. There were also others, e.g. *vatnfasta*. Sanmark 2004, 242.

(the bites), he has to pay three *aurar* for that to the bishop. If it happens to him again that he eats meat on Friday he must pay a fine of three *merkr* to the bishop.

If he has paid that fine twice and will not respect Friday or our Christianity, then he has forfeited every penny of his property; but he may go to confession and do penance. If he is not willing to (do this) he must leave the realm of our king.

If someone eats horse meat,[59] he must pay three *merkr* for it to the bishop, every man who speaks our language, and go to confession and do penance. If a man's slave eats meat on Friday or at forbidden times, then he should be flogged or a fine of three *aurar* must be paid to the bishop.

If the bishop or his representative accuses someone of eating meat on Friday or at forbidden times, and he denies (it), then the bishop's representative should go home to him and summon him before the assembly and bring action against him. If he denies (it), he should swear to it with a three-man oath.

If someone eats meat during Lent, then he has to pay a fine of three *merkr* for it to the bishop, unless he eats out of necessity and has no other food. Then he should go to three of his neighbours and offer them exchange of food. Then it is well if he gets (other food), but if he gets nothing, he may eat meat, thus saving his life; because it is better for him to eat a dog than that a dog eats him.[60]

If someone eats horse meat during Lent, then he has forfeited every penny of his property, and he must leave the realm of our king. But if the bishop's representative accuses him of this, he (the accused person) should swear against it with a three-man oath. But if this oath fails he will be outlawed.

If a man's slave eats without his master's consent, then his master should sell him out of the realm of our king and use the price for his own benefit and not eat together with him; but if he does, then he has to pay forty *merkr* for it. And if the bishop's representative accuses him of this, then he should swear against it with a three-man oath.

## 21 Magnus abolished part of this

Now the next thing is that every child which is born in our country is to be nurtured *Olav:* unless it is born with such deformities[61] that the face turns around where the neck should be or the toes turn to where the heels should be, then that

59 The eating of horse meat was prohibited because it was considered as a heathen practice. Sanmark 2004, 222–4. But the ban was not equally strict throughout the Nordic countries. Even in Norway there were local differences. Kværness 1996, 79–81. See also TJ's comment to paragraph 20.

60 To eat dogs, cats, or horses intentionally was considered the severest crime, with exile as punishment. But if the man is in an emergency, the principle of necessity could be applied, as reflected in this proverb-like saying. The same phrase is found in the *Borgarþing* law (I 5) and the *Eiðsivaþing* law (I 29), which indicates either a common origin or a later exchange of regulations between the provincial laws.

61 Children born with deformities are mentioned in Latin literature. Norwegian church law may have been inspired by Augustine. Jenny Jochens (1995, 2) suggests "constant inbreeding" as the cause of physical deformities. It is possible that some of the descriptions should be read in connection with medieval theological-mythological ideas on possible consequences of a violation of the abstinence regulations.

child should be brought to church and baptized and be put down in the church and left there to die.

*Both:* But every child which is born after Christmas Eve should be baptized before the preparatory fast[62] begins. If it is born during Lent, it should be baptized at Easter season. If it is born after Easter season, it should be baptized before the Feast of St John the Baptist (June 24th).[63] Every child which is born after Michaelmas (Sept. 29th) should be baptized before Christmas Eve.

The priest from whom people buy services must baptize unless he is hindered by valid excuse. If the child falls ill so fast that they cannot reach that priest, then the priest whom they may find first must baptize; no priest may refuse without being liable to a fine of three *merkr* to the bishop.

Now the child is so weak that one cannot reach a priest in time, then the men who bring the child with them shall name it, dip it into water and speak these words over it: "I baptize you N. in the name of the Father, and of the Son, and of the Holy Ghost". Then it may be buried in the outer part of the churchyard.

*Magnus:* If they cannot get water, they should baptize in whatever liquid they may find. But if they do not find any liquid they must spit in the palm of their hands and make the sign of the cross on its breast and between its shoulders.[64] And this baptism can even be performed by a woman, if a man is not available.

*Both:* Now if it is not baptized before the first time limit, a fine of three *aurar* is to be paid to the bishop, and the child should be baptized, even if it is (done) later. But if he will not let it be baptized, and keeps an unbaptized child in his house over two time limits, then he is liable to a fine of three *merkr* to the bishop and must have the child baptized. If he still refuses and keeps an unbaptized human being in his house for twelve months, then he has forfeited every penny of his property. But he may go to confession and do penance. But if he will not, they will both[65] have to leave the realm of our king.

## 22 Here King Magnus has provided permanent outlawry for a crime which King Olav made a three *merkr* case

If a man exposes his child,[66] heathen or christened, and lets it perish, and he is convicted of this, then he has forfeited peace and property, and we call that the great murder.[67]

62 Septuagesima, nine weeks before Easter.

63 Here some words seem to be missing; we should expect prescriptions about children who were born after the Feast of St John the Baptist and before Michaelmas. See the *Eiðsivaþing* Christian Law (I 8).

64 In this baptismal rite for emergency situations the chrism is replaced by spittle. These rites are basically concerned with exorcism, and the purpose is to drive out the devil and make the child ready to receive the Holy Ghost.

65 Ambiguous, either referring to the parents (so Fr. Brandt) or to the father and the child. Larson 1935, 50, note.

66 Exposure of children was forbidden a few years after the introduction of Christianity.

67 The murder of a heathen child was considered to be worse than that of a baptized child, because it was believed that a human soul was lost when a person died unbaptized. See the *Borgarþing* Christian Law (AM 78, 4to), I 3. See also TJ's comment to paragraph 22.

If a slave lets his child die, heathen or christened, then his master should have him flogged within five days or else have taken him to the king's men; and he may sell him out of the country if he wants to, and not eat together with him. But if he does, he must pay a fine of three *merkr* to the bishop.

If the bishop or his representative accuses a man of letting his child die, heathen or christened, and he (the accused person) denies (it), then he should deny (clear himself of) this murder[68] in the same way as any other (murder). If this oath fails he is outlawed. And if the bishop or his representative accuses a man of having buried a heathen child in hallowed earth and this turns out to be false when the matter is investigated, then he who brought the accusation must pay for that those three *merkr* to the bishop which he had intended the other one to pay.[69]

If a man comes as heathen to our country and says that he will go where there are priests and become baptized, then one should give him food, but let him eat alone. But if he travels past churches or priests and does not let himself be baptized, then the bishop's representative has to arrest that man and take him before the assembly; then it is well if he lets himself be baptized. If he will not, then the assembly should grant him legal protection for five days (in which) to leave the realm of our king, and no night give him food in the same place where he was the night before. If people give him food longer (than that) and eat together with him, they must pay a fine of forty *merkr* for it.

Always, when the fine for violation of Christian Law exceeds three *merkr*, the king is owed half of it, and the bishop the other half.

Every man who sits for three winters not paying his dues to the bishop or the priest[70] and disobeys the injunctions we have added for our Christianity, he will have forfeited every penny of his property.

## 23 Concerning burial in the churchyard[71]

Now the next thing is that every human being who dies shall be brought to church and buried in hallowed earth, except *údáðamenn*, traitors to the king, murderers, violators of a peace pledge,[72] and thieves, and people who commit suicide.

Those people whom I have now enumerated should be buried in the foreshore where the tide and the green sod meet.

Dead bodies may not remain in a house longer than five days except in case of emergency. If it remains longer, the one responsible must pay a fine of three *aurar* to the bishop and bring the dead body to the church. But if he will not, and leaves the corpse at home to decay, then he has forfeited every penny of his property. But

68 According to the rule in Ch. 132.

69 According to the retaliation principle (*ius talionis*, "an eye for an eye and a tooth for a tooth"), ultimately derived from the Old Testament (Exod. 21:24; Lev. 23:20; Deut. 19:21).

70 See Chs. 9 and 15.

71 Burial practices characteristic of Christian graves are: east-west oriented graves, inhumation burials, and absence of grave-goods. Sanmark, 265 and 281 with further references.

72 People violating agreement confirmed by oaths, such as reconciliation after blood revenge, disposal of land, or giving slaves their freedom. This ban was part of canonical law. Jacoby 1986, 201.

he is still entitled to go to confession and do penance. If he will not he must leave the realm of our king.

If he lives so high up in the mountains or far out among the islands that those things prevent him from bringing the dead body forward – that it is impossible to cross the sea or the mountain – then he should bring it to an outhouse and suspend it and not let it lie on the ground.

If someone buries a dead body into a mound or under a heap of stones,[73] then he has to take it up and pay a fine of three *aurar* for it to the bishop and bring the body to church and bury it in hallowed earth.

If someone falls ill and wants to send for a priest, let him send for the priest from whom he buys services;[74] and if he asks for the Extreme Unction,[75] then the priest should go to him and anoint him. *Olav:* and receive two *aurar* for the Unction. *Both:* But if he has a sudden illness and can reach another priest before (the priest from whom he buys services), then that priest should go to him and give him the Extreme Unction *Magnus:* without payment. And if he does not go, then he is liable to a fine of three *merkr* unless he is prevented by a serious hindrance or (the needs of) his parishioners, and witnesses know. He should anoint every man who paid his tithes to him and said, while he was able to speak, that he wanted to be anointed.

*Both:* If someone is dead and his heir goes to the priest and asks him to come and sing over the corpse, then he (the priest) has to go and sing that which he is obliged to. *Olav:* And for that he should receive half an *eyrir*, people call that a funeral fee.

*Both:* Now when the dead body is brought to church, then the priest should go towards it and sing over the body according to the appropriate ritual and put it into a grave *Olav:* and receive a burial fee.[76]

*Both:* But if the priest will not perform those services, then the heir of the deceased should take *Magnus:* the tithe \ *Olav:* the burial fee / and buy the chant of the Mass with it for his soul.

If the priest is not at home, one should nevertheless lay the body in earth; and when the priest comes home, they must drive a stake down to the coffin and pour hallowed water into it and he should sing funeral service over (the grave). No priest may go without necessity into the parish of another priest[77] in order to earn money. If he is identified and convicted of this, then he must pay back to the priest who is entitled to claim money there, and pay for it a fine of twelve *aurar* to the bishop.

Whenever people die and the heir wants to make an ale feast, whether he wants to make it on the seventh day or in the morning of the thirtieth day (after the funeral) or even later, people call that inheritance ale. If people give an ale feast

73 Burying a corpse in a mound was considered to be honourable in heathen times, burying under a heap of stones was not.

74 I.e. the priest in his local parish.

75 The sacrament given to dying people.

76 Payment for religious services in connection with death and burial.

77 A priest was normally not allowed to earn money from other parishes than his own.

and call it a soul's ale, they should invite the priest from whom they buy services, they should invite him with at least two others.[78] And the priest should attend the inheritance ale or the soul's ale as a matter of course, unless he is hindered. If he refuses to attend he will lose his tithe \ *Olav:* fee, / so much of it as was due for twelve months from that levy district in which the feast was given. This *Magnus:* tithe \ *Olav:* fee / should he receive who is the heir after the person for whom the banquet was given and be offered for his soul's health.

*Both:* If there are several feasts, he should go first to the one to which he was first invited and stay there the first night. And the next morning (he should go) to the second. *Both:* If there are three gatherings and he can go to them and back from them in one day, then he should bless all these feats. But if he cannot, he should go to the second feast and drink there so long as there is enough ale.[79]

## 24 Both decreed this

Now the next thing is that none of us shall ever marry his kinswoman. If a man is identified and convicted of having a wife more closely related than the law allows, then he is liable to a fine of three *merkr* to the bishop and must dismiss that wife and go to confession and do penance. We are allowed to marry our kinswomen in the seventh knee and the seventh degree (of kinship). And those other women who are widows[80] of our kinsmen, in the fifth knee and fifth degree. Likewise those women who are related to each other, the wife he had before and the one he marries.

If a man takes a wife more closely related than those whom I have now indicated, *Magnus:* or takes the wife of another man or a wife in addition to the one he has already, *Both:* then he is liable to a fine of three *merkr* to the bishop and must dismiss that wife and go to confession and do penance. If he will not they must both leave the realm of our king. If the bishop or his representative accuses a man of having a wife more closely related to him than the law allows, and he denies (it), he may refute it with a three-man oath.

There are other women who should be even more highly respected by us, whom we commit a crime against if we become intimate with them. Now the first is a man's mother, the second (his) sister, the third (his) daughter, the fourth (his) stepmother, the fifth his daughter-in-law, the sixth (his) brother's wife, the seventh (his) son's daughter, and all those other women to whom one is equally closely related, whom men happen to commit crimes against. *Magnus:* These are (those who are equally closely related) stepdaughters, a brothers' daughters, a sisters'

78 According to the *Eiðsivaþing* Christian Law (I 49) the priest and his wife should be invited, and a third person (probably the deacon). The priest was supposed to sit in the high seat, and his wife beside him.

79 This law makes it clear that the initiatives to these ale feasts were taken by the population, which strongly suggests that these gatherings belonged to pre-Christian traditions. Sanmark 2004, 213.

80 The original has *frændkonur* ('kinswomen'), which seems to be an error. What is meant is probably *frændleifar* ('widows of kinsmen'). Hertzberg 1895, 212.

daughters and a daughter's daughters, the mother's mother and the father's sisters, the mother's sisters and the father's mother and the sister of a man's wife.

*Both:* But if someone is identified and convicted of having slept with a women that closely related to him, then he is outlawed together with that woman, and they must leave the realm of our king. *Magnus:* until they have done such penance as the bishop instructs them to, *Both:* and have forfeited every penny of their property both in land and movables, the king is owed half of it, and the bishop the other half, *Magnus:* unless the king or the bishop wants to mitigate (the punishment) when they come home again.

*Both:* If the bishop or his representative accuses someone of having committed that crime, and he denies (it), let him refute it with a six-man oath.[81] Twelve men of his own rank[82] should be appointed; he has to choose one of them, and he himself should be the second, and the third his nearest kinsman, and three who can be held to account for pledge and promise[83] in our language. That oath must be taken in front of the church door. If that oath fails,[84] then he is guilty of that crime. *Magnus:* But even if the oaths fail he may be allowed to prove his innocence with trial by ordeal before he is finally (judged) guilty. *Both:* And every man who undergoes trial by ordeal (from guilt), whether by taking oaths or going to trial by ordeal, and is found guilty, is entitled to legal protection from the church door for five days.

## 25 That a man shall have one wife only

Now the next thing is that each of us shall have only one wife, whom he has bought with the bride-price and according to agreement. But if he buys the bride-price for two women, then he has to dismiss the woman whom he bought last and pay a fine of three *merkr* to the bishop and go to confession and do penance. But the child which he begets with the woman he took last, should inherit from no man except from his freedman[85] only. If he will not dismiss that woman he took last, they must both leave the realm of our king and they will have forfeited every penny of their property.

If a man has a female slave beside his wife and keeps her in his house as a concubine, or any mistress he may keep beside his wife; if he is identified and convicted of this, then he must pay a fine of twelve *aurar* to the bishop and go to confession and do penance and he has to dismiss that wife.

## 26 Concerning spiritual kinship

There are six kinds of spiritual kinship which we should respect as highly as we do our kinswomen. Now the first is the one who holds the child when it receives

81 Cf. Ch. 133.

82 I.e. of the same social standing.

83 I.e. persons of age.

84 I.e. is not taken or taken in an incorrect way.

85 A slave who has been given his freedom by his master. See Ch. 4.

the sign of the cross,[86] the second the one who lifts it up from the (baptismal) water, the third the one who takes it out of the white robe,[87] the fourth the one who holds it under the bishop's hand (at confirmation),[88] the fifth the one who loosens the ribbon (worn at confirmation),[89] the sixth the one who leads the mother into the church.[90] In this last case there is such kinship between the priest and the woman only, but in all the other five cases there is the same spiritual kinship with the father and the mother as with the child.

If anyone is identified and convicted of having his spiritual kinswoman (as his wife), then he must pay a fine of three *merkr* to the bishop and dismiss the woman and go to confession and do penance.

## 27 Concerning weddings[91]

Wives are to be taken at proper and not at improper times. But if a man buys a wife with bride-price and according to agreement at an improper time, or at times when the bishop has forbidden us to take wives, (that is) the night before Sunday or Friday or Wednesday, or those nights when fast-days follow the next morning, or holy day or preparatory fast, (that is) the three weeks before the Feast of St John the Baptist (June 24th) and the three weeks before Michaelmas (Sept. 29th) and the three weeks before Christmas *Magnus:* \ *Olav:* / and in the thirteen Christmas days; if a man takes himself a wife on any of those days that I have now enumerated, then he has to pay a fine of three *aurar* to the bishop. But if he takes himself a wife during Lent, those nine weeks when the bishop observes the fast, and in the Easter week, which is the tenth (week), he must pay three *merkr* to the bishop.

## 28 Concerning soothsaying and incantations[92]

Now the next thing is that we are not to pay attention to soothsaying, incantations[93] or wicked sorcery.

Whoever is identified and convicted of soothsaying and telling fortunes, he is an outlaw and he is not entitled to legal protection; and he forfeits every penny of his property, half of it goes to the king, and the other half to the bishop.

Any man who pays attention to soothsaying and is found guilty of this, he has to pay a fine of forty *merkr*, half of it goes to the king, the other half to the bishop.

Other men who practice sorcery and witchcraft and are identified and convicted of this, they must leave the realm of our king.

86 The *prima signatio*, ON *prímsigning*, took place immediately before baptism.
87 It was supposed to be taken off one week after baptism.
88 It was the duty of the bishop to perform confirmation.
89 The white ribbon worn across the forehead to protect the holy oil. It should be taken off and burnt three days after confirmation.
90 The first time a woman comes to the church after having given birth to a child.
91 On the following restrictions see also Steinsland 2005, 439.
92 Landro 2010, 228–9.
93 ON *galdrar*, derived from the verb *gala*, 'scream with a loud voice', esp. when performing sorcery.

Men should not indulge in such practices. If they do, they have forfeited every penny of their property; but they may be allowed to go to confession and do penance.

If the bishop or his representative alleges that a man practices soothsaying or incantation or sorcery, but he denies (it), then there are certain fixed ways of doing this (i.e. denying).[94]

If a man is accused of practicing soothsaying, (then he may) deny (it) with a six-man oath. Twelve men of his own rank[95] should be appointed, among these twelve men he should choose one, he himself should be the second, the third his nearest kinsman, and (in addition) three who can be held to account for pledge and promise;[96] (that oath) leads to outlawry if it fails.

*Magnus:* But if a man is identified and convicted of having sworn a false oath and takes other men with him (into perjury) then he is liable to a fine of fifteen *merkr*, and three *merkr* for each of those who swore with him, if they did not know it was perjury. But if they knew before swearing, then each of them must pay a fine of fifteen *merkr* just as he himself.

*Both:* If a woman[97] is accused of practicing incantations and witchcraft, then six women should be appointed, housewives whom people know to be good, three to each side of her, they should bear witness that she knows neither incantations nor sorcery. If that testimony fails her, then it leads to outlawry, and then the king is owed half of her property and the bishop the other half. And her heir must bring her out of the realm of our king. [*NRA 1 B, AM 146 4to, and AM 78 4to add:* If a woman is accused of being a witch or a man-eater, then that should be pronounced against her from three houses,[98] after having been rumoured in the district. If she is found guilty, she must be taken out to sea and executed by an axeblow to her back. But if she denies (it), then she should claim trial by ordeal, (let a priest) bless water and cauldron, and she must put her hand in it. Then it is good if she is cleansed (from guilt). If a man speaks against her from a house, calling her a witch and man-eater, then that is slander and gossip.[99] If she is cleansed from that, then he (who accused her) shall put his feet where he wanted hers to be.]

## 29 Concerning sacrifices

Sacrifices are also forbidden to us; we are not allowed to worship any heathen god, or (to do so on) burial mounds[100] or (with) stone altars.[101] If a man is identified and

94 There were different rules for men and women in cases of sorcery. For men a six-man oath was required, for women the decision of a commission was required.
95 See note 82.
96 See note 83.
97 Women were more severely punished for practicing sorcery than men.
98 If this was done, the matter was considered to be known throughout the local community.
99 On the punishment for slander (ON *róg*) see Ch. 137.
100 They were associated with ancestral worship and considered heathen.
101 The meaning of the term *hǫrgr* is not entirely clear and has probably changed over time. It seems to have been used to denote cultic objects of stone as well as of wood. Sanmark 2004, 167, 174, and 175 with further references.

convicted of this [*NRA 1 B, AM 146 4to and AM 78 4to add:* that he builds burial mounds or houses and calls them stone altars, or he raises a pole and calls it libel pole,[102] whatever he does of this kind, he has to pay a fine of three *merkr* to the bishop and go to confession and do penance], then he has forfeited every penny of his property; he should go to confession and do penance. If he will not, he must leave the realm of our king.

## 30 Concerning *údáðamenn*

All evil deeds[103] are forbidden; none of us may have sexual intercourse with cattle. And if a man is identified and convicted of this, then he should be castrated. *Both:* and he must leave the realm of our king as an evildoer and never come back. *Magnus:* The officials who have their districts there, both on behalf of the king and on behalf of the bishop, they should have him castrated. *Both:* But the man who owns the cattle must drive it into the sea and make no further use of it.[104] If he does, he must pay a fine of three *merkr* to the bishop.

If the bishop or his representative accuses a man of having sexual intercourse with cattle, and he denies (it), then the bishop's representative should go home to him and summon him before the assembly for that evil deed; if he offers (to clear himself) [*NRA 1 B: Magnus:* with a six-man oath, *Olav:* a three-man oath], *Both:* he must have taken that (oath) within ten weeks of oath days, because there is a deadline for all oaths taken according to the laws.

In taking these oaths one should proceed in the following way: One must go home to the man who is to witness that the oath is taken and notify him to appear after five nights at the church where he will take the oath. Then it is well if the other goes there (to that church) and hears him take the oath. But if the other does not go, then he should take that oath with a witness present. [*NRA 1 B adds: Olav:* And he should appoint two men . . . he himself be the third, those two men must be impartial,[105] one . . . who can be held to account for pledge and promise. *Both:*] He should take that oath in front of the church door, lay a gospel-book on the threshold and take the book up from the threshold, then it is well if he takes the oath in the proper way. If that oath fails him, he is an outlaw and deprived of all personal rights; (but) he may be legally protected for five days after he leaves the church door.

102 The most famous example of this special form of insult can be found in *Egils saga Skallagrímsonar* (Ch. 57), in the description of Egil raising a libel pole against King Eric Bloodaxe and Queen Gunnhild.

103 Cf. Lev. 18:23 and 29; 20:15 and 16.

104 This may have been an attempt to prevent the spread of pollution. The overriding aim of the biblical food regulations in Norway seems to have been the prevention of ill health. Sanmark 2004, 226. See also TJ's comment to paragraph 30.

105 ON *valinkunnr*, 'from a chosen family', i.e. not related by kinship to either party; the word may also mean 'independent; highly respected'.

In this way all oaths should be taken which are offered (to refute charges) in case of violations of our Christian Law.

## 31 Concerning *svidda*[106] and forbidden food[107]

. . . [108] is also forbidden for us to eat. If a man is identified and convicted of having eaten meat of animals that have died in this way, then he must pay a fine of three *aurar* to the bishop and go to confession and do penance.

We speak about animals having died of themselves when no one knows what caused their death. But people (may) eat that which wolves bite and kill. People (may) also eat that which the bear strikes or dogs bite. People (may) also eat that which drowns in running water, falls down from mountains, and that which is strangled by the halter. It goes for all flesh of animals having died in this way, that salt and water should be blessed and sprinkled on the meat, and it should then be hung up until the blood dries up. It is allowed to sell (the skin) and divide the money such that the owner keeps half of it himself, but for the other half he has to buy wax (for candles) and send it to the church from which he buys services.

## 32 Magnus made this new provision[109]

All men who violate pledges of peace and security[110] given between people in cases of killing, they are *úbótamenn* having forfeited their rights to peace and property, land and movables, odal-land as well as other land.

Those men who are killed as thieves and robbers, whether they plunder on ships or on land, and also (those who are killed) for murder and sorcery or for sitting out at night to call forth trolls and thus promote heathen worship, and those men

106 Etymologically, it can be translated 'self-dead', which probably indicates 'dead by disease'. The word may be normalized *svídái*, see Hertzberg 1895, 621; Noreen 1970, 100 (§ 110.3, Anm. 4). More important historically is the explanation given in this chapter: "animals having died of themselves when no one knows what caused their death". In the *Borgarþing* law (I 5) the term is defined as "not killed by the works of the human hand", and consequently forbidden to eat.

107 The penitential handbooks from the early Middle Ages and the more comprehensive Canon Law collections from the 11th century onwards pervade with dietary regulations inspired by Mosaic law. The issue was dealt with at the so-called Council of Jerusalem (Acts 15), where the Old Testament regulations were confirmed. Augustin considered these regulations as temporary, with no binding force for later generations of Christian. The only important thing was to know the cause of the animal's death, to be sure not to eat animals dead by disease. This interpretation is found both in the *Gulaþing* Law and in the Icelandic *Grágás*. Apart from biblical traditions these regulations are likely to have been used as a measure to stop non-Christian ritual feasting. Sanmark 2004, 217, 221 with further references. See also TJ's comments to paragraphs 20 and 31.

108 In the MS. only part of an M is legible. A conjecture takes it to be the first letter of *'*mortit*' from Lat *morticinus* 'dead by accident or disease'. Hertzberg 1895, 453; Jacoby 1986, 201–2.

109 It seems to have been an attempt to secure domestic peace, esp. to reduce the extent of blood vengeance. A partly similar provision may be found in the *Frostuþing* law.

110 This is the subject of Ch. 320.

who make themselves hired bandits[111] to kill people against whom they have no charges and take money for it, except (for being men whom) the king lets be punished for the purpose of peace and cleansing the country for miscreants.[112]

And likewise those men who take women by force or (carry off) other men's women or betrothed women, or people's daughters without the consent of those who are entitled to make decisions about their marriage, or without their own (consent), no matter how their wishes are later when marriage is decided upon; and likewise those who take revenge on these *úbótamenn* or claim compensation from them, if witnesses know, they are all *úbótamenn* having forfeited peace and property, land and movables; but those who protect their property and kinswomen against them are protected by the law. All the others are not liable to wergild, whether they are hurt or killed, to the king or to the kinsfolk.

All courts which are to be established in cases of killing[113] and adultery for those women whom we are legally entitled to defend and revenge,[114] they must all be set according to the law and legal protection granted until the first day of payment (of compensation).

And whoever disregards lawful judgement[115] before payment day or on the first payment day without compelling reason, he loses legal protection, and he is a violator of peace pledge and has forfeited his right to peace and property.

That is compelling reason if a man is ill or wounded or has such serious reasons, as good men testify, that he could not be present.

The first instalment[116] (of compensation) should be paid within the same month and be brought home to him (who is to receive it) and offered to him in front of two witnesses. And the other should receive it, or someone who represents him, unless he who is to receive it wants to make it easier for the other (who is to pay).

In all other cases[117] where people establish courts (to judge) between them, then he who disregards the judgement is liable to a fine of eighteen *aurar* to the plaintiff – and he should respect the judgement as before – and fifteen *merkr* to the king; and the king or the sheriffs should claim it on behalf of both, the other (the plaintiff) should first be paid his dues according as the court has decided.

111 Persons who were paid to commit murder, enticed with money like fishes with flies (hence *flugumenn*).

112 A papal decree from Alexander III to the Archbishop of Nidaros and his suffragan bishops stated that murderers should do penance for at least seven years, except when they killed lawfully, i.e. having been instructed by the king to do so in order to promote justice (*pro iusticia facienda*).

113 Courts consisting of twelve men, six from either party, whose purpose it was to achieve conciliation (hence the term *sættardómr*), stipulate the compensation and the time for payment. Sunde 2007, 316–20.

114 See Ch. 160.

115 I.e. that the compensation is not paid in due time.

116 In Skåne (now part of SW Sweden, then part of Denmark), compensation for murder was to be paid in three instalments with an interval of four months. The first instalment was to be paid by the killer himself; he was allowed to demand the second from his father's side and the third from his mother's side. Wührer 1966b, 331.

117 This refers to private courts of arbitration.

The compensation to both should be distributed in proportion to the value of the property.

But if he will not respect the judgement, the sheriffs must summon him before the assembly and declare him an outlaw unless he pays what the court has decided.

If a man comes to terms with him who has slept with his wife, then he who has the wife should assure (that the agreement is kept). But if the other sleeps with the wife of the former a second time, then he is a violator of peace pledge just as much as he who kills after agreement (of good terms) has been made.

If a man kills his son, or a son his father, whether he is a Christian or a heathen, or (if he kills) his mother, or brother, or daughter, or sister, then he is an *úbótamaðr*, as provided above,[118] unless he is insane, and people know that he is out of his wits.

If two men have sexual intercourse[119] and are identified and convicted of this, then they are both *úbótamenn*. And if they deny (it) while it is still rumoured in the district, let them confirm their denial by carrying hot iron. But if they are found guilty, then the king is owed half of their property, and the bishop the other half.

If people fight in church or in a consecrated churchyard, then they are *úbótamenn*; and the bishop should have three *merkr* for it and (in addition) what is needed for the churchyard, and the king the rest; but if there is not more left in the property (than that which is paid to the bishop for re-consecration of the churchyard), then the king and the bishop must divide it in two equal parts (each taking one half), unless they want to show greater mercy to them (the *úbotamenn*).

If a man has been declared an *úbótamaðr*, and the plaintiff has neither the power nor the knowledge to summon him by sending forth the arrows,[120] he is nevertheless an *úbótamaðr*.

## 33 Concerning saddle horses[121] for the bishop

Now the next thing is that when the bishop goes ashore from his ship in order to consecrate a church or provide other services to people, whether he goes a long or a short distance, then the householders should provide him with eighteen saddle horses, but thirty if he goes to consecrate a primary church (*fylkis* church). If they will not provide him with saddle horses, every one (of those who refuse to do so) is liable to a fine of three *aurar*.

If the bishop or his representative charges someone with having done something inappropriate, by violating some part of the Christian Law, for which the bishop is entitled to a fine, and he (the accused) denies (it), then the bishop's representative should go home to him and take those two of his neighbours who live nearest to him (as witnesses), then it is well if they are willing to follow him. If

118 See the older provision in Ch. 164.
119 Cf. Lev. 18:22 and 29. See TJ's comment to paragraph 32.
120 The message stick was formed like an arrow.
121 Cf. Chs. 11 and 14.

they refuse, he has to call on them formally (to follow), then they are each liable to a fine of three *aurar* to the king's representative. But he (the bishop's representative) should himself find witnesses and go to the house of the other one (the accused) and summon him before the assembly for this case and charge him there. He (the accused) should defend himself by swearing a three-man oath. But if he will not comply with the law or come to the assembly, then he is liable to a fine of twelve *aurar* to the king's representative. Our bishop and his representative and all priests must bring their legal actions in the way that I have now told.

## The Gulathing law in a theological and church history perspective. A commentary essay by Torstein Jørgensen

### Some general observations

When Christianity first gained a foothold in the Nordic countries it arrived as a powerful factor of change which on the one hand caused quite immediate effects and on the other initiated a gradual and long-lasting process of alteration. One of the contexts in which the new impulses, at a quite early stage, left visible traces for later times to investigate were the Christianity "books"[1] to be found in the early provincial Scandinavian laws. There is every indication that the different Scandinavian regions had their own more or less independent legal practice, shaped by tradition from pre-Christian times, although the contents and provenance of these practices remain blurred behind a lack of historical evidence. Still, when looking more closely at the preserved texts of the laws mentioned, these appear in a number of respects as a juxtaposition of indigenous traditions and foreign impulses, within which the imprints of the then current ecclesiastical ideas from abroad are especially visible.[2] There can be no doubt that the texts on the latter point bear the mark of the hands of some qualified theological expertise, reflecting the status of international theological learning at the time.

In this commentary essay we will take a closer look at how the formation of the Norwegian Gulathing Law had its *Sitz im Leben* in one of the 11th and 12th century missionary frontiers of Western Christendom. A principal question to be asked therefore is to what extent and on which particular points the Christianity Book of this law reflects the current ecclesiastical ideas of how to spread Christianity into new territory and to transform this country into a Christian society in line with the rest of Western Christendom.

The preserved text of the Gulathing Law reveals two stages of the formation of the text, i.e. the Olav provisions, referring to the promulgations allegedly agreed upon by King Olav Haraldsson the Saint (1015–30) and his missionary bishop, Grimkjell, at the council of Moster in 1024 or 1022,[3] and the Magnus provisions added by King Magnus Erlingsson (1161–84) in agreement with

1 In the vernacular of Old Norse: *kristindómsbelkir*.

2 For the discussion about provenance, influence from the British Isles and the continent see Knut Helle, *Gulatinget og Gulatingslova*, Leikanger: Skald, 2001, 23–47; *How Nordic are the Nordic Medieval Laws?* Ditlev Tamm and Helle Vogt (eds.), Copenhagen: Copenhagen University Press, 2005; Torgeir Landro, *Kristenrett og kyrkjerett: Borgartingskristenretten i eit komparativt perspektiv*, PhD dissertation, Bergen: University of Bergen, 2010, 11–14, 187–209, 227–29; Sverre Bagge, *From Viking Stronghold to Christian Kingdom: State Formation in Norway c. 900–1350*, Copenhagen: Museum Tusculanum Press, 2010, 179–82, 195–202.

3 See G 10 and 15: "The next thing is that we shall maintain all those churches and observe those decrees about Christianity which Holy Olav and Bishop Grimkjell laid down at the Moster assembly".

Archbishop Øystein Erlendsson and Earl Erling Ormsson the crooked.[4] This means that the period during which this law was formulated covers a timespan of at least 150 years.

In this period Norway saw a development from a newly planted mission church within a largely pagan environment into a well-developed church organization in line with contemporary churches in the rest of north-western Europe in a setting which defined itself as Christian. The different stages of this process are in several places indicated *expressis verbis* in the text but it is difficult to determine exactly when the different provisions became part of the law. More specifically, it is impossible to say anything more particular about the extent to which the practices and ideas mentioned in the law gained ground in the actual conduct of the people, let alone their minds. Yet we can assume that this has taken place as a gradual process which must have gone on over a longer period of time. However, without some degree of internalization into the ways of thinking and beliefs of the majority of those involved, the new Christian Law codes would hardly have achieved the status they did and become as widespread as they actually were. The measures for the conversion of souls as prescribed in the law are, however, not to be interpreted in terms of modern ideas of individual choice. Conversion to and adaptation of new beliefs and ethos was basically an object of collective processes and decisions. But collective units consist of individuals, and for collective internalization of new ideas to take place individual involvement is always a part of the process.

We have few surviving documents from the Church specifically focusing upon its possible mission strategy on the Christianization of Scandinavia, or about the principles of the new Christian societal order to be established in these lands.[5] The closest we come to this seems, as far as Norway is concerned, to be the texts of the books on Christianity in the provincial laws. In an indirect way these texts display interesting aspects of and glimpses into what elements the 11th and 12th century Church regarded as essential in the formation of Norway as a Christian kingdom.

Although our main focus here will be on the Gulathing Law we will on some points make side glances at relevant paragraphs in the three other Norwegian provincial laws – the Frostathing, the Borgarthing and the Eidsivathing laws, for comparison and complementary perspectives. We will also take into account some texts and studies about similar processes on the continent and the British Isles from earlier periods, more for the detection of parallels in content rather than explicit causal connection, which is difficult to prove.

One important aspect to note is that at the stage when Christianity was introduced in Norway on a more formal basis it was implemented as a joint effort by King and Church in close collaboration.[6] On this point the Norwegian process of law formation seems to have been in perfect line with similar processes

4 G 2.

5 From a wider spectrum of different sources one can, however, derive more general ideas and conclusions about missionary motives, methods, and strategies. Tveito 2004.

6 Bagge 2010, 195–202.

elsewhere in Central Europe, Britain, and the rest of Scandinavia.[7] The new laws were, however, to be resolved by the assemblies of a regional *þing*.[8] A disputed matter has been about what kind of role the leading local representatives and householders having full legal rights[9] played in these regional processes of law formation. Whereas earlier research tended to emphasize the influence of local people, recent studies have – in our mind convincingly – argued that the dominant powers behind these laws were those of the Crown and the Church.[10] In this essay, in which our commission is to look at the Christianity book of the Gulathing Law in a theological and church history perspective, a main focus will therefore be on the traces of traditional and contemporary ecclesiastical thinking and strategies. Among the very few surviving texts that document direct contact between the papacy and Norwegian kings in the 11th century, a papal diploma from Pope Gregory VII to King Olav Kyrre from 1078 gives some evidence about the process of increased central ecclesiastical impact from the papacy itself on Norwegian legislation in this particular period. In this letter the pope, by addressing the king as "you who live in the outskirts of the world . . . have fewer men to teach you the Christian religion", asks the king to "send some young and noble men from your country to the Apostolic See that they, under the wings of the apostles Peter and Paul, in a proper way can be taught the holy and divine laws" so that after their training these men can "preach to you what is required in the order of Christianity".[11] The letter gives an indication on how the contemporary Gregorian ambitions during the period of the investiture controversy and the contemporary impetus on Canon Law in learned centres like Bologna and Paris from this time onwards put their marks also on the distant North.[12] And it gives a likely picture of how learned ecclesiastical personnel, some after direct contact with the papal curia, some after studies at ecclesiastical centres abroad, had a hand in the Norwegian legislation process in the period.

7 Archbishop Wulfstan of York (c. 950–1023), for instance, is known as a prominent author of law texts. Abbot Ælfric of Eynsham (c. 950–1010) also played an important, but more indirect role in the shaping of society in accordance with Christian norms. Inka Moilanen, *Writing the Order: Religious-Political Discourses in Late Anglo-Saxon England*, PhD dissertation, Bergen: University of Bergen, 2011, 95–106, 153–243. For wider parallels on the continent see Patrick Wormald, *Legal Culture in the Medieval West: Law as Text, Image and Experience*, London: Hambledon Press, 1999, 32. On Visigothic law see Lynch 1938, 137–40; and on Bavarian law see Eckhardt 1927, 56–68.

8 See Glossary s.v. Assembly.

9 The vernacular term *bóndi* was a householder of a certain rank with full legal rights, in Norway mostly a landowner and free farmer.

10 Landro 2010, 23–4, 210–26.

11 DN 6. No 1. The original Latin text goes as follows:

> de uobis tamen qui quasi inextremo orbe terrarum positi estis . . . quanto uos eorum qui in christiana religione uos instruant . . . rogamus uos sicut et regi Danorum denuntiauimus ut de iuonioribus et nobilibus terrę uestrę ad apostolicam aulam mittatis. quatenus sub alis apostolorum Petri et Pauli sacris ac diuinis legibus diligenter edocti, apostolicę sedis aduos mandata referre, non quasi ignoti sed cognati et Christianę religionis ordo postulauerit apud uos non quasi rudes aut ignari sed lingua ac scientia moribusque prudentes digne deo predicare.

12 Sigurðsson et al. 2008, 37–60.

Each of the four Norwegian laws mentioned was in force only in the area belonging to the respective provincial assemblies. As a consequence, some variations in the status of the law continued to exist between the regions even after Norway was united into one kingdom. The joint enterprise of King and Church took place on what in modern terms can be described as a national level. The best and earliest evidence of such an initiative is the already mentioned event of the so-called Mostra-thing in the year 1024 (or 1022). For this, according to the sources, King Olav Haraldsson, Bishop Grimkjell, and other leading men of the realm met at Moster on the south-western Norwegian island of Bømlo (which was not a location of a traditional *þing*), holding something that may have been a preparatory meeting, where they agreed on some basic principles for the new Christian order of society. These were again to be presented to the proper provincial assemblies.[13] However, the actual references in the preserved text of the Gulathing Law to provisions made by King Olav and Grimkjell at Moster can only with considerable reservations be taken as historical.[14] The important point to note for us here is that the texts of the four laws give a general impression of a harmonious relation between King and Church at the stage when these laws were developed, which stands in contrast to the later conflict between *sacerdotium* and *regnum*, and to the bitter and long-lasting tension between royal and ecclesiastical power regarding the making of a common law for all Norway, and the inclusion of church matters in this law, during the last decades of the 13th century onwards.[15]

As the following investigation will show, the endeavour of Christianizing Norway, as elsewhere, can broadly speaking be described as a threefold task:

- Conversion of souls.
- Formation of society in accordance with Christian ideals and norms.
- Clearing and cleaning new land of pagan practices as part of a geographical and spiritual incorporation of these lands into the territory of Christendom.

And, it was a task in which both Church and King had a common interest. As we will see in the following both are referred to as executors of church law. As a general rule fines up to 3 *merkr* for minor violations of the law should accrue to the bishop, whereas fines for more severe crimes exceeding that amount should be shared half-and-half between bishop and king.[16]

13 Birkeli 1995, 165–7.

14 For the discussion on this matter see Landro 2010, 189–91.

15 King Magnus the Law-Mender's Law of the Realm was approved by the four provincial assemblies 1274–76, and an agreement between King and Church on the demarcation line between royal and ecclesiastical jurisdiction was concluded in 1277, stated in the *Compositio Tunsbergensis*. For the research history on the latter document: Seip 1942; Sandvik 1986, 563–85; Riisøy 2004; Hamre 2003, 381–431; Orrman 2003, 446–7, 451; Bagge 2010, 297–316; Jørgensen 2013a, 209–36.

16 G 22.

## *The law and conversion of souls*

In its radical form conversion includes a basically new life orientation. The sociologist and theologian Peter L. Berger explains the phenomenon of conversion as a process in which the appearance of *new plausibility structures* is a crucial element.[17] By this term Berger implies a situation in which new existential questions appear on the horizon, to which the old schemes of explanation fall short of giving meaningful answers. In such a situation the human mind is generally open to adopt new outlooks on life, new beliefs and new standards of behaviour. To what extent this applied to the change of religion that took place in Norway in the early Middle Ages is difficult to say. Sources dealing more explicitly with the inner conviction of groups or individuals involved in the process are almost non-existent.[18] There is no doubt, however, that some of the passages of the laws mentioned do have a focus on the issue of conversion, that is on the transition to and adaptation of new religious beliefs and practices. The more detailed doctrinal content of the new beliefs was, of course, primarily a topic of internal church documents. Nevertheless, on a number of points the different sections of the law on church and religion certainly do reflect current theology adapted to individual and social practice.

## *The formation of a new Christian society*

The provisions of the Christian book of the Gulathing Law consist mainly of more or less detailed instructions about the conduct of a Christian life. These were supposed to be followed by individuals as well as by the people as a whole and they appear in this way as a strong formative power of a Christian society.[19] The law included promulgations about a new organizational order of the week and year with the observance of Sundays and feasts with rituals, liturgies, prayers, and regular participation in the Holy Communion, fasting and food, new procedures for dealing with the dying and the dead, tithes and duties for the support of priests and maintenance of churches and churchyards. Further the law contained new regulations for sex and marriage in regard to accepted and prohibited degrees of consanguinity and affinity and in regard to accepted and prohibited periods for the contraction of marriage and sex to take place. And they present a new religious understanding of oaths and testimonies including the practice of priests to consecrate the divine judgement of the ordeals of carrying hot iron or putting hands in boiling water.

17 Berger 1969.

18 Some glimpses of the actual beliefs of people in the period of religious transition can probably be found in some of the oldest skaldic poems, such as a so-called *lausvise* by Hallfred Vandrædaskald, who allegedly operated at the time of King Olav Tryggvason 950–1000. For a modern Norwegian translation of the poem see *Gjør døren høy: Kirken i Norge 1000 år*, Torstein Jørgensen, Ingunn Montgomery, and Jan Schumacher (eds.), Oslo: Aschehoug, 1995, 18.

19 For parallels on the British Isles regarding the legislation of Ælfric of Eynsham and Wulfstan of York see Moilanen 2011.

As we will see in the following, the law on a number of points provides clear evidence of learned personnel acquainted with contemporary theology and ecclesiastical legislation having taken part in the process. There are, however, no explicit references whatsoever in the text of the law either to particular passages from the Bible, to theological works, or to foreign laws. The only references one can find to foreign church legislation are of an indirect and general nature, in formulations such as "violating articles of Christian Law",[20] which are probably to be read as an allusion to Canon Law. As our analysis of the different articles will show, some learned level of knowledge to the Bible, to current theology and to foreign legislation is indirectly reflected in the text.

When it comes to allusions to the Bible in the Gulathing Law these include both the Old and the New Testament, but there is a difference between the two that we need to note. Whereas the laws of the Old Testament had their historical context in the state of old Israel, with the aim of forming a theocratic society in accordance with religious and divine norms, the community of the Church, which was the context of the New Testament, was of a different and more spiritual kind, consisting of believers in the Christian faith regardless of political citizenship or ethnic background. Thus, the parallelism of the Nordic provincial laws was in many ways closer to the historical setting of the Old Testament than to that of the New Testament in the fact that they were meant to form a civil-religious society under a common king, *in casu* a Christian kingdom.[21]

### *The law as a clearing of new Christian land*

One aspect closely related to that of the law as a main factor in the formation of a Christian society is the territorial dimension of this expansion as it was looked upon in theological terms. This has hardly been in focus in studies on the Christianization of Scandinavia, but to some extent the aspect has been touched upon in scholarly works on Christian missions elsewhere in Western Europe such as the Carolingian Empire and the British Isles and Ireland. The main perspective is that of a conquest of new land under a Christian sovereign and under the divine protection of the Christian God together with a total eradication of pagan cult and practices. Thus, the Carolingian emperors referred to their subjects within their

20 "[M]isgort einnhvern lut i kristins doms brote", G 33.

21 For a similar observation regarding the biblical background of English legislation see Wormald 1999, 32:

> The Bible was the law book of the heavenly kingdom, and Christ was of course regularly depicted as a judge holding a book. Moreover, the Bible contained, in the Pentateuch, what King Alfred called "seo æ (*The* Law)", the model legislation which Moses had derived from God. Thus barbarian *lex scripta* could emulate Moses, could testify to the new status of kings as Christian rulers, and could identify their subjects as another holy people like the Israelites.

lands as "fideles dei et nostri", and a common term for Christendom was "populus Christi".[22] The focus on land also applies to Irish laws and jurisdiction.[23]

It seems that this aspect was motivated by an Old Testament rather than a New Testament idea about people and land.[24] A fundamental element in the Old Testament understanding of land was that of the covenant between God and the people of Israel, selected by God among all peoples on earth, and for whom a chosen land was granted. On this very land and among this people the Kingdom of God on earth was understood to be realized as expressed in the Pentateuch, especially Deuteronomy 12–26, Leviticus 17–26 and the so-called Book of Covenant in Exodus 21–23. However, by the turn of the first millennium Western Christianity, infiltrated as it was in political processes and structures, displayed a similar idea about itself, that is as the chosen people of the new covenant. When studying Western legislation of the time it is difficult not to read this too as some kind of a resonance of the Old Testament legislation about the Jewish land as the place for a cultic union between God and his chosen people void of heathen elements.[25] On this point Norwegian law also fits into the general pattern.

## Comments to relevant paragraphs

In the following, we will make our comments on the different provisions (chapters) of the Christianity Book of the Gulathing Law in the order they occur in the text. We will omit paragraphs with little theological relevance.

### *The beginning of the law and bowing to the East*

The opening words of the very first provision of the Gulathing Law read:

> That is the beginning of our laws that we should bow to the east and pray to the holy Christ for good harvest and peace, that we may retain our settled land and keep our liege lord in health. Let him be friend to us, and we to him. And let God be a friend to all.[26]

A unified people paying reverence to the one true God in loyalty to the ruling king summarizes in brief the essence of the idea of a Christian kingdom in the medieval West. Thus, apart from the statutory promulgation on bowing to the east the introductory words of the Gulathing Law appear as an echo of the previously

22 For the two terms see: Reinhold Schneider, 'Karl der Grosse – politisches Sendungsbewusstsein und Mission', in *Kirchengeschichte als Missionsgeschichte* II, H. Frohnes, H.-W. Gensichen, and G. Kretschmer (eds.), *Die Kirche des früheren Mittelalter, Erster Halbband*, Munich: Chr. Kaiser Verlag, 1978, 228, 235; Steinen 1932, 207–80.

23 Corráin et al. 1984, 382–438, especially 394–400.

24 Rieber 1949, 99–166; Douglas 1966/2002, 2002; Hardinge 1972.

25 Wormald 1999, 75–6.

26 G 1.

mentioned reference by Carolingian emperors to the people as *fideles dei et nostri*, and also as a variant of similar introductory formulations in English and other Scandinavian laws.[27] This theological and legal relation between God, monarch, and people laid the foundation for a most beneficial alliance between King and Church in their joint enterprise of organizing bigger kingdoms.

It is of great interest to note that a decree to bow to the east is found at the very beginning of this law. This can be understood in no other way but as a declaration that the Norwegian people submit to "Holy Christ", whose glory comes from the east, as the supreme lord.

A more advanced understanding of the theological symbolism embedded in the concept of the east was probably something that was confined to the clergy and to the better oriented among the laity. At the point of time when this motif was included into Nordic laws,[28] however, the idea of the east had a long tradition throughout the history of the Church with roots all the way back to the Old Testament. According to the Old Testament the east is the cardinal direction from which God's glory comes.[29] Accordingly, the expectation of the coming of Messiah included the perspective of his appearing from the east. Thus the temple in Jerusalem was built in an east-west direction from the Temple Square towards the Mount of Olives.

During the time of the Ancient Church and early Middle Ages, baptism rituals, in accordance with this basic biblical idea, instructed the catechumens first to renounce the devil by turning to the west and then, by turning to the east, profess their faith in Christ. An excerpt from the Byzantine rite shows this very illustratively:

> after this he [the priest] says to them [the baptism candidates]: Turn to the west, raise your hands, what I say, you say also: I renounce Satan and all his works and all his service and all his angels. . . . Then again he says to them: Turn to the east and lower your hands, behave with reverence, what I say, you say also: I adhere to Christ.[30]

27 Sven-Erik Pernler, 'De svenska kyrkobalkarnas inledningsord (The Prefaces of the Swedish Ecclesiastical Codes)', in *Kyrkohistorisk årsskrift 1984*, Ingun Montgomery (ed.), *Publications of the Swedish Society of Church History 1:84*, Uppsala: Almquist & Wiksell, 1984, 61–99; Edward and Guthrum, 1: "To love one God and renounce heathen practices", *The Laws of the Earliest English Kings*, F. L. Attenborough (ed. and tr.), New York: Russell & Russell, 1922/6, 103; Æthelred V.1 and 34: "To love and honour one God, and observe one Christian faith and renounce all heathen practices", *The Laws of the Kings of England from Edmund to Henry I*, A. J. Robertson (ed. and tr), Cambridge: Cambridge University Press, 1925/2009, 79, 89; Canute I: "Above all else love and honour one God, unanimously uphold one Christian faith, and love King Canute with true fidelity", *The Laws of the Kings of England* . . . , 155.

28 The same motif also introduces the Borgarthing Law, B I 1, but is not mentioned in the Eidsivathing or Frostathing Laws. There is no mention of bowing to the east in any of the Swedish provincial laws. See Pernler 1984, 61–99.

29 Ezekiel 43:1–5, especially v. 4: "And the glory of the Lord came into the house, by the way of the gate whose prospect is toward the east". The Hebrew word '*kedem*' means 'east, origin'.

30 Whitaker 1970, 110–11.

Similar formulas seem to have been a common feature in most of the baptismal rituals from these centuries.[31]

In the Nordic setting this perspective of geographical orientation is perhaps most conspicuously reflected in the new practice of Christian burials, according to which the dead bodies were placed on their back in the grave with their head pointing westwards and feet eastwards, so that on the day of Christ's return they could sit up facing His coming. The erection of church buildings also adopted the general east-west construction of Christendom with the altar, which represented God's presence in the church, placed at the eastern end, and the congregation facing it with their backs towards the west.[32]

A different piece of Nordic evidence from another kind of source that points towards the east as showing from whence the Christian God reveals himself can be found in Snorri Sturluson's saga about King Olav Haraldsson's encounter with the local pagan chieftain Dale-Gudbrand. The climax of the story, which deals with a contest of power between the Nordic god Thor and the Christian God, occurs exactly at the moment when the sun rises above the horizon at the same time as one of Olav's men clubs down the statue of Thor and Olav shouting: "Look up now, look to the east where our God is coming with a great light".[33] It is naturally the case that Snorri wrote his sagas at a time when Christianity was well established in the Nordic countries,[34] but his account about St Olav and Dale-Gudbrand was probably based on older oral material and gives, as such, at least some support to the idea of the east, in the relevant laws, as a motif adopted in Norway during the period of Christian consolidation.

## *Freedom for slaves*

During the period of Christianization Norwegian society – like most European societies of the time – was highly hierarchical. At the very bottom of society was the class of slaves, or thralls[35] as they were called in Norwegian. In provision 4

31 For instance the Syrian-Orthodox rite: "The priest dips the child into the baptismal font facing east, the child facing west", and the Armenian rite:

> Next he orders the catechumen to turn to the west, and he adjures him three times to say as follows: We renounce you, Satan, and all your deceitfulness and your wiles, and your service and your paths and your angels. . . . Then he shall turn towards the east, confessing the one Godhead of the Holy Trinity.
>
> Whitaker 1970, 94, 75–6.

32 Cf. Hippolytus' metaphor of the church as a ship: "Her prow points to the east, and her stern to the west". Hippolytus, *de antichristo*, 59; in Jacques-Paul Migne, *Patrologia Graeca*, 10.777C–779A. Translation into English from *The Christian Theology Reader*, Alister E. McGrath (ed.), 3rd ed., Oxford: Blackwell Publishing, 2007, 81.

33 'Olav den helliges saga', *Norges kongesagaer*, Bd. 1: Snorre Sturluson, *Kongesagaer*, Første del, Oslo: Gyldendal, 1979, 315–19.

34 First half of the 13th century.

35 *þrælar*.

the Gulathing Law prescribes that one slave is to be given his freedom every year on the first Sunday of the assembly of the law district. Nothing is said as to how this person should be selected, but the costs are instructed to be shared equally among the delegates by a joint amount of 6 *aurar* which equalled half the price of a slave.[36] In the following provision 5 it is stated that the same should be done in each *fylki*[37] of the Gulathing, and that the release should be executed before Christmas Eve every year. The fact that failing to comply with the law entailed a fine to the bishop (of 12 *aurar*) is a clear indication of this being basically an ecclesiastical promulgation.

The imposed benefaction of releasing slaves was a practice with roots all the way back to some of the oldest writings of the Old Testament. The promulgation to set slaves free every sixth year as stated in Exod. 21:2–3 and Deut. 15:12 is part of the divine Torah-legislation of the Jewish society.[38] And as such the principle was also part of the very scriptural basis of the Church throughout the ages. An example of realization of the principle in a historical setting closer to that of the Norwegian provincial laws was King Æthelstan's ordering his reeves to release a slave every year.[39]

## *Ale feast*[40]

Another practice with religious connotations attached to it was the ale feast, mentioned in provisions 6 and 7. The main goal of ensuring the community's continued existence and prosperity by good harvest and peace was stated already in the first paragraph of the law. In provisions 6 and 7 this is connected to the celebration of two annual feasts, the former in the autumn before All Saints' Day,[41] the latter on Christmas Eve. Feasts of beer drinking were common elements in the Old Norse culture and religion. The established feasts of the law appear as a replacement of these feasts, now put under the supervision of the Church by the ale being "blessed with thanks to Christ and the Virgin Mary for good harvest and peace", with fines paid to the bishop and king for people shirking their duties but with the possibility for them to go to confession and do penance.

## *Episcopal services and tithes*

The two provisions 8 and 9 of the Christianity Book of this law – dealing with payment for episcopal services – show how the promulgations of the law in the course of the 11th and 12th centuries were the result of a process of development

36 The other half was supposed to be paid by the slave himself, see G 62.
37 Sub-district or county.
38 See also Lev. 25:47–54 and Jer. 34:12–19.
39 *The Laws of the Earliest* . . ., 127. See also Foot 2011, 136–40.
40 *ǫlgerð*.
41 Starting at sunset on 31 Oct. and ending at sunset 1 Nov., i.e. at a time of the year when the crops and supplies for the winter were stored.

from an early stage attributed to King Olav the Saint and a later stage attributed to King Magnus Erlingsson. In the older Olav text of provision 9 a certain annual tariff of 1 *ertog*[42] is prescribed for the bishop to claim for every 40 persons within the law district. Adam of Bremen, who wrote his famous history book around the year 1070,[43] indirectly confirms the text of the Gulathing Law on these points, by stating his finding the price for these duties among the Norwegians to be too expensive: "Baptism, confirmation, consecration of altars and ordination to holy orders, all these things both they [the Norwegians] and the Danes must buy expensively".[44] The three first Norwegian bishoprics of Nidaros, Selje,[45] and Oslo were established during the reign of King Olav Kyrre (1067–93). Prior to that the bishops seem to have been operating in close contact with the royal court and in different parts of the country with no permanent see or residence.

Nothing is stated about what services the Gulathing assembly expected from their bishop but in general a bishop's particular duties consisted of the ordination of priests, consecration of churches and churchyards and the confirmation of children.[46] But the law does state that the bishop is to visit each *fylki*[47] of the law district once a year to perform his duties. There he is to summon an assembly and set a date for the settled amount to be paid. This ordinance, thus, seems to have been promulgated after the establishing of permanent bishoprics.

The later Magnus text of provision 8 obviously reflects a stage when the remuneration system according to set tariffs, in Old Norse called the *reiða*-system, was replaced by a system of tithes. This was a system evidently initiated by the Church and in Norway allegedly introduced by King Sigurd the Crusader (1103–30)[48] after his visit to the Holy Land.[49] In Norway the tithes were divided into four equal parts; one for the bishop, one for the poor, one for the church and one for the priest.[50] The procedures to be followed by the bishop for the collection of the tithes seem, according to the Magnus text, however, to have been more or less the same as the ones prescribed in the Olav text.

The paying of tithes was a principle that only gradually got a foothold in the teaching and practice of the Church. And again we see that the Old Testament rather than the New Testament came to stand as model for an aspect of legislation for a society in which religion was part of the political structure.[51] Among the

42 Approximately 1/3 ounce. See Glossary s.v. Monetary system.

43 *History of the Archbishops of Hamburg-Bremen: Adam of Bremen*, tr. Francis J. Tschan, new introduction by Timothy Reuter, New York: Columbia University Press, 2002.

44 Ibid., chapter 31.

45 In 1170 moved to Bergen.

46 A general main aim was to consolidate a proper organization of the young Norwegian church.

47 G 9.

48 In the last decade of his reign the bishopric of Stavanger was established, and from this point of time the Gulathing Law district covered two dioceses.

49 See Kolsrud 1958, 182; Wisløff 1966, 128; Helle 2001, 18, 21–2.

50 In Denmark the tithe was divided into three parts; one for the bishop, one for the priest and one for the church.

51 Gen. 28:22, Lev. 27:30, Num. 18:26, Deut. 14:22, 2 Chron. 31:5.

many places where tithes are mentioned in the Old Testament,[52] Lev. 27:30–2 is probably the most central:

> All tithes from the land, whether the seed from the ground or the fruit from the tree, are the Lord's, they are holy to the Lord. . . . All tithes of herd and flock, every tenth one that passes under the shepherd's staff, shall be holy to the Lord.

The earliest community of the Church, which was a purely religious unit, was also in need of some kind of proper support for the clergy, as stated by St Paul in his 1st letter to the Corinthians: "those who serve the altar shall live by the altar. In the same way the Lord has decided that those who preach the Gospel shall live by the Gospel".[53] In the New Testament, however, provisions for the sacred ministers were instructed to be supplied by spontaneous offerings.[54] The earliest formal ecclesiastical legislation on tithes can be traced back to the letter of the Episcopal Assembly of Tours in 567 and the canons of the Council of Mâcon in 585. In the capitularies of Charlemagne of the late 8th century the principle of ecclesiastical tithes was also codified in civil law.[55] The Council of Mainz in 813 confirmed the arrangement of tithes by an explicit reference to the Old Testament: "Decimas Deo et sacerdotibus Dei dandas, Abraham factis, Iacob promissis insinuate, et omnes sancti sacerdotes conmemorant".[56] The same scheme appears also in 10th century English laws, as stated in the law of King Athelstan (924–39): "Let us remember how Jacob the Patriarch declared: 'Decimas et hostias pacificas offeram tibi'", and "as Moses declared in God's Law: 'Decimas et primitias non tardabis offere Domino'".[57] Similar ordinances are also to be found in the laws of

52 See also Gen. 28:22, Num. 18:26, Deut. 14:22, 2 Chron. 31:5.

53 1 Cor. 9:13b–14.

54 1 Cor. 16:1–2, 2 Cor. 9:7.

55 See *New Catholic Encyclopedia*, 2nd ed., vol. 14, Washington, DC: The Catholic University of America Press, 2003, 92.

56 "Tithes for God and God's priests, Abraham made, Jacob promised to serve, and all holy priests remembered", C.16, qu.7, c.6, *Corpus Iuris Canonici*, I, *Decretum Magistri Gratiani*, Aemilus Friedberg (ed.), Leipzig 1879/Graz: Akademische Druck- und Verlagsanstalt, 1959, col. 802.

57 Athelstan's law has a quite detailed ordinance on tithes:

> I, King Æthelstan, with the advice of my Archbishop, Wulfhelm, and my other bishops also, inform the reeve in every borough, and pray you in the name of God and all His saints, and command you also by my friendship, that in the first place ye render tithes of my own property, both in livestock and in yearly fruits of the earth, measuring, counting and weighing [them] in accordance with the strictest accuracy. And the bishops shall do the same with their own property, and my ealdormen and my reeves likewise. 1. And I desire my bishops and the reeves to give this order to all those whose duty it is to obey them, and that it [the payment] be rendered on the legally appointed day; and that shall be the day on which Saint John the Baptist was beheaded. 2. [see quotation in the text: "tithes and offerings to thee", and "to offer tithes and first-fruits to the Lord is not to be delayed"]. 3. It behoves us to remember how terrible is the declaration stated in books: "If we are not willing to render tithes to God, he will deprive us of the nine [remaining] parts, when we least expect it, and moreover we shall have sinned also".
>
> I, Preamble, and I, 1–3, *The Laws of the Earliest* . . . , 123.

King Edmund I (939–46),[58] Edgar (959–75),[59] Æthelred (978–1013/14/15),[60] and Canute (1016–35).[61]

At the time of the formulation of the Magnus text of the Gulathing Law the principle had been clearly stated in *Decretum Gratiani* as a principle of divine law: "Decimas a populo sacerdotibus ac Leuitis esse redendas, diuinae legis sanxit auctoritas".[62] The Norwegian legislation about tithes appears at this stage, therefore, to be more or less perfectly in line with the current processes of intensive work on Canon Law. Failure to comply with the law was punished in the first instance with quite heavy fines to the bishop,[63] but after three years' negligence the culprit was to be sentenced to forfeit all his property of land and movables, half of it accrued to the bishop, the other half to the king.

### *Building and maintenance of churches and fences*

In provisions 10–13 the law gives instructions for the building and maintenance of churches and fences around them. On this matter the law reflects a system of collective responsibility similar to the one we saw regarding payment for episcopal services. So also on this point we see an adaptation of an important ecclesiastical issue to local conditions. Again the established community of the *fylki* is pointed out as the basic administrative unit also regarding responsibility for churches and fences. The actual text of the provisions mainly deals with instructions about whom the responsibility for the churches and church fences should rest upon, about the different kinds of sanctions to be imposed in cases of failure and about deadlines for repairs to be made. Further, the text renders an insight into the ecclesiastical landscape at the time when the law was compiled. Within each *fylki* there should be a main church. In addition there were quarter churches, eighth churches, parish churches, and private churches as part of a hierarchical system related to the size of the areas they were supposed to service. What we see here is a stage when the parochial geography seems to have been about to find its form, which means that the latest version of the text here probably can be dated to the beginning of the 12th century. The fact that the text refers exclusively to wooden churches[64] is also an indication of the same dating, that is from a time before the first stone churches were built in the early 12th century.

58 The Laws of King Edmund I, 2, *The Laws of the Kings of England* . . ., 7.

59 The Laws of King Edgar, II, 3, *The Laws of the Kings of England* . . ., 22–23.

60 The Laws of King Æthelred, VI, 17, *The Laws of the Kings of England* . . . , 97.

61 The Laws of King Canute, I, 8, *The Laws of the Kings of England* . . . , 165.

62 "Tithes for priests and Levites are an obligation of divine law, sanctioned by the authorities", C.16, qu.1, c. 47, Friedberg I, col. 775. The code is attributed to a decree of Pope Paschal II (1099–1118). See also *Decretales Gregorii IX*, C.14, X de decim. III, 30, Friedberg II, col. 561: "Quum decimae non ab homine, sed ab ipso Domino sint institutae, quasi debitum exigi possunt".

63 In case of one year's negligence, the fine was 3 *merkr* (c. 214 g pure silver), for two years' 6 *merkr*.

64 All are described with wooden corner posts which was a basic element in stave churches.

Another two interesting pieces of information in provision 12 are the injunction on the responsible groups of people never to leave the church vacant and the reference to them as "the men who own the churches". This implies that the people in the areas of the quarter, eighth, and parish churches collectively are appointed as the owners of the church and that they are to provide the necessary means for the sustenance of the priests.[65]

When it comes to the provisions in articles 11 and 13 about the erection and maintenance of fences around the churches, which is a responsibility imposed on the same groups of people as in the case of church building, the Norwegian law on this point copies the tradition from everywhere else in Western Christendom. The church was a sacred building, and the ground around it allotted for burials was regarded as sacred land to be separated from other land, and in which certain rules of behaviour and protection applied. In the Gulathing text, however, no mention is made about the Old Testament principle[66] of the church and the fenced land around it as a refuge from violence and asylum for people on the run such as to be found, for instance, in the other Norwegian laws and in English laws.[67]

### *Consecration and supervision of churches*

The ordinance of the brief provision 14 deals with the consecration of churches and churchyards which, in accordance with traditional and current theology, was a duty of the bishop.[68] The text prescribes that the service in this matter is to be bought from the bishop at the price of 12 *aurar* for consecration of the churchyard and 3 *merkr* for the consecration of both church and yard. From this we can deduce that the text stems from a period prior to the introduction of tithes.

### *Supervision of churches, priests' duties, and observation of mass days*

The following provisions 15–19 contain regulations regarding the role and duties of priests. In these sections we also see traces of the different stages in the development of the text. For instance, the initial more or less standard reference to King Olav the Saint's and Bishop Grimkjell's agreement at the Mostra-thing of provision 15 is immediately followed by the words: "and we agreed to later", which is in clear terms an allusion to the formulation of the law as a process. And in the following sentence, stating that "Our bishop must now[!] appoint to all churches . . . priests" must be read as an indication that there was a period prior to that when such appointments were made otherwise, in all likelihood by

65 For further information about this and about procedures for investiture, see comment to the following article 15.

66 1 Kgs. 1:49–51.

67 See F II 10; B I 8.1–4; E I 37; and the Law of King Alfred the Great 2.1, *The Laws of the Earliest . . .*, 65; and the Laws of King Edmund II, 2; and the Laws of King Æthelred VIII, 1, *The Laws of the Kings of England . . .*, 9 and 117.

68 c. 9, 12, 25 D. I. de cons., Friedberg I, col. 1296–7, 1300.

the previously mentioned lay owners of churches and other lords. The change of system mirrors the arrival of the results of the investiture controversy in Norway which took place in the first half of the 12th century.

One of the main duties for a priest was, of course, to celebrate mass, and according to the Gulathing Law, to keep control of the church year as well as to keep the population informed about it. In provision 19, which probably reflects an early stage of the Norwegian church organization, priests are instructed to carve message sticks in the form of small crosses to be distributed to the farms of their parish on the day before mass-days in order to summon them to come to church.[69] These crosses were to be carried around by the farmers themselves, the one to other, to "all houses from which there is smoke". Householders who blocked the process by not taking the cross to the next farm were liable to a fine of 3 *aurar* to the priest who had carved the stick. Provision 15 also contains instruction about sanctions against priests who over a period of one year misled their congregation about fast-days and holidays, in the form of quite heavy fines of 3 *merkr* to the bishop.[70] The same provision also gives a little glimpse into the way local priests were included as integrated figures of the local community:

> Our priests should enjoy the same personal rights as any one of us enjoys with respect to any one else in this country . . . for we have abolished punishing them by beating, because we enter into marriage relations with them or let them teach our sons.[71]

Provisions 16–18 contain promulgations on what kind of work was forbidden and what could be allowed on Sundays and holy days, as well as long lists of holy days to be observed and celebrated throughout the ecclesiastical year. On this point we also see the process of development of the text. In provision 16 the punishment for slaves violating Sunday regulations is to be flogged or to pay a fine of 3 *aurar* to the bishop. In provision 18 nothing is said about flogging, and the fine is reduced to one and a half *eyrir*.[72]

## *Fasting*

A religious practice closely related to observation of holidays was that of fasting. Provision 20 decrees that every seventh day "we shall abstain from eating meat" and that "we call that (day) Friday". In cases of ignorance about the day,

69 See also E I 10.1, 5–6, 11.1–2; B I 13.2; F II 22.

70 For a parallel in English laws, see Treaty between King Alfred/Edward and Guthrum, Ch. 3.1. *The Laws of the Earliest . . .*, 103, 105.

71 The text here illustrates how the social status of the local clergy rose in the course of the latter part of the 11th and beginning of the 12th century.

72 These penalties correspond to Ine's Law, stating that "If . . . the slave works [on Sundays] without the cognizance of his master, he shall undergo the lash or pay the fine in lieu thereof". Ine's Law, 3.1, *The Laws of the Earliest . . .*, 37.

the violator is not liable to pay a fine, but go to confession and do penance. But in cases of repeated violation the culprit is to be fined 3 *aurar* to the bishop. And if he continues violating the regulation, after having paid the fine twice, he, as the law states, "has forfeited every penny of his property, but he may still go to confession and do penance". The only exception relates to the long lasting period of Lent, when eating of meat is to be accepted if a person "eats out of necessity and has no other food". In such cases even the eating of dog meat is accepted, for as the law says, "it is better for him to eat a dog than that a dog eats him".

### *Forbidden food*

In addition to the prohibition against the consumption of meat during days and periods of fasting the same provision 20 also contains regulations against horse meat and meat from animals that had died of themselves. As for the prohibition against horse meat the law is categorical:

> If someone eats horse meat, he must pay three *merkr* for it to the bishop, every man who speaks our language, and go to confession and do penance. . . . If someone eats horse meat during Lent, then he has forfeited every penny of his property and he must leave the realm of our king.[73]

The text reveals no information as to why this was forbidden, and a twofold explanation is possible here. The closest solution is to read this rule in light of the ban on *blót* stated in provision 29. The pagan Nordic ritual of the *blót* consisted of the sacrifice of horses, the drinking of horse blood and the eating of horse meat. Thus, the prohibition may be motivated by a need to abolish practices connected to pagan cult. But for the learned clerics, who had a hand on the law formation, the Old Testament prohibition against eating "Every animal that has hoofs, but is not cleft footed or does not chew the cud"[74] may also have played a role.

Meat from animals that had died of themselves is dealt with in provision 31. Such meat, which is specified as "meat . . . of animals having died of themselves when no one knows what caused their death", is forbidden to be eaten. At a first glance this is in perfect agreement with Old Testament Law: "You shall not eat anything that dies of itself".[75] But the possible Old Testament impact on this point of the Gulathing Law is ambiguous. The interpretation of the term 'died of itself', or *morticina* which is the Latin term, is not the same. The Gulathing Law allows eating meat from animals that "wolves bite, . . . the bear strikes or dogs bite", or that "which drowns in running water, falls down from mountains and that which is strangled by the halter". The same is categorically forbidden in the Old Testament, saying "you shall not eat any meat that is mangled by beasts in the field,

73 G 20.
74 Lev. 11:26–27.
75 Deut. 14:21.

you shall throw it to the dogs".[76] The Gulathing Law seems on this point to have been only partly in accordance with the Norwegian Borgarthing Law, which in provision V.5 defines animals that die of themselves as "not killed by the works of the human hand".[77]

The regulations about forbidden food, as we can read them in the Old Testament, were not included in the New Testament. At the famous council in Jerusalem, where all the leading apostles were present, and which is reported in Acts 15, it was decided that, when it came to Old Testament prescriptions about unclean food, Christians were only instructed to "abstain from what has been sacrificed to idols, and from blood and from what is strangled".[78] And St Mark is even less reserved by lifting the subject to a spiritual level: "Do you not see that whatever goes into a person from outside cannot defile, since it enters, not the heart, but the stomach, and goes out into the sewer".[79]

The issue of forbidden food illustrates, however, to the full the very long road that existed from the historical setting of the Old and New Testament to that of the 11th- and 12th-century Norwegian provincial laws, and with no indications in the text it is difficult to establish clear conclusions about the actual historical motives behind these rules.[80]

## *Baptism*

The main act to mark the conversion of an individual from paganism to Christianity was baptism.[81] Ever since New Testament times, baptism was the true initiation rite for people who wanted to adopt Christian faith, understood as it was as a sacramental burial with Christ to his atoning death for men's sin and resurrection with him to a new life under God's grace.[82] When all the four Norwegian laws in explicit terms state the invariable obligation for every child born within the realm to be baptized they were in full compliance with a unanimous Christian tradition. In the text of the Gulathing Law this is stated as follows: "Every child which is born in our country should be . . . brought to church and baptized".[83] On this point the Norwegian legislation is in line with similar provisions in old English laws.[84]

76 Exod. 22:31.
77 For a more detailed discussion of this issues in the Norwegian provincial laws see Landro 2010, 94–107.
78 Acts 15:29.
79 Mk. 7:18–19, see also Col. 2:16.
80 For a wider discussion of the ecclesiastical food prescriptions in the early Middle Ages, such as in the penitential, see Landro 2010, 83–91; Sanmark 2005, 203–24.
81 G 21. See also B I 2; E I 8; F II 1.
82 Rom. 6:4: "By our baptism, then, we were buried with him and shared his death, in order that, just as Christ was raised from death by the glorious power of the Father, so also we might live a new life".
83 G 21.
84 See for instance, Ine's Law, Ch. 2, *The Laws of the Earliest . . .* , 37.

All the Norwegian laws also operate with four or five set time limits within the course of the ecclesiastical year for new-born children to be brought to baptism. The instruction on this point in the Gulathing text goes:

> But every child which is born after Christmas Eve should be baptized before the preparatory fast [Septuagesima] begins. And if it is born during Lent, it should be baptized at Easter season. If it is born after Easter season, it should be baptized before the Feast of St John the Baptist [June 24th]. Every child which is born after Michaelmas [Sept. 29th] should be baptized before Christmas Eve.[85]

The weight that the provincial laws attributed to baptism is also reflected in the provisions regarding emergency christening. In the Gulathing district the law provided that unbaptized children who were so weak that they could die before reaching a priest, should be baptized by the man responsible for it, or by a woman if a man was not available. He – or she – should

> name it, dip it into water and speak these words over it: "I baptize you N. in the name of the Father, and of the Son, and of the Holy Ghost".

The older layers of the same law add:

> If they cannot get water, they should baptize in whatever liquid they may find. But if they do not find any liquid they must spit in the palm of their hands and make the sign of the cross on its breast and between its shoulders.[86]

Although the rite of baptism is definitely New Testament and Christian; the procedures and formalities around it, as promulgated in the Gulathing Law, contain striking parallels to the Old Testament. One aspect is that baptism is imposed as an obligatory initiation rite for everyone within the borders of the kingdom to submit to in the same way as circumcision was in the Jewish society of the old covenant. Both rites were also supposed to take place within rather short deadlines after birth, in the Old Testament eight days,[87] in the Norwegian laws within set time limits in the course of the ecclesiastical year.

The provisions of the law on baptism of unbaptized people coming to the country from pagan regions also demonstrate the urgency and importance that the legislators attached to this sacrament. Such people could be travellers, traders, or immigrants of different kinds. Within the territory of the Gulathing such a person was instructed to see a priest as soon as possible and be baptized. As long as he was still unbaptized he was entitled to be offered food and accommodation. But

85 G 21. In Ine's Law the deadline is 30 days after birth. Ine's Law, Ch. 2, *The Laws of the Earliest . . .*, 37.

86 G 21. For parallels see E I 2.1; B I 2.2–4; F I 3.

87 Gen. 17:10–14.

if he was unwilling to be baptized he was to be granted a deadline of five days to leave the country, and it was not allowed for him to be accommodated in one and the same house for more than one night.[88] On this point Old Testament law also provides a parallel: "Any uncircumcised male who is not circumcised in the flesh of his foreskin shall be cut off from his people, he has broken my covenant".[89] Thus, in the same manner as circumcision in the Old Testament baptism was in the Norwegian legal context more than an initiation into a spiritual community of co-believers. It was also an entrance into a political society.

We have no indication in these texts, or in any other, about what kind of instruction and teaching was connected to baptism in Norway in this early period. But there is every indication to assume that a strong symbolic act like baptism executed by a team of professional religious personnel cannot have taken place in a total intellectual vacuum. At least, baptism as the actual principal initiation rite of Christianity must have been understood as a submission to Christ as the highest Lord – with all its implications – as stated in the last part of the already cited first paragraph of the Gulathing Law:

> That is the beginning of our laws that we should bow to the east and pray to the holy Christ for good harvest and peace; that we may retain our settled land and our liege lord in health. Let him be a friend to us, and we to him. And may God be a friend to all.[90]

Although it is not possible to point out a direct line of historical impact, one can in these words hear a resonance of Carolingian ideas of order of Christian society with given relations of supremacy and obedience between people, emperor/king, and God, as expressed in what has been interpreted as Charles' own gloss in *Libri Carolini* to an Augustinian text:

> *Der Schöpfer wird als solcher bezeichnet im Hinblick auf die Geschöpfe, ebenso wie der Herr so heisst im Hinblick auf die Knechte.*[91]

And if we turn to England we find the same fundamental principle stated in the very first provision of King Canute's laws:

> The first provision is, that above all else they would ever love and honour one God, and unanimously uphold one Christian faith, and love king Canute with due fidelity.[92]

88 G 22.

89 Gen. 17:14. See also Ezra 10 and Nehemiah 13. Cf. also Canute's Proclamation of 1020, 10, *The Laws of the Kings . . .*, 143.

90 G 1.

91 "The Creator is referred to as such with regard to creatures, just as the Lord [King] is so called with regard to the subjects". Schneider 1978, 228; Steinen 1932, 207–80.

92 The Laws of King Canute I, 1, *The Laws of the Kings of England . . .*, 155. See also ibid.: The Laws of King Æthelred V, 1; 79 and VII, 1; 109.

### *Deformed children and the exposure of children*

As already mentioned, all the four Norwegian provincial laws contain an overarching rule that all citizens of the realm were to be baptized. However, in cases where the baby suffered from serious deformities the question was more complex. The laws therefore contain more specific regulations on this matter. The provision of the Gulathing law is quite short. If the deformity of the child is so severe that

> the face turns around where the neck should be or the toes turn to where the heels should be, then that child should be brought to church and baptized and be put down in the church and left there to die.[93]

Whether the motive behind this instruction was that the child was so deformed that it could not possibly survive, or that it was regarded as some kind of a monster, is impossible to determine on the basis of the formulation itself.

If, however, we look at the two laws from Eastern Norway, the Borgarthing and the Eidsivathing Laws, both of these are more specific, and in the former of these both arguments are mentioned in more detail. First, this law deals with cases of severe deformity such as

> When the mother is unable to feed the child, when the heels are where the toes should be, or the toes where the heels should be, if the chin is between the shoulders, the nape of the neck on the chest, the muscle of the lower leg on the front side, the eyes in the back of the head, if the child has the flippers of a seal or the head of a dog, these children are to be placed in the unholy place, in heaps of stone, the haunt of the devil, where neither men nor cattle walk.[94]

Our interpretation of this passage is that the law here considers these children as some kind of monsters, affected by supernatural evil powers before birth and as representations of evil in the Christian community. The solution to the problem was to give these creatures back to the devil by leaving them in heaps of stone where “neither men nor cattle walk”.

Second, in cases of less severe deformities the same law prescribes a different procedure. Children born with faces like shells or pods who were unable to ingest food and were doomed to die anyway, should be brought to church to be blessed with the sign of the cross, put in front of the church door and watched over by the closest next of kin until the spirit left them. Further, they were to be buried in the churchyard, their soul prayed for, and finally left to the kind of hope that God might bestow upon them.[95]

93 G 21.
94 B 1.2.
95 B 1.3.

The Eidsivathing Law also distinguishes between two kinds of deformities in babies; the human and the monstrous, but with provisions that differ from those of the Borgarthing Law. Babies identified as human beings, despite severe deformities, are to be nurtured, brought to church, baptized, shown to the bishop, and then the bishop's advice followed regarding the child.[96] When it comes to babies regarded as monsters, "without the head and voice of a human being" these may

> be brought to church if [the parents] want it and let the priest baptize it if he is willing to, dig a grave on the churchyard, put the child in it, put a slab of rock over it so dogs or ravens cannot get to it, but not let earth fall on it until it is dead, and let it live as long as it can.[97]

The main concern in all the three laws was an obligation to baptize children regardless of deformities. In cases where the deformity prevented the child from being fed, the laws instructed the parents to bring it to the church to die there. But, as we have seen, there was one exception, namely the cases of babies identified as monsters. Regarding such cases the provisions of the Norwegian laws vary and, as in the case of the Eidsivathing Law, to some extent simply leave the decision about course of action to the parents' or the priest's discretion.

### *Exposure of children*

The old Scandinavian custom of carrying unwanted babies out into the wilderness to let them die there[98] could not be tolerated within Christian society. In provision 22 of the Gulathing Law this is stated in clear terms:

> If a man exposes his child, heathen or christened, and lets it perish, and he is convicted of this, then he has forfeited peace and property, and we call that the great murder. And if a slave lets his child die, heathen or christened, then his master should have him flogged within five days or else have taken him to the king's men, and he may sell him out of the country if he wants to, and not eat together with him.[99]

The headline of the paragraph contains an interesting specification that the sanction of outlawry and confiscation of all property for these crimes is a new and harder punishment introduced by King Magnus Erlingsson to replace the older Saint Olav legislation of payment of a fine for the same kind of misdeed. Most likely the Church has had a hand in this since human life for the Church was a holy thing, and since we know that King Magnus was working in close contact

96 E I 5.
97 E I 6.
98 Helle 2001, 189–90.
99 G 22.

with church authorities. The Borgarthing Law also levies loss of all property, outlawry, and expulsion from the realm for killing babies. But this law adds a remark worthwhile noticing, namely that murdering a heathen baby is more severe than killing a baptized child since the death of an unbaptized person would also imply the loss of a soul.[100]

Any direct biblical parallel to the Norwegian laws on this point is difficult to find. But a little passage in Lev. 20:2–5 deals with a similar issue, namely that of giving Jewish children away to a pagan god. The prescribed punishment is similar to that of the Norwegian laws, namely eradication from the people of God.

### *Burials and treatment of the dying and the dead*

The general rule for burials according to the law was that every citizen of the realm was to be buried in hallowed soil (i.e. in consecrated churchyards), but there were exceptions. Provision 23 of the Gulathing Law lists these exceptions as applying to murderers; truce breakers; thieves; and persons who have committed high treason, suicide, or crimes that could not be compensated for; in addition to pagans as mentioned in provision 22. The dead bodies of the criminals mentioned are compelled to be put on the foreshore "where the tide and the green sod meet".[101]

The law also operates with a deadline of five days for the kinsmen of the dead to bring the corpse to church for burial. Violation of the law on this point entailed a fine of 3 *aurar* to the bishop, and in cases where the kinsmen refused, confiscation of all property and outlawry. But even on this point there were exceptions. In cases where people lived "high up in the mountains or far out among the islands" the kinsmen are instructed temporarily to keep the body by placing it in an outhouse, suspending it, and avoiding letting it lie on the ground.[102]

The same paragraph continues by specifying the duties of the priest in connection with the dying and the dead. This section of the text consists of more or less pure ecclesiastical ordinances reflecting the current state of church law. First of all the law emphasizes, under the threat of heavy fines in cases of omission, the invariable duty of priests to come to dying persons when called upon and administer the last rites. The same is imposed regarding the indispensable obligation of priests to come and "sing over the body . . . according to the appropriate ritual".[103] On this point we also see the two identified stages of the development of the law in the way that the Olav-text operates with payment to the priest for his services according to set tariffs whereas the Magnus-text represents a stage when the services mentioned are covered by the tithes.

100 B I 4.2.
101 G 23.
102 Ibid.
103 Ibid. For a more detailed presentation of death rites in Scandinavia in the Middle Ages see Sundmark 2008.

### *Matrimonial affairs*

Matrimonial affairs are dealt with in two sections of the Gulathing Law, the Book on Christian Law and the Book on the Marriage of Women.[104] The two sections reflect the two formative sources of the law, namely the influence of Canon Law and indigenous tradition.

The relevant provisions 24–27 on the issue in the Book on Christian Law appear on the whole as an application of ordinances from Canon Law about prohibited degrees of relation between groom and bride, on monogamy and on proper and improper times for the contraction of marriages. Similar more or less explicit references to Canon Law are also to be found in English laws from around the year 1000.[105]

The provisions of the Gulathing Law on marriage affairs are formulated from the standpoint of the man, with him as the subject and the woman as the object. Much of the text, especially that of provision 24, consists of lists of different women in specified prohibited degrees of relation to a man. The overall rule of the law is that it allows marriages, as the text puts it, "in the seventh knee and the seventh degree", and forbids all closer relations.[106] From this we can conclude that the Gulathing Law on this point reveals a stage of legislation prior to the Lateran IV narrowing of prohibited marriages from the seventh to the fourth degree of consanguinity and affinity.[107] In cases of consanguinity the Canon Law principle was to count links between the two parts of the wedding couple and their common ancestor.[108] Siblings, thus, were related in the first degree of consanguinity, first cousins in the second degree and so forth.[109] The Gulathing text does, however, operate with both the Canon Law term of 'degree' and the Old Norse term of 'knee',[110] but unlike Canon Law the Old Norse counting of knees started with first cousins as the first knee. In this text, however, the two terms are used synonymously, either erroneously or deliberately as an adjustment of

104 *Kvinnebortgiftingsbolken*, G 51–56.

105 The Laws of King Æthelred, V, 10 and VI, 11–12, in *The Laws of the Kings . . .*, 83, 95, and The Laws of King Canute, I, 7, in *The Laws of the Kings . . .*, 163.

106 The law does, however, allow marriages with widows of relatives within "the fifth knee and the fifth degree".

107 Johannes B. Sägmüller, *Lehrbuch des katholischen Kirchenrechts*, vol. 2, Freiburg: Herder, 1914, 176.

108 If the number of links were not the same on both sides one counted the links of the person with the more distant relation to the ancestor. Freisen 1893/1963, 435. See also Jørgensen and Saletnich 2004, 48. Salonen 2013, 181–6.

109 For Canon Law legislation on marriage and sexual relations throughout the Middle Ages see *Corpus Iuris Canonici*, II: *Decretalium collectiones*, Friedberg II, col. 661–732, 1065–8.

110 The use of the word 'knee' to describe consanguine relations seems to have deep roots in Germanic tradition; Cf. '*tertio genuculo propinqua*' by St Boniface (Archbishop of Mainz ?–754), *Die Briefe des heiligen Bonifatius and Lullus*, Michael Tangl (ed.), 2nd ed., Berlin: Weidemann, 1955 (1916), Ep. 50, 83–84, and '*cneowe*' in old English Law, The Laws of King Æthelred, VI, 12, in *The Laws of the Kings . . .*, 94.

the Norse tradition to Canon Law.[111] In line with this, the general reference to what "the law allows"[112] is perhaps more likely to be interpreted as referring to Canon Law rather than to the Gulathing Law itself. The prescribed sanction for violation of the mentioned restrictions on marriages is for the man to dismiss the wife, to pay a fine of 3 *merkr* to the bishop, to confess and do penance. In cases of refusal the law obliges both the man and the woman to "leave the realm of our king".[113]

In the Gulathing Law we find no explicit distinction between *consanguinitas* (kinship) and *affinitas* (in-law relations) like in Canon Law. But the law does distinguish between more serious and less serious violations of the law which, with some variation, reflects Canon Law distinctions. Thus, in addition to the general regulation about prohibited degrees the Norwegian text presents a list of women to be "more highly respected" and with whom sexual relation is regarded as a crime of the most severe kind.[114] These women are: a man's mother, sister, daughter, stepmother, daughter-in-law, brother's wife, son's daughter, and in addition, as added by the later Magnus-version: stepdaughter, brother's daughter, sister's daughter, daughter's daughter, mother's mother, father's sister, mother's sister, father's mother, and wife's sister. A first point to note here is that the Gulathing Law follows Canon Law by promulgating an indispensable prohibition of marriage and sexual relation between partners related by descent in the direct line.[115] The other women on the list are all women connected to the man in the first or second degrees of consanguinity or affinity. The seriousness of violating the law by having sexual contact with the women mentioned is reflected in the prescribed punishment. Both layers of the law impose outlawry for both the man and the woman, expulsion from the king's land, and the confiscation of all their property in land and movables, which was to be shared half-and-half between king and bishop. The Magnus text does, however, add that the culprits may return from their expatriation when they have completed the penance imposed on them by the bishop and that the king or the bishop may then also mitigate the economic loss. Grading of penalties in accordance with the degree of the incestuous relation is a feature also to be found in English laws.[116]

In addition the Canon Law principle of spiritual kinship[117] as an impediment for legal marriages is included in the Gulathing Law. In the late Middle Ages,

111 See Glossary under Kinship, and Helle 2001, 182.

112 G 24.

113 Ibid.

114 *Úbótamál*, i.e. a crime which in principle could not be compensated.

115 *Linea directa*, Plöchl 1962, 322.

116

> If anyone commits incest, he shall make amends according to the degree of relationship, either by the payment of wergild or of a fine, or by the forfeiture of all his possessions. The cases are not alike if incest is committed with a sister or with a distant relation.
>
> The Laws of King Canute, II, 51, *The Laws of the Kings . . .*, 201–2.

117 *Cognatio spiritualis*. For the historical development of this impediment see Weigand 1994, 8–17.

when the regulations of this matter were fully developed, Canon Law operated with twenty-one forms of this impediment,[118] most of which applied to persons with some kind of a sponsor role in connection with baptism or confirmation.[119] In provision 26 of the Gulathing Law only six kinds of spiritually related persons are mentioned. Of these, three are persons holding the child at different stages of the baptismal ritual, two are persons with similar roles to the child by confirmation, and the last one is the person who introduces a woman to church after child birth. In the first five cases mentioned, spiritual kinship is established between the sponsors and the child as well as with its parents.[120] In the last case spiritual kinship is only between the woman and the man who introduces her to church. The small number of possible cases of spiritual kinship in the Gulathing text is indicative of this text being a product of 12th-century legislative processes.

In provision 25 we find a promulgation of New Testament rules[121] regarding monogamy in quite categorical terms: “Now it is the next thing that each of us shall have only one wife”. If a man disobeys the law on this point by taking a second wife, the law requires the dismissal of the second wife and imposes a fine of 3 *merkr* to the bishop, confession and penance. No exception is allowed even if the contraction of the second marriage had been contracted by the customary payment of bride-price. In cases of refusal the law obliges both the man and the second wife to forfeit all their property and to leave the realm. It is also forbidden for married men to keep a female slave as a concubine or any mistress. The punishment of such misdemeanour is however milder, 12 *aurar* to the bishop together with confession and penance. In contemporary English laws we find a similar promulgation in the Laws of King Canute.[122]

Provision 27, which deals with proper and improper times for the contraction of marriages, is a clear reflection of the ecclesiastical principle of *tempus clausum* (closed season) or *tempus feriatum* (forbidden season). During these days or periods people were supposed to dedicate themselves to prayer, penance, repentance, almsgiving, and self-denial as preparation for the following solemnity days. During the closed times all kinds of celebrations and festivities, including that of weddings, were forbidden. The biblical basis for so detailed regulations as those listed in the Gulathing text is, however, quite vague. The biblical evidence consists of rather general statements about observance of sexual continence in situations of contact with the holy and as preparation for religious feasts and periods of prayer.[123] The most ancient traces of the same concern in the history of the Church date back to the mid-4th century Council of

118 For instance, spiritual *paternitas/maternitas* was established between godfather/godmother and the baptized child and spiritual *fraternitas* with their children.

119 Schmugge et al. 1996, 73.

120 Cf. The Laws of King Æthelred, VI, 12, in *The Laws of the Kings* . . . , 95.

121 Cf. Mt. 19:5–6, Mk. 10:8–9, 1 Cor. 7:2, Eph. 5:31.

122 Canute I, 7, *The Laws of the Kings* . . . , 163.

123 Exod. 19:14–15, 1 Sam. 21:4–5, 1 Cor. 7:5.

Laodicea which in one of its canons simply states that "Marriages and birthday feasts are not to be celebrated in Lent".[124] Throughout the following centuries the regulation of *tempus clausum* seems to have achieved general dissemination in the Christian West, in the first instance applying to the Lenten period, and then extended over the Advent and other festal periods.[125] The *tempora clausa* mentioned in *Decretum Gratiani* are Quadragesima, Septuagesima, the Easter octave, three weeks before the Feast of St John the Baptist and the period of Advent till after Epiphany.[126]

On the whole, the Gulathing Law follows Gratian, and is a clear indication that its regulation on this point was included in the law around the mid-12th century. In fact, the Gulathing Law is a little more specified than Gratian. The list of forbidden periods in the Gulathing Law are: nine weeks before Easter and the Easter week; nights before Sunday, Friday, Wednesday; and nights followed by fast-days or holy days from the morning, three weeks before the Feast of St John the Baptist, three weeks before Michaelmas, three weeks before Christmas, and thirteen Christmas days. The general penalty for neglecting the regulation in these periods was a fine of 3 *aurar* to the bishop. But if anyone broke the law by contracting marriages during the nine weeks of Lent, or in the course of the Easter week, the culprits were levied a heavy fine of 3 *merkr* to the bishop.

If we compare the Gulathing Law with the other three Norwegian provincial laws we find that their regulations on forbidden times with small variations are very much parallel to those of the Gulathing Law. The most conspicuous variation in the Eidsivathing and Borgarthing laws are that these laws speak about sexual intercourse instead of weddings and the Frostathing Law about both.[127]

When it comes to the ecclesiastical issue of mutual consent from both wedding partners for a marriage to be valid[128] nothing is mentioned in the Book on Church Law of the Gulathing Law.[129] On this point the Gulathing Law differs from the Eidsivathing and Frostathing Laws in which the principle of mutual consent is stated.[130] However, as so clearly expressed in the Gulathing Book on the Marriage of Women[131] the institution of marriage was in Norway in the 11th and

124 *A Select Library of the Nicene and Post-Nicene Fathers of the Christian Church*, 2. Series, Vol. 14: The seven ecumenical councils, Philip Schaff and Henry Wace (eds.), New York: Christian Literature Publishing Co., 1900, Canon 52.

125 www.biblicalcyclopedia.com/T/tempus-clausum.html.

126 C.33, qu.4, c.8–11, Friedberg I, col. 1249.

127 E I 21; B I 7; F III 9.

128 See, for instance, C.27, qu.2, c.1 and 2, Friedberg, I, col. 1063. The principle was further developed in the Decretals of Pope Alexander III (1159–81). Schmugge 1986, 68–9.

129 The only mention we find of the individual will of women in the Gulathing Law is in connection with its condemnation of men taking other men's wives, fiancées, or daughters by force "without the consent of those entitled to decide about their marriage or without their own consent". G 32.

130 E I 22.1, 6, 8 and 23.1; F III 22.

131 G 51–6.

12th centuries still primarily a matter of contracts between families. Thus, the individual will of the partners was in the marriage process only one point to be taken into account and, as it seems, regard to individual will had in the Gulathing Law to yield to national tradition.[132] Altogether, however, the Gulathing provisions regarding marriage affairs give an illustration that more than anything else shows how civil law and church law were intertwined in Norwegian legislation in the 11th and 12th centuries.

## *Soothsaying, sorcery, and* blót

The following provisions 28 and 29 deal with the issues of soothsaying, sorcery, *blót*, and pagan cult in general. As already mentioned the goal of purifying the country of pagan customs and cult was a central element of the project of building a Christian Norwegian kingdom in the 11th and 12th centuries.[133] Again the overarching theological perspective was the idea of the Christian Church as the chosen people of the new covenant between God and man which in this period was identified with Western Christendom.[134] We have already discussed the regulations of the law against unclean food and on the expulsion of people who refused to be baptized as part of this overarching perspective.[135] But more than anything else idolatry in terms of different kinds of direct contact with pagan or evil supernatural powers was a seriously disturbing and undermining factor. The biblical ban on any kind of such contact, whether in the form of divination, fortune telling, enchantment, or sorcery, is categorical.[136] As acts of idolatry all such abominations were to be eradicated from the land of old Israel, by way of expelling practitioners from the realm.[137]

The biblical perception of witchcraft and sorcery as destructive representations of supernatural powers and as channels for these forces to execute their evil and devastating acts on the good order and wellbeing of society was introduced and seems to have gained universal acceptance in Western Christendom. Both

132 In King Canute's law the will of the woman is explicitly stated: "And no woman or maiden shall ever be forced to marry a man whom she dislikes, nor shall she be given for money, except the suitor desires of his free will to give something". Canute II, 74, *The Laws of the Kings . . .*, 213.

133 This is also a frequent motif in old English laws. Cf. the treaty between Edward and Guthrum: "In the first place they declared they would love one God, and zealously renounce all heathen practices". Edward and Guthrum, Introduction § 1, *The Laws of the Earliest . . .*, 102. More or less the same wording is repeated for instance in Æthelred V, 1 and 34, VI, 1, *The Laws of the Kings . . .*, 79, 89, 91.

134 See the previously mentioned under *The Law as a Clearing of New Christian Land*. See also Wormald 1999, 32ff., 75, 78; Jørgensen 2013b, 240–2.

135 See comments to provisions 20–2.

136 Cf. the 1st commandment of the Decalogue, "Thou shalt have no other gods before Me", Exod. 20:2; Deut. 5:6.

137 Deut. 18:10–14. See also Exod. 22:18, 20, Lev. 19:26, 2 Kgs. 21:6, Gal. 4:20, Rev. 21:8.

in English legislation[138] and in all the other three Norwegian provincial laws[139] contact with such beings was strictly banned. The fact that the same description of magic rituals seems to have been repeated in ecclesiastical sources throughout Latin Christendom has led to the conclusion that parts of the Nordic regulations on the matter is more a reflection of common ecclesiastical jurisdiction than a description of actual behaviour in the law areas.[140] However, the phenomena of soothsaying, interpretation of omens, the *blót* ritual, and other acts of pagan cult are abundantly testified as actual and practiced customs in other Old Norse sources.

So, what were the actual provisions on the issue in the Gulathing Law? The forbidden practices mentioned in provision 28 refer to soothsaying, *galdr*-song, and sorcery, all of which deal with the exercise of some kind of magic. Also, it seems that for practitioners of these acts all three are regarded as equally serious.

The ability to foresee somebody's future, and even more to affect it, is an extraordinary capacity of supernatural origin, in early Nordic society generally related to pagan gods, especially Odin, and other supernatural beings. Thus, to act as fortune-teller, and especially to divine the future,[141] but also listening to fortune-tellers was strictly forbidden. The sanctions on those found guilty were extremely heavy. For performers of soothsaying the sanction was simply outlawry and the confiscation of all one's property, half of which accrued to the king and half to the bishop. For listening to soothsaying the penalty was 40 *merkr*, falling in the same proportions to king and bishop. The division of the penalty shows that the offence was regarded as a violation of both civil and church law. The size of the latter penalty might seem disproportionately large if compared to those imposed on other serious crimes, and is a clear indication of the gravity attached to this offence by the legislators.

The phenomenon of *galdr*-song[142] refers to a special kind of incantation or uttering words in a loud voice for the purpose of casting evil on somebody. Accordingly,

138 For instance in the Treaty between Alfred/Edward and Guthrum:

> If wizards and sorcerers, perjurers or they who secretly compass death . . . be met with anywhere in the country, they shall be driven from the land and the nation shall be purified; otherwise they shall be utterly destroyed in the land.

11, *The Laws of the Earliest* . . . , 109, and Æthelstan II.6 on witchcraft, sorceries, and deadly spells, *The Laws of the Earliest* . . . , 131. The text from Alfred/Edward and Guthrum is almost word by word repeated in Æthelred VI.7, *The Laws of the Kings* . . . , 93. See also Edmund I.6, *The Laws of the Kings* . . . , 7, and Canute, II. 4, *The Laws of the Kings* . . . , 177.

139 E I 45 and 46; B I 16.2–9, F III 15.

140 Landro 2010, 217–18. Examples of this are the following formulations in the Borgarthing Law, describing a female sorceress "who performs magic on cow or calf, woman or child" by putting "hair, legs of frogs, nails or other items into people's bed clothes", the one who "bites a finger or toe off from her child . . . in order to live longer" or "the mistress or master who brings up their child as a heathen". B I 16.4–7.

141 ON *seiðr*.

142 ON *galdr*, derived from the verb *gala*.

it can be described as a special way of exercising sorcery. The sanction prescribed for practitioners of this atrocity, whether they were men or women, was outlawry and expulsion from the king's lands. The same punishment was imposed also on listeners and followers with the moderation that they were granted the opportunity to confess and do penance. However, in cases where a woman was found guilty of being a so-called 'sorceress and man-eater', which must have been the worst kind of a witch, the punishment was to bring her to the shore, kill her by a chop in the back, apparently for the purpose of leaving the corpse to be swallowed by the sea. In this practice we see an example of the same way of thinking as in the cases of other unholy persons not to be allowed to be buried in churchyards.[143]

### *Trial by ordeal*

The process prescribed in the Norwegian law material to determine whether the accused person was guilty or not includes trials by ordeal,[144] compurgation,[145] and witness statements. It is of interest to note that all three practices are mentioned here in one and the same provision 28 of the Gulathing Law. Trial by ordeal was an ancient judicial procedure by which the accused was subjected to some kind of bodily pain or torture and tested under priestly supervision as to whether the defendant escaped the ordeal without being harmed or not. If harmed, the defendant was found guilty, if unharmed he or she was innocent. The biblical basis for this praxis is rather flimsy. Only in Num. 5:11–31 do we find a more detailed description of a process to be administered under the supervision of a priest to a wife accused of adultery. The ordeal consisted of the drinking of cursed bitter water, which in the case of guilt would cause her belly to swell and her thighs to rot.[146]

In contemporary early medieval ecclesiastical sources the practice was referred to as *iudicium dei*[147] as it was based on the belief in God's determining intervention in the trial. The centuries between the reign of Charlemagne and the pontificate of Innocent III, that is from 800 to 1200 AD, form what Robert Bartlett calls the "heyday" of the practice of the ordeal in Western Europe.[148] This means that the Gulathing Law provisions on the issue fit well into the bigger picture of Western European legislation of the time. In 1215 Pope Innocent III at Lateran IV

143 See comments to provision 23.

144 For a more comprehensive analysis and discussion of the judicial practice of ordeal see Robert Bartlett, *Trial by Fire and Water: The Medieval Judicial Ordeal*, Oxford: Clarendon Press, 1986.

145 Formal judicial practice of oath-giving.

146 The ritual of the bitter water, in Talmudic literature referred to as *Sotah* (Errant wife). Arnost Zvi Ehrman, 'Sotah', in *Encyclopaedia Judaica*, 2nd ed., vol. 19, Detroit: Macmillan Reference USA in association with the Keter Publishing House, 2007, 32–3.

147 See Bartlett 1986, 5: 'judgement of God', in Norwegian 'Guds-reinsing', G 24.

148 Bartlett 1986, 13. For parallels in English laws see Ine 62, Edward and Guthrum 9, Æthelstan II.21, *The Laws of the Earliest* . . . 57, 107, 139, and Æthelred III.7 and V.18, Canute I.17, *The Laws of the Kings* . . . , 69, 85, 167.

issued a ban on priests who participated in judicial trials by ordeal.[149] However, as early as the latter half of the 12th century we find legislative measures against clerics being submitted to ordeals, also in the case of Norway.[150] The effect of the Lateran IV provision was that the very foundation under the practice itself was undermined since priestly supervision had been one of its constitutive elements. The result was that the practice was soon also banned in secular legislation in several European countries in the wake of the council.[151]

Both of the most widespread kinds of ordeals, namely those of putting hands in boiling water and carrying hot iron,[152] are mentioned in the Gulathing Law. In provision 28 the ordeal of putting hands in boiling water was prescribed for women accused of the earlier mentioned atrocities of being a "witch or a man-eater". Only accusations based on rumours[153] from at least three households in the village were to be taken into consideration under the law. In provision 32 the ordeal of carrying hot iron is mentioned as a possibility to prove innocence for men facing rumours in the district of homosexual acts.[154] The Gulathing Law does not contain any detailed descriptions of the actual process of the ordeals. But we think it reasonable to assume that they were performed as variants of procedures prescribed in English laws which clearly show how religion and law were interconnected on this issue.[155]

149 Lat. IV, canon 15. For the discourse on and critique against ordeals in the 11th and 12th centuries, see Bartlett 1986, 86–94.
150 'Canones for Den norske kirkeprovins', in *Norske Middelalderdokumenter*, Bagge 1973, 60. The dating of the manuscript is disputed, but the majority of scholars suggest the period 1160s–70s. See ibid., 54.
151 Bartlett 1986, 100–1.
152 In Anglo-Saxon legislation the hot-iron ordeal, the hot and cold water ordeal, and the so-called *corsnæd* were the commonest forms. *Corsnæd* was a form of ordeal that seems to have been confined to the clergy by which the defendant swallowed a morsel of barley bread or cheese. 'Notes to the laws of Ine and of Alfred', *The Laws of the Earliest . . .*, note 37, 187. We have found no traces of the latter practice in Norwegian laws. Unlike Norwegian laws, English legislation also included a distinction between the simple and threefold ordeal to be implemented depending on the severity of the offence: in cases of the simple hot-iron ordeal an iron ball weighing one pound had to be carried three feet, if the ordeal was a triple one, the iron weighed three pounds and was to be carried nine feet. Similarly in cases of the simple boiling-water ordeal the accused person had to lift out a stone suspended a *span* deep, i.e. the length of a hand stretched out, about 9 inches, and an *ell* deep, i.e. the length of the arm from elbow to the tip of the middle finger, about 18 inches, if the case was a threefold one. Ibid. 188.
153 Cf. the Canon Law principle of '*fama*'. Statements from only one house were to be rejected as 'slander and gossip'.
154 In G 24 trial by ordeal is referred to in general terms.
155 See for instance, Æthelstan II, 23:

> If anyone engages to undergo an ordeal, he shall come three days before to the mass-priest who is to consecrate it, and he shall feed himself on bread and water and salt and herbs before he proceeds thither, and he shall attend mass on each of the three days. And on the day he has to go to the ordeal, he shall make an offering and attend communion; and then before he goes to the ordeal, he shall swear an oath that according to the public law he is innocent of the accusation. § 1. And if the ordeal is by water he shall sink to a depth of one-and-a-half *ells* on the rope. If

### *Oaths*

In the Gulathing Law, as in medieval legislation in general, there is an overarching connection between the two phenomena of ordeal and oath in the sense that both include an element of '*iudicium dei*'. The very basic substance of the oath was the invocation of God himself as witness and guarantor of the truth of the oath.[156] Thus, the practice of taking oaths in court was, like the institution of ordeals, also a matter of theological and ecclesiastical relevance and concern.[157]

The phenomenon of oath-taking has archaic and multicultural roots.[158] The Anglo-Saxon verb '*swerian*' (to swear) indicates a magic origin of the practice, originally meaning "to recite mystic charms and spells in a strange sing-song kind of chant".[159] Correspondingly, the meaning of the Old Frisian verb '*swera*' was simply to sing in the service of religion.[160] Thus, some kind of phenomenological connection to the previously mentioned magical *galdr*-song is likely to be observed here. Further, a fundamental feature of the oath pointed out by phenomenologists of religion is that it is based on belief in the blessing or cursing power in the sworn words, in that the person taking an oath exposes him- or herself to the saving or destroying power – magic or divine – called upon to try the truth of the oath.[161]

In the Old Testament we find oaths mentioned in a number of contexts. Most common is the so-called 'promissory' oath whose intention was to seal solemn pledges for the future such as treaties and agreements between individuals, groups of people, or between man and God.[162] In this sense, we also find examples of God swearing by himself.[163] But, also the category of the 'assertoric' or 'reaffirming' oath occurs in the Old Testament. The aim of this kind of oath was to free oneself

---

the ordeal is by iron three days shall elapse before the hand is unwrapped. § 2. And every man shall precede his accusation with an oath, as we have already declared, and everyone who is present in both parties shall fast according to the command of God and the archbishop.

*The Laws of the Earliest* . . ., 139, 141. For further information see ibid., 187–9.

156 Sägmüller 1914, Band 2, 283–6.

157 Latin terms: *iuramentum* or *ius iurandum*. C.22, qu.1, c.1–17, Friedberg, I, cols. 862–66, C.22, qu.2, c.1–3, Friedberg, I, cols. 866–67, C.22, qu.5, c.12–13, Friedberg, I, col. 886.

158 Known in Assyrian by the term '*mamuti*', in Arab '*bai*'. Elmar Klinger, 'Vows and Oaths', in *The Encyclopedia of Religion*, Mircea Eliade (ed.), vol. 15, New York/London: Macmillan, 1987, 301–2. According to Cicero "An oath is an assurance backed by religious sanctity; and a solemn promise given, as before God as one's witness, is to be sacredly kept". *De officiis* 3.104. For further information about the concept of oath in medieval Norwegian legislation see Ole-Albert Rønning Nordby, *The Judicial Oath in Medieval Norway. Compurgation, Community and Knowledge in the Thirteenth Century*. PhD dissertation, University of Oslo, Oslo: Unipub, 2018.

159 Klinger 1987, 302.

160 Ibid.

161 "Der Eid als feierliche Bekräftigung einer Aussage erhält seine Qualität durch den ihm zugrundeliegenden Glauben an die Segen und Fluch bewirkende Macht des Wortes. Entsprechend hat die Religionsphänomenologie den Eid neben Schelt- und Fluchworten gerechnet". Hoch 1999, 1122.

162 Thus, Jos. 9:15, 18–21, Gen. 31:44–53, 1 Sam. 14:24.

163 Gen. 22:16–17, Ps. 89:36, Am. 4:2, 6:8.

from charges as part of a legal procedure,[164] and as such a parallel to the practice of oath-taking prescribed in the Gulathing Law.

The New Testament seems to reveal a two-sided view of the oath. On the one hand, we find several references to oaths without any reservation, such as to God's own oaths in the Old Testament,[165] or to the apostle Paul taking God as witness to the truth of his statement.[166] On the other hand, we have Jesus' words in his Sermon on the Mount in which he exhorts his disciples not to swear at all.[167] In particular, Jesus appears to be critical of the Pharisees and their way of swearing.[168] The patristic fathers of the Ancient Church – especially those from the Greek world – express a generally negative attitude to oaths, but not in absolute terms.[169] In the Latin West the church fathers accepted oaths rendered in the name of God, but forbade Christians to swear by any idol or any object of creation.[170] This latter principle and the following summary of the issue by Augustine laid the ground for the Church's teaching in the following centuries: "Peccat et graviter qui falsum iurat; non peccat qui verum iurat; sed nec ille peccat qui non iurat".[171]

In all the Germanic kingdoms that replaced the Roman Empire the use of the assertoric oath in the sense of a purification oath with oath-helpers was a common element in legal proceedings. The general picture is that the institute of the purification oath in the same way was accepted and included as a main element also in the regulations of ecclesiastical law and trials, generally referred to as *purgatio canonica*.[172] Another general feature in the early medieval West is that the issue of oaths, and especially the sanctions entailing perjury, became a matter primarily to be dealt with by Church Law. According to Theodor of Orléans – and Gratian – perjury was reckoned among the worst of crimes equal to murder and fornication.[173] In provision 28 of the Gulathing Law, the punishment for

164 1 Kgs. 8:31–2:

> If any man trespass against his neighbour, and an oath be laid upon him to cause him to swear, and the oath come before thine altar in this house, then hear thou in heaven, and do, and judge thy servants, condemning the wicked, to bring his way upon his head; and justifying the righteous, to give him according to his righteousness.

See also Gen. 22:10–11.

165 Lk. 1:73, Acts 2:30, Heb. 6:17.
166 2 Cor. 1:23, 1 Thess. 5:27.
167 Mt. 5:33–7.
168 Mt. 23:16–22.
169 Landau 1982, 383–4. Especially, swearing was forbidden if somehow connected to pagan cult.
170 Thus, Tertullian allowed swearing by the fortune of the emperor, but not by his genius. And according to Hieronymus, Jesus in the Sermon on the Mount did not prohibit oaths in the name of God, only oaths connected with invocations of the Heavens, the earth, or any part of creation. Ibid., 383.
171 "Gravely sins the one who swears falsely; the one who swears true does not sin; but also the one who does not swear, does not sin". Ibid., 383 (Sermo 180.4).
172 Ibid., 384.
173 (Kapitular c.26) ibid., 385, C.22, qu.1, c.17, Friedberg I, col. 866.

perjury in the older layer of the text is outlawry, the younger layer, the Magnus-text, prescribes a heavy fine of 15 *merkr*. The general ecclesiastical sanction was excommunication.[174]

## Blót *and pagan cult*

Provision 29 deals with the traditional ritual of *blót* and the building of cult sites connected to the veneration of pagan gods. A main element in the *blót* ritual consisted, as already described in our comment to provision 20, in the sacrifice of horses and the consumption of horse blood and horse meat. Further, the ritual was performed by smearing blood from the sacrificed horse onto idols and the pillars of the high seat of the chieftain or master of the house, and by the blood being drunk by the participants.[175] From the perspective of the Church the *blót* ritual was an exquisite example of idolatry that had to be eradicated from the land as part of the already mentioned overarching aim of purifying the country of all heathen practices. Thus, a strict ban was levied on the ritual in all the four Norwegian provincial laws.[176]

Other forbidden practices specified in this text are the performance of cult activity on pagan grave mounds or on special stone altars in the countryside and the raising of magic libel poles for casting evil spells on one's enemies. The cult activity on grave mounds is assumed to refer to the traditional pagan custom of sitting outdoors at night, in Norwegian known as '*utesete*',[177] possibly on grave mounds and at crossroads to wake the dead or call on their spirits,[178] or, as stated in provision 32, "sitting out at night to call forth trolls and thus to promote heathen worship".

The sanctions mentioned in this provision seem to reveal the two layers of the text of the Gulathing Law. The older layer of the law simply states that violators have forfeited every penny of their property whereas the younger layer imposes a penalty of 3 *merkr* to the bishop. Both versions open the possibility of going to confession and doing penance. In cases of refusal, culprits were to be expelled from the king's realm.

## *Bestiality with cattle*

It is somewhat surprising that we find the phenomenon of bestiality the topic of a separate provision of the Gulathing Law. The background is probably to be found in the headline of the actual paragraph 30, which simply says that it deals

174 Sägmüller 1914, 286.
175 Steinsland 2005, 274–305.
176 B I 16.9; E I 24; F III 15.
177 B I 16.2.
178 Steinsland and Sørensen 1994, 87. Other literary sources reveal that this practice was especially associated with female fortune-tellers. For instance, in *Vǫluspá*, the Nordic figure *vǫlva*.

with men who commit outrage, i.e. a sexual act of the most abominable kind. In early medieval tradition, both on the continent and on the British Isles, sexual intercourse with animals was a topic of the church penitential rather than the law.[179] The basic attitude to the act was, however, the same, based as it was on the categorical condemnation of bestiality in the Old Testament.[180] Among sexual sins listed in the penitential, sins against nature like sodomy and bestiality were regarded as the worst, before incest, adultery, and fornication.[181] The same ranking order was confirmed by Gratian in his *Decretum*.[182]

In the Gulathing Law both the ban on the offence and the prescribed punishment for it are in line with the categorical condemnation of the penitential and legislative tradition: "None of us may have intercourse with cattle. And if a man is identified and convicted of this, then he should be castrated". Among the other three Norwegian provincial laws a similar statute is included in the Frostathing Law,[183] whereas the Eidsivathing and Borgarthing laws keep silent about the issue. In cases when the accused denies it, the Gulathing provision instructs him to swear a solemn oath at the church door, but if the oath failed, the punishment was outlawry[184] with "*fimtargrið*", a set grace period of five days to leave the country.

The act of bestiality, however, was not only believed to pollute the perpetrator, but also the cattle exposed to the act. Consequently, it was not permissible to use any part of the animal. It had to be driven into the sea under the threat of a 3 *merkr* fine to the bishop in case of neglect to do this.

## *Some additions by King Magnus on severe crimes*

The somewhat summary provision 32 contains a number of regulations mainly aimed at securing peace within the realm in particular for the purpose of reducing the practice of blood vengeance. It is reasonable to read the Gulathing statutes here as a reflection in Norwegian law of the at the time widespread ideas of *pax dei*[185]

179 For the attitude to and dealing with bestiality in the Church in the Middle Ages, see Salisbury 1994, 61–80.

180 Exod. 22:19, Lev. 20:15.

181 Jeffrey Richards, *Sex, Dissidence and Damnation; Minority Groups in the Middle Ages*, London/New York: Routledge, 1991, 30: For habitual offenders entailing 15 years of penance. See also James Brundage, *Law, Sex, and Christian Society in Medieval Europe*, Chicago: Chicago University Press, 1990, 245–51.

182 C.32, qu.7, c.10–14, Friedberg I, cols. 1142–3.

183 F III 18.

184 The Frostathing Law has a similar note about oath-taking, but mentions also the ordeal of hot iron. Ibid.

185 The peace of God. The concept dates back to the period of the dissolution of the Carolingian Empire when the higher clergy introduced the concept as a spiritual protection against random assaults from people of power on church property and poor or defenceless citizens. Huber 1983, 622–3.

and *treuga dei.*[186] In both of these institutes we see a combination of theology and law in which Church and King operate in close cooperation. The legal institutionalization of *pax dei* was generally based on solemn pledges confirmed by oaths under the threat of excommunication. In the Gulathing variant of the principle, therefore, this promulgation is introduced by a general ban on everyone who violates "pledges of peace and security given between people in cases of killing". The securing of peace on these terms was a basic prerequisite for the maintenance of law and order in the realm. So, breaking the law on this point was considered a crime of the most serious nature resulting in the perpetrator becoming a so-called *úbótamaðr.*[187] The punishment for a person sentenced as *úbótamaðr* was the loss of all property, outlawry, and expulsion from the king's lands.

Following the general introductory words to this paragraph, the text lists a number of examples of such crimes, all of which are of the kind that they undermine the very existence of an orderly society. The criminals mentioned are: men who lose their lives as thieves and robbers, those who sit out at night in order to call on evil powers,[188] hired assassins who kill people whom they themselves are not in legal conflict with, those who take other men's women by force against the consent of the guardian or that of the woman herself, and all those who avenge these culprits or claim compensation from them. In addition, the text mentions men who kill relatives in the first degree of consanguinity, men who have sex with one another, those who fight in church or churchyard, and above all those who in different ways violate legally settled judgements.

When it comes to the distribution of confiscated property from the listed evildoers the text here gives few details about the portions which accrued to king, bishop, or the offended party. Only regarding the cases of homosexuality and executors of violence on sacred ground is the law more specific. In the former case king and bishop share the property half-and-half, in the latter case the bishop is entitled to 3 *merkr* plus what is needed to restore the churchyard whereas the rest goes to the king.

## Concluding remarks

In this essay we have confined ourselves to the Church Law section of the Gulathing Law. This choice of focus is justified by the fact that this part of the law more than the rest was shaped – not only on indigenous Norwegian ground – but in a process of interaction between traditional Norwegian law and foreign impulses. An overarching point for us has also been to explain how the aim of the law was more that of change and creation of a new society rather than that of preservation

186 The truce of God. This legal institute arose in the first half of the 11th century as an unconditional ban on exercise of blood revenge and feuds in specified periods, such as Lent, Advent, and certain days of the week. Ibid., 623.

187 A person having committed a crime that could not be compensated for.

188 See our comment to provision 29.

of the old. The 150 years' period of the formation of this law coincides with the inclusion of Norway into the world of Western Christendom and the consolidation of Norway as a Christian kingdom fully in line with other Christian countries under the Roman Church. In this process the influence of the on-going contemporary efforts on the part of the Church to manifest its policy and interests over those of secular rulers was crucial.[189] Law formation on national ground was an important part of this picture. For the Church a major goal was to establish the highest possible degree of agreement between Canon Law and national legislation.

Thus, the period when the Church section of the Gulathing Law was enacted coincided with the time when Canon Law, in the course of the 11th century, gradually adopted the form of a fixed and solid body, and more substantially by the mid-12th century by the compilation of *Decretum Gratiani.*[190] The level of knowledge among the leading clerical expertise in Norway about the Canon Law processes abroad is difficult to determine. However, despite the fact that the Gulathing Law contains no references to specific articles of Canon Law,[191] foreign legislation, the Bible, or theology in general terms, the resonance of current Church Law principles is clearly visible throughout the investigated text.

189 See our introductory comments on the rivalry during the 11th and 12th centuries over the division of power between *regnum* and *sacerdotium*, within which law-formation and the drawing of a demarcation line between civil and ecclesiastical jurisdiction was a main aspect.

190 Also known as *Concordantia discordantium canonum*.

191 In provision 33 we find a reference to 'church law' in general terms.

# II The book on contracts

## 34 Here begins the book on contracts[1]

Now the next thing is that none of us should take goods away from others, nor should we take the law into our own hands. Every man is entitled to a test in court in (matters concerning) his own possessions. But he who takes something from others should bring it back and pay a fine of a ring[2] to the king for unlawful seizure, and (he from whom something was taken) should demand his rights later according to the law.

If a man has a lawsuit against another, and the latter will not pay what he is instructed to, then the former should summon[3] him to be present at his home, call on witnesses and demand compensation from him. This compensation should be demanded three times like any other debt.

If he still refuses to pay, then he should be summoned before the assembly and be charged with robbery and contempt of law. Then men should outlaw him with respect to the man who charged him and to all other men present at the same assembly until he offers compensation at the assembly or where many men come together, and presents payment there.

## 35 Concerning home summons and pecuniary claims

Now the next thing is that if someone has money due from another, and witnesses know,[4] then he (the creditor) should summon him to be at his home for presentation of the claim and the testimony of witnesses, a householder (should be summoned) at his high seat, a single man (should be summoned) at (the home of) his heir, if he lives in the same *fylki*, or else at the place where he (the single man) stayed during Christmas Eve, with as short respite as he likes, at most fifteen

1 The ON term *kaup* covers a fairly wide range of meaning: 'bargain; agreement; contract; deal', etc. In essence it involves contribution from two sides.

2 Preferably in gold or silver. The standard fine to the king was twelve *aurar* silver.

3 Cf. next chapter.

4 This chapter states the rules for civil action concerning attested claims. Sunde 2007, 314–20.

nights in advance. Now he must say this so that he (the summoned person) will be at home when he comes there.

The whole day is available for appointment, whether he arrives early in the day or later (when it is still) daylight and (he is) unhidden. He should then present testimony on lawful[5] home summons immediately and then present witnesses to the amount of money due to him from the other.

If the other refuses to pay, he should claim it from him and charge him with robbery unless he pays at once. If the other answers "I do not know the law, but I accept what the men at the thing assembly declare to be law", then he (the former) may summon him to meet before the thing assembly after five nights at least, five times five at most, provided that he (the latter) knows when this assembly is to meet. But if he does not know, one must wait until he knows.

Whoever needs to summon an assembly may do so if he wants to.

If their case is treated at the assembly, then the plaintiff should present witnesses that lawful summons has taken place; then the men at the assembly have to give judgement in the case, and award him the money due. But if they do not want to give judgement, then they are liable to pay fifteen *merkr* if he demands judgement from them.

Now, if they do not reach agreement in the quarter assembly, the case may be referred to the *fylkis* assembly, with two witnesses.

But the one of them who thinks that he has still not got justice according to the law, can refer the case from the *fylkis* assembly to the *Gulaþing* only if one quarter of the men leaves the assembly, declaring (it) to be law what he claims; then the appeal is valid, otherwise it is not.

And whenever all agree that the man has claimed his money and his witnesses have been found satisfactory, then they should award him his money.

But if he (the debtor) did not meet the demand by asking for judgement from the men at the assembly, then he is liable to pay a ring to the king, and the amount of money to the other (the creditor) should be doubled. But if someone (the debtor) refers his case to the judgement of the men at the assembly, he escapes the (payment of the) ring. Then he (the creditor) should present at the assembly the witnesses (neighbours) who heard him demand his money as the law prescribes; then it is well if the other will pay that money at the assembly or appoints a day (for its payment) and settles the matter there.

But if he does not want to pay, then the creditor, if he has claimed his money according to law, should call on the men at the assembly, and likewise on the king's representative and as many householders as he considers necessary, to go to the debtor and seize twice as much as he (the creditor) (first) claimed, and a ring[6] to the king. The creditor is entitled to six *aurar* for distraint (as compensation for difficult acquisition).

5 I.e. correct, as prescribed by law.

6 A fine for unlawful seizure or holding of property. Cf. also Ch. 77.

Now people resist and defend themselves with point and edge, then they will be outlawed and deprived of all personal rights; but all others (will be) protected by the law, those who prosecute at law and observe the law. But if they do not give up resistance, their leader is liable to a fine of forty *merkr*, and each of the others (the followers) three *merkr*. He is the leader whom the creditor says is so.

If people refuse to go from the assembly to seize the money claimed, then each of them is liable to pay a fine of three *aurar* to the king. If the king's representative will not go, he should forfeit what fines were due to him.

## 36 Concerning leased and borrowed things

Now there are borrowed things[7] and leased things[8] and things awarded by the court and debt promised by handshaking and debt to be paid on an appointed day and all that debt which witnesses know of, that should all be sued for by formal demand. Whenever a day is set for the payment of the debt, then you have to present your witnesses on that day as if you had summoned him (your debtor) to (be present at) his home.

Now he who is to receive the money does not appear, but he who is supposed to pay is present; then he (the latter) should offer the money on that day; if there is someone present who has been authorized by witnesses to receive these money, then he should hand over (the money) to them. But if none such is present, he has to declare himself absolved from the hire and possession and responsibility, if it was borrowed before,[9] and he should have it who had it before and remain responsible for his negligence until the owner claims (the money), then he (the former) should hand it over to him.

## 37 Concerning appeal to an organ of arbitration[10]

Now the next thing is that if a man has money due to him from another man which witnesses do not know of, then the latter should be summoned to his home, and the former should demand the money he (the latter) owes him. He (the debtor) must either promise (to pay) the money *Olav:* or meet the demand with a request for arbitration, unless he will be prosecuted for ignoring the demand. The plaintiff must accept the request for arbitration from whoever offers it, provided he (the latter) is a free man and of mature age, if the one whose duty it is to offer it is not present.

In every case when arbitration by court is offered within the fences, the court of arbitration should meet after five days before the door of the defendant.[11] The

7 Cf. Ch. 49.
8 Including debts for which the loaner had to pay interest; cf. Ch. 42.
9 I.e. if interest should be paid.
10 This chapter deals with procedures in lawsuits about non-attested claims.
11 I.e. the person prosecuted.

court must be set for a time that will not fall on a Sunday or a Mass-day,[12] otherwise his (the plaintiff's) prosecution is invalid if it had begun.

The court of arbitration has to be set before the defendant's door and not behind his house. The plaintiff may not place his arbiters nearer to the house than it is possible for the defendant to place his arbiters between the door and the arbiters of the former and (leave space for) a cart-load of wood to pass between the arbiters and the door.

Now it is well if the defendant comes out (of his house) and accepts arbitration; otherwise the plaintiff should go into his house with two witnesses and summon him to appoint arbitrators against him (the plaintiff).

Now their court of arbitration has been set. Then the defendant should challenge the court of arbitration produced by the plaintiff. If he (the plaintiff) has chosen, among his arbiters, agnates or cognates or relatives closely related to him by marriage[13] or someone who has a lawsuit[14] against the defendant, then they have to stand up and leave the court, and others, impartial men, should take their place, if available. If such men are not available, his (the plaintiff's) court is invalid.

If he has chosen a landed man among his arbiters, or the son[15] of a landed man, one who is younger then forty years, or the king's representative, then he loses by default[16] and will never be allowed to bring up the case later. These men may never come so near to the court that their voices can be heard.

Now the plaintiff is to challenge the defendant's court of arbitration as the defendant challenged the plaintiff's court of arbitration.

When the courts of arbitration of both parts have been challenged and neither part can render the court invalid for the other, then the plaintiff must present testimony to home summons that he summoned him (the defendant) properly to be at his home to hear his (the plaintiff's) claim and (he should) further (present) witness that he demanded his money. Then those who are appointed arbiters have to pass judgement and order him who denies the debt to take an oath just as great as the one he has to take according to the law when denying the payment of the amount which was requested from him.

And one (oath) will (do to) deny (the debt of) one *eyrir*, two (one of) two *aurar*, three (one of) three *aurar*; then (it) should be denied with a three-man oath until the debt rises to half a hundred, that is to seven and a half *merkr*[17] or more, then he should repeat the three-man oath: lay a holy book on the threshold,[18] take it up again and the other men should take the same oath.

Men should conduct the arbitration in such a way that no one should (be allowed to) rise or leave, except on necessary errands; in that case he has to leave

12 See Chs. 17 and 18.
13 ON *námágar*, see Ch. 239.
14 Or at least had something due from the other.
15 See also Chs. 206 and 200.
16 Because he shirks from his duty to attend the case until it is concluded.
17 I.e. sixty *aurar*, amounting to half of a so-called "big hundred" (120).
18 The oath was taken on a liturgical book or the Bible in front of the church door. Cf. Ch. 30.

his gloves or weapons or some other valuable thing and tell his needs, and he must return to the arbitration court immediately. But if a man rises from the court and leaves it before they are all agreed on the case, then the one who had him in his court loses his case by default.

If a man claims money due to him and the debtor does not submit to arbitration, then he should go outside the fence or on to the edge of the shore[19] and then go back to the house and present his claim once more.

But if the other still does not submit to arbitration, (he should) ask the other to stay at home in the morning the next day, and he should present his claim a third time. He will need four witnesses at the third demand. If he will not then submit to arbitration he is liable to a fine of eighteen *aurar* to the king, six *aurar* for each request.

From then on the plaintiff should summon the debtor to the assembly and present all those witnesses there, those witnesses which he would have presented to the court of arbitration.

If the defendant still refuses to pay, the men at the assembly should award the plaintiff what is due to him, he (the plaintiff) must demand that they set out and take from the defendant eighteen *aurar* to be given to the king, but to himself (the plaintiff) twice as much as the amount he sued for *Magnus:*[20] or (let him promise to swear) the oaths demanded by the laws.

But if he will not do anything of this he acknowledges his debt; then the plaintiff must call two witnesses to this[21] and summon him before the assembly for robbery and present two men there as witnesses that the debtor refused both to pay the money and defend his case with oath; then the men at the assembly should award him his money and (add) a ring of twelve *aurar* to the king.

But if he will neither pay at the assembly nor promise to pay, then the plaintiff should call upon the king's local representative or sheriff and as many householders as he thinks necessary, to go with him and take from the defendant twice as much as was due to the plaintiff from him. But anyone who refuses to go with him is liable to a fine of three *aurar* to the king. But one man shall swear for (i.e. deny the debt of) one *eyrir*, two men for two *aurar*, three for three etc. (see earlier), until the other men (the oath helpers) take the same oath.

## 38 Concerning debts to which there are no witnesses

If a man who had to pay a debt dies, but he is alive to whom it was due, then the latter cannot get his money unless he presents witnesses, for no one should swear before the breast of the deceased (i.e. on behalf of him).

19 The edge of the shore was legally equal to the fence enclosing cultivated land.

20 Magnus has removed the rules regulating the procedures in the courts of arbitration in this case, when the decision was about an oath of denial; instead, the defendant should promise to take the oath immediately.

21 Thus making it an acknowledged debt.

But he (the heir) should swear that "there was no such debt, as far as I knew". Thus he swears before his own breast (i.e. to what he knows himself) and not before the breast of the deceased.

## 39 If debt becomes time-barred to witnesses

If a debt remains unpaid for twenty winters or longer than that, then this debt is too old for testimony.[22] But the creditor may still compel the debtor to an oath (of denial); because the case remains open[23] if the plaintiffs are capable.[24]

## 40 Concerning bargains attested by witnesses and handshake

Now all bargains should be kept that are confirmed with handshake, and those that witnesses know of, when such men make bargains who are their own masters, unless someone sells illegally or there is fraud involved, then the bargain is to be cancelled and the other (the buyer) should have his payment returned.

None of us shall sell to another false or fraudulent things; but he who commits fraud, is liable to pay a fine of three *merkr*. That is all fraud which men consider as such; if a man buys sand or dirt when he believes that he is buying meal or butter, and (if he buys) everything which it is not possible to tell what it is by looking at its outside.

All bargains made with handshake should be kept if it is possible to keep them.

It cannot be kept if you sell to a man what you have already sold to another man. But when he who bought it last has it in his hands, then he may set up a court of arbitration for his bargain. He who bought it first should have the thing bargained, if his witnesses are found satisfactory by the court. Then there has been a fraudulent bargain to the one who bought it last, and he should call upon impartial men to witness.

That is also a fraudulent bargain if someone buys what the seller did not possess anything of, unless it was sold with the consent of the owner. The buyer should call on him who sold it to him, and have his money returned. If the latter will not give it to him, then the buyer should summon to his home and present his witnesses that "you let that thing go according to the law", and claim your money from him and charge him with robbery.

22 Only the testimony became time-barred. It was thought that the witnesses' memory was not reliable after twenty years. But the creditor might prosecute the debtor according to the rules of Ch. 37.

23 Lit. 'lies in salt', i.e. 'is safely stored, retains its vigour'; meaning that the claim is not prescribed. Sunde 2011b, 227.

24 I.e. the case is not time-barred if the plaintiff correctly follows the accepted rules of procedure.

## 41 Concerning a hired cow

Now a man lends a cow, then he who hires her shall be responsible for the cow in every respect, and deliver her back in the same condition as he received her, except that she is older.

Now he should, according to proper agreement, keep the cow until Rogation Days[25] the next spring – then the cows should be on their road home – unless they have agreed on another time when he hired the cow.

If that cow is dead, but the owner had part of another in pledge, he must have that cow, because one cow should replace the other.

If his cow is alive he should have his own. But if she has incurred injuries, be it only a horn broken or the tail torn off, then he who hires must pay for those injuries. If he does not want to hire the cow any more, he must go to see the owner, if he is in the same *fylki*, and offer him the cow. But if he is not in the same *fylki* he must drive the cow home and let men come and look at the cow, that she is unhurt and fit to be received by the owner; then he should declare himself free from the responsibility and take care of the cow as he does of his own cattle, and take the yield from the cow and have her there grazing, being responsible for his own negligence only.

Now he who owns the cow has left the country and appointed another man as his representative, then he who has hired should offer the cow to the representative, if he is in the same *fylki*, (but) to the heir in case there is no representative, if he who had hired the cow does not want to have it any longer.

## 42 Concerning interest[26]

Now someone borrows gold or silver from another man, or whatever kind of money he borrows, then he should pay such interest on the money as was decided upon until he terminates the loan in a legal way.

On that interest which accrues he should pay no interest, except if such interest had been decided and agreed upon from both parts.

## 43 Concerning the rent of livestock

Now a man places his livestock with another man for foddering[27] according to proper contract; then he (the latter) is responsible for any negligence on his part.

That is his negligence if he or the men for whom he is responsible as a guardian underfeeds or kills (the cattle). That is also his negligence if the herdsman fails to find (one of) the cattle before it is dead, likewise if a bear hurts it, a wolf bites it or it falls down from a cliff, and the herdsman is not present, then it is his negligence.

25 Cf. Ch. 18.

26 The church forbade taking interest on loans. This prohibition was ultimately based on the Bible, Exod. 22, 25.

27 Esp. during winter.

But if it falls down from a cliff and he shows it to people before flaying it, then it is not his negligence. That is also his negligence if it drowns in a well and no one looks after it;[28] and it is his negligence if it dies from starvation or the halter strangles it. But if there is a swivel in the tether or a pole (which makes it possible for the tether to twist and slide freely), then it is not his negligence.

Now you should fodder it until it is able to find food outdoors; then you should go to see the owner and ask him to take care of his cattle, and show to people that it is capable of feeding itself, and declare yourself free from responsibility for it.

If someone accepts to fodder or graze a horse by contract, and wolves bite it outdoors, then it is negligence unless other people have their horses outdoors.

Now someone accepts to fodder cattle by contract, then he will be responsible as for cattle taken to foddering during winter.

No one must be held responsible if a cow fails to become pregnant when he has a bull among his cattle.

Now a man has been promised a cow as payment for what is due to him, a cow which is not reduced either in value or rent, then that cow must not be older than eight winters and not younger than having had her second calf, in good condition and with unhurt teats, and having calved in the winter (before).

## 44 Concerning hidden flaws

Now someone buys a horse or livestock from someone else; the buyer has the responsibility as soon as he leads it away.

When people buy live animals, no one should sell it to others with fraud or hidden faults.

That is a hidden fault if it sucks itself. The seller must swear to it that he knew of no hidden fault if the buyer discovers it within the first month, or (if he does not swear) have it (the animal) himself.

## 45 Concerning responsibility for single articles of value

Now a man buys from someone else something unseen, then the seller bears the responsibility until the article comes into the hands of the buyer or the man whom he has authorized, in the presence of witnesses, to receive the article, unless they agree on something else in the presence of witnesses.

## 46 Concerning home summons[29]

Now there comes into the *fylki* a man whom you want to sue for some reason, and he has no heir in the *fylki* and did not stay there during Christmas Eve, then you should ask him about his home.

28 This rule can be traced back to Mosaic law (Exod. 22, 10–15). Jacoby 1986, 202–3; Tamm 2002, 303.

29 This chapter deals with what in legal terms is called venue.

If he names it he should be summoned to appear there; he may not say that he lives with a landed man unless that is the case.

But if he refuses to name his home, this must be witnessed, and he may be summoned to appear at any farm whatever, except at your own, and then be sued there.

That is also correct summons of any man when he is summoned to appear where the bargain took place.

A single man should be summoned in the same way as a householder to the place where he has taken residence for one year. But if there is no such place he must be summoned to the place where his heir lives, if that is within the same *fylki*; otherwise to the place which he names within the same quarter, unless he says (he lives with) a landed man.

## 47 Concerning lawsuits and home summons

Now legal actions are to be suspended when the levy is in service and until the ships have been on land[30] for five nights. Legal actions shall be suspended during Lent. Ecclesiastical cases[31] may always be prosecuted, and new cases which turn up.

Nothing should be prosecuted on holy days except home summons.

A man may summon another man to his (the latter's) home on behalf of another as for himself, if he has been authorized in the presence of witnesses to do so.

Every free man of legal age should bring his own action within the country. But if a man leaves the country, then the one whom he has authorized thereto, in the presence of witnesses, has to take care of his property for three years. Then he (the latter) should have the right to bring lawsuits and defence on his (the former's) behalf. If he goes to Greece[32] he who is his nearest heir should look after his property.

A woman must be prosecuted in the same way as a man if she is single; but she may choose to assign her right of lawsuit and defence (to another person). She may not assign it to a landed man or to a man more prominent than her opponent. A man may bring her lawsuit as his own if he has been authorized thereto with witnesses.

Now a man wants to prosecute somebody for something, but another plaintiff has already brought an action against the same man; then he who was the last to begin must yield unless the first prosecution is fraudulent,[33] because the defendant cannot answer two at the same time.

## 48 If a man sells illegally

Now two or more men own something together, then one of them sells it without asking those who own it together with him. If his fellow owners want to nullify

30 Where they were placed on rollers.

31 Violation of the Christian Law.

32 The Greek Empire (capital: Constantinople).

33 I.e. that the first suit is a mere pretence.

the sale, it should be decided by drawing lots. If he wins who sold, it must go his way. But if the others win, who wanted to nullify (the sale), then they have to declare it void within the first month after having heard of it.

## 49 If a man lends something to another

Whoever receives a thing lent to him should be held responsible for it and bring it safely back.

If he will not, it must be recovered as an acknowledged debt.[34] That is all acknowledged debt which witnesses know of.

Now a man lends (to another) what was lent to him and it is damaged, then the owner should claim it from whoever of the two he wants to. It is always like this when a man sells the property of another, then he (the latter) should claim it from whom he wants to, from him who sold or from him who bought.

## 50 Concerning pledges

Now a man deposits an object to another man as security for something, then he who receives it bears the responsibility.

If they have appointed a day to redeem the pledge, then he should offer it on that day and bring witnesses. But if then no one redeems it, the owner has forfeited his ownership.

Now a man has money due from another and takes something in pledge, be it land or other property. Now he (the former) sells the pledge to another man, then he who owned the pledge should present witnesses within twelve months that it is his pledge if he is within the *fylki*. But if he is not within the *fylki* he must have redeemed the pledge within the first twelve months after he has come home to his *fylki*; otherwise he will have no right to renew the claim later.

Now a man gives the same thing in pledge to two men, then he must have the pledge who got it first, when witnesses know; but is it fraud to him who got it last.[35]

34 Acknowledged debt, cf. Ch. 35.

35 I.e. he loses it.

# III The marriage of women

## 51 Women's marriage[1]

Now the next thing is that we should know how to buy women with bride-price, so that a child becomes entitled to inherit. Then the man must pledge himself to pay (at least) twelve *aurar*, (which is) the bride-price paid by a poor man, and have witnesses thereto, and he must have bridesmen[2] and she bridesmaids,[3] and (he should) give her a present in the morning after they have been together during the night, such a present as he promised her in the betrothal. Then that child which is born later is entitled to inherit.

Now the next thing is that a man wants to enter into a marriage requiring more expenses (than twelve *aurar*).[4] Then the father must himself betroth his daughter if she is a maid, but her brother if her father is deceased. If the father does not want to marry her off to the man to whom he had betrothed her, then the fiancé has to summon him home and appoint a day on which he wants to have his betrothed.

If he (the father) will not let him have her, he (the fiancé) should claim[5] his betrothed and summon the other to the assembly, charged with robbery. Then the men of the assembly have to outlaw him. The girl has no say in the matter, when (i.e. even if) she does not run away.

He who controls the marriage may withhold the betrothed woman from her betrothed man twelve months. That may annul the betrothal, that one of them (the betrothed woman or the betrothed man) contracts leprosy.[6] But if someone sleeps

1 On the institution of marriage in legislation see Vogt 2010, 235–40, 253–8.

2 The bridesmen followed the bridegroom in the wedding and sat beside him. According to the *Bjarkøyjar réttr* there should be two bridesmen and two bridesmaids.

3 The bridesmaids followed the bride in the wedding and sat beside her.

4 I.e. when betrothal and wedding are celebrated separately and not at the same time (as in the previous paragraph).

5 Cf. Ch. 35. A decree from Pope Alexander III to the Archbishop of Nidaros and his suffragan bishops states that if the betrothed hesitate to move in together, the church may coerce them to marry, provided that there are no obstacles or they (the betrothed) do not agree to postpone marriage.

6 ON *hǫrundfall*. It is unclear whether this term refers to leprosy or impotence. See Robberstad 1981, 347.

with his betrothed he has to pay a compensation,[7] fixed by law, to her heir, and then marry her.

A widow may betroth herself and take advice from her kinsfolk, then she may not break the contract. But if it is without advice from the kinsfolk, she may break it and (must then) pay a fine of three *merkr*[8] for breach of promise to the one who had affianced her.

Every man should have his betrothed woman, if he who has the right to give her in marriage affiances her. But if someone betroths to another man a woman whose marriage he does not control, then he must pay a fine of three *merkr* to him who had become betrothed to that woman.

Now two or more brothers[9] have to decide for their sister, then one of them betroths her to a man; now the others want to break (the betrothal); then they should settle by drawing lots who is to decide; if it is the one who betrothed, it must be kept; but otherwise not, and (then the former must) pay a fine of three *merkr* for breach of promise.

If the betrothed man or woman falls ill or is wounded, then they have to wait twelve months, (and) then do one of two things: either let the engagement remain valid, with those injuries that have come into it, or annul the betrothal.

He who has the right to give her away in marriage (i.e. her father or brother) may not do so (i.e. give her away to someone else) until twelve months have passed, unless he (the earlier fiancé) accepts it; neither may the latter take another woman (as his betrothed woman), unless he (who had the right to give the former woman in marriage) accepts it.

Now a man does not want (to marry) his betrothed woman, then (he who has the right to give her away) should summon him home to receive (her) and appoint a day for this; then he has to summon him to appear before the assembly for having avoided his betrothed woman; the men of the assembly must outlaw him and he is called a runaway from his betrothed woman.

In the same way they should appoint a day for a woman if she pledges herself to a man and does not arrive on the appointed day to marry the man whom she had pledged herself to. If she will not come on the appointed day she must be summoned to appear before the assembly for having fled from her betrothed man, and she must be outlawed in the assembly, and she has to leave the country and is called a runaway from her betrothed man.

Every man should take care of his betrothed when an army invades our country, if she is entrusted to his care in the presence of witnesses. But if he refuses and will not take care of his betrothed, then he thereby breaks the betrothal.

Now a betrothed woman is taken captive, then her betrothed man is obliged to go after her and pay three *merkr* to release her, but the heir (must pay) whatever more it takes.

7 To the aggrieved person for defamation or physical insult, cf. Ch. 200.

8 Earlier: six *aurar*. Cf. Chs. 72, 78, and 146.

9 This rule corresponds to the rule for common property in Ch. 48.

Now a man takes another man's betrothed and marries her and they both agree to this, then he who had affianced her first should summon him to the assembly who got her last; then the men of the assembly have to outlaw both of them. But if she declares that this (marriage) was not what she wanted, then she is free of this.

## 52 How a husband should manage his wife's property

No man may remove his wife's property out of the country unless she is willing. He should manage all of their property to the benefit of both of them.

Neither of the two may by word or deed spoil what belongs to the other.

Every man has the same right to compensation in his wife's case as in his own.

## 53 Concerning entrance into co-ownership[10]

A wife must not deny her husband co-ownership.[11] Now a man marries a maid; they cannot enter into co-ownership without the consent of their nearest heirs. But if they have children to inherit from them, they may enter into [such co-ownership as they want to.[12]

Now a man marries a widow and she has children who inherit from her, and they are minors; and he nevertheless wants to enter into co-ownership with her, then the paternal relatives of the children should be summoned, and the ownership has to be arranged in proportion to the size of the wealth, land (in comparison) to land, movables to movables, and his means be valued (so as to ensure) that they are greater than his wife's.

Now it cannot be annulled when it has been established in this way. But if they form their ownership differently, then it may be annulled by his heir or hers, whichever of them wants to, in such a way that he goes to the assembly before they have been together for twenty winters [*Deichman 11 8vo:* nine winters] and declares the co-ownership annulled. And if it is not annulled before they have been together for twenty winters, then he can never bring the matter into court later. [*Deichman 11 8vo adds:* Everywhere when man and wife enter into co-ownership, that ownership should be kept in accordance with what lawful witnesses know. And if co-ownership between spouses is lawful and is passed on to heirs or minors after either one of them, then it devolves upon them (i.e. the heirs etc.) according as their co-ownership was arranged. This bridal gift should be at

10 The meaning of this chapter is disputed. Some believe that actual ownership was formed, others hold that the income only was concerned in the agreement. Larson 1935, 74, note 12 with further references.

11 This did not mean that the husband was more entitled to dispose of his wife's property than before, but it implied a different distribution of property after the death of one of the spouses.

12 *Deichman 11 8vo:* joint company (with equal shares) if there are children to share with; but if there are collateral heirs to share with, then that part (of the two, i.e. the joint company and the collateral heirs) which lives longer owns two thirds and the collateral heir(s) one third, and the odal should be dealt with as prescribed in the statute book.

the wife's disposal.] Everywhere when spouses enter into co-ownership they have to announce it before assembled people.[13]

Now two spouses live together for twenty winters or more than twenty winters, then their co-ownership is implied by the law, if it was not determined before. Then she owns one third of their property, and he two thirds. But if co-ownership was established but not publicly declared within twenty winters, then it is to be considered non-existent.

## 54 Concerning bride-price

Now the gift that was given to a woman shall be at her disposal, no matter how their marriage may come to an end. *Olav:* Bride-price must be paid for all that property a maid brings with her into the marriage, and *eyrir* (should) match *eyrir*, but for a widow's property only one half (*eyrir*). The bride-price[14] must remain in force in all cases except two: if the wife dies childless or if she leaves him without cause.

*Both:* No man should punish his wife with blows at the table or at drinking-parties. But if he beats her in the presence of a great number of men, he must pay her such compensation as he may demand for himself, and likewise the second and the third time (he does this). *Olav:* Then she has the right to leave him, taking with her (her) husband's gift and the property set aside to balance the portion.[15]

But if a man wants to be divorced[16] from his wife, he has to announce it so distinctly that each of them can hear the other's voice, and (he must) have witnesses present.

## 55 Olav and Magnus (concerning transfer of a debt to another)

Now a man claims a debt from another who is within the same *fylki*. If he (the latter) transfers him (the former) to another man (i.e. pays a debt by transferring the claim to a third man), then he has paid that debt on his part if there are witnesses to the arrangement.

## 56 How large a purchase may be made by a woman

A minor can neither make a purchase nor conclude a valid bargain. Neither can a slave make any bargain, except about his own knife. Nor can a freedman who has not given his freedom ale, make any bargain that exceeds the worth of an *ertog*.

13 I.e. at the assembly or at the church, in an alehouse or on a fully manned vessel.

14 I.e. this balancing of bride-price and portion.

15 "[H]usband's gift and property . . . to balance the portion", ON *gjǫf* and *gagngjald*, were contributions from the bridegroom; cf. Ch. 51.

16 The church forbade marriages arranged in such a way that the husband reserved for himself the right to divorce whenever he wanted to. The punishment in this case was excommunication.

That must also be known, how large a purchase may be made by a woman.[17] A freedman's wife may make a bargain (to the amount) of an *ertog*, if her husband has given his freedom ale. But his son's wife (to the amount) of half an *eyrir*, the wife of a householder may bargain (to the amount of) one *eyrir*, the wife of a freeholder (to the amount of) two *aurar*, the wife of a landed man a bargain (to the amount) of half a *mǫrk* (i.e. four *aurar*).

If they make a larger purchase, it may be cancelled within the first month. But if he (who has the right to cancel) is not at home, then it has to be cancelled within the first month after he has come home.

17 This clearly shows the differences in class and social standing.

# IV Freedman's law

## 57 Freedman's law

Now the next thing is that a man buys a slave from another man. They make their bargain according to the law. The seller should bear the responsibility until the moon has been waxing and waning, that the slave does not suck cows, and that he is not epileptic[1] or does not have a stitch in the side or any other dangerous disease (pestilence) and that he carries out his urine and keeps his clothes clean, and he (the seller) must bear the responsibility for all hidden defects for the first month. If there is such a defect, the bargain has to be cancelled during the first month, with witnesses present.

If the slave has a natural child, then he who sold the slave should provide for the child. But if the slave has work for his own benefit, it should be used to pay for the maintenance of the child. If the slave lives openly with his wife, then the buyer must take care of the child she is carrying, but the other (i.e. the seller) (has to take care of) all those (children) who were there before.

That is also a hidden defect if a bondwoman is pregnant and the buyer did not know. Then he who has the child with her should bear the responsibility when she goes to childbed, if it causes injury or death to her, until she is capable of carrying two buckets of water from the well.

Then the buyer must take care of the child and let its mother follow it to the place where the seller is, and offer him the bondwoman and hand the child over to its father. He (the seller) should lend out the bondwoman if the other needs her to ascribe paternity to someone. Then he has disposed of the child according to the law, and he must have witnesses present.

Every man has to pay (the) legal fine for his slave as for himself, if the slave sleeps with a woman.

The heir is entitled to receive compensation for a woman, unless she is married.

He shall be the father of the child whom the mother says is father. Now she ascribes paternity to a slave, then they have to summon his master home and bring

1 Epilepsy as a cause for cancelling the bargain of a slave was already mentioned in Hammurabi's law and the law of the Gotlanders.

home summons witnesses; he must take a three-man oath for his slave, or receive the child. But if he will do neither of the two things, then the child must be laid down there and the responsibility be passed on to him. He should dispose of the child of a free woman in the same way as (he disposes of) the child of a bond-woman. Now she ascribes paternity to a free man, then they have to summon him home for declaration of the claim and receiving the child. He (the plaintiff) must go to that place at the time the other had been summoned to be home and bring his home summons witness. The mother of the child should ascribe paternity to him; she must claim the legal fine she is entitled to and demand from the man she said was the father, that he receive the child. For no one must expose a child on the street and offer it to a man there.

Now it is well if he answers yes; then it is his child, born of a bondwoman;[2] but if he answers no and says that he has nothing to do with it, and will neither pledge himself according to the law nor receive the child, then the child should be laid down there, for his no is worth nothing unless he offers a three-man oath and promises to take it (the oath) there immediately.

(If he promises to take an oath,) then the plaintiff must take the child away with him, and the oaths may be valid for ten weeks of oath days.[3]

A three-man oath shall (be the oath of denial) for each case of sleeping with a woman, unless the man is so closely related (by birth or marriage) to the woman that it amounts to a crime,[4] then it is a six-man oath.

Now if he takes the oath he swears the child off his hands, then neither he nor his relatives bear any responsibility for it.

Now the child resembles him, and he realizes that he has perjured himself, then he has to go before assembled people and acknowledge the child as his own and pay to Christ for having perjured himself, then it is his child, born of a bondwoman.

Now he has promised the oath but will not take it, then he must pay to the other (half an?)[5] *eyrir* (to the value of) six ells (wadmal per *eyrir*) for each month the other fosters his child. A failure to take this oath should be prosecuted as any other (such failing) within the first twelve months, otherwise it is as if it were taken according to our rule of law.

Now if he who did not take the oath does not claim his child during the first twelve months, then the other should foster it as his slave or his bondwoman, for none of us must foster a slave as he would a calf to another man's profit.

Now he will come (to the child) when it is grown up and acknowledge it as his own, then he should redeem it with such a sum as impartial men stipulate that the slave is worth without considering the work for his (i.e. the slave's) own purposes.

2 See Ch. 104.
3 See Ch. 135.
4 Cf. Ch. 24.
5 The amount is not stated, but Hertzberg (1895, 758) suggests half an *eyrir*. Ch. 115 stipulates the cost of fostering a minor to half a *mǫrk* per year.

Now a man acknowledges his child and brings it to church before it has (lived) three Christmas Eves and gives it freedom, then it enjoys the same right as its father,[6] when he brings it up in his family. In the same way the child's kinsman may give it freedom on the father's behalf, and if he brings it up in his family, then the child enjoys the same right as the father has.

## 58 Concerning legitimization (of a natural child)

Now a man may improve the conditions of his son and legitimize him, if he wishes and he who is the nearest heir consents. If he has sons and their mother is bought with bride-price, if only one is of age and he consents, then he gives his consent for all those who are still minors as well as for those who are unborn. He who owns the odal with them must consent to the odal-rights. The legitimizer (the father) should give a party with ale brewed from three *sáld* of malt according to the measure used in *Hǫrðafylki* and slaughter a bull three years old. He must flay the skin off the right foreleg and make a shoe of it and place the shoe beside the ale cask. He who legitimizes the man has to be the first to put on the shoe, then he who is legitimized, then he who grants him inheritance, then he who grants him the odal, then the other kinsmen.

No one shall give away the inheritance of another, a fraudulent contract is not valid.

The father must put on the shoe when he legitimizes his son, and his son of age must do likewise. That is full legitimization. If there is no son, then he who grants him inheritance must put on the shoe. Then he who grants him the odal must put on the shoe.

He (the father) should state that "I conduct this man to the property that I give him, and to wergild and gift, to seat and to settle, to fines and to (payment of) wergild, and to all personal rights, as if his mother had been bought with bride-price".

A brother and a sister may legitimize a brother with themselves, and a father's brother a brother's son. A nookling and a scrubling[7] should be legitimized in the same way as a son of a bondwoman. Other kinsmen may be legitimized and granted inheritance in the way that I have now said, if the nearest heir consents. He whom the father gives his freedom before he has (lived) fifteen Christmas Eves may also be legitimized; but all those who are in the same class as him with respect to inheritance must give their consent.

Now he should have everything to which he is legitimized, as long as they are living who stepped into the shoe with him; later, after they have passed away, he should take both, inheritance and odal. He must announce his legitimization in public every twenty winters until he has received an inheritance. Then the inheritance should testify for him for the rest of his life and ever after.

6 I.e. it is entitled to receive equally big compensation (if offended) and has the same social standing as the father.

7 Cf. Ch. 104.

## 59 Concerning testimony

Every lawsuit shall be adjudicated according to witnesses and legal remedies. If only one man bears witness for a man, it does not count, but two count for ten, if the man does not suspect counter-witness.

To these witnesses no counter-witnesses must be produced: home summons witness[8] and witness to summons to the assembly[9] and witness to a claim[10] and witness to legal excuses and witness to a demand for the surrender of odal-land[11] and witnesses that men bear to quarrels at drinking-parties.[12]

If someone claims money from another man, then he (the latter) may defend himself against the claim in this way: by saying that he has paid the debt and naming his witnesses then present. If the witnesses are within the *fylki*, they should be given notice (in time) adjusted to the distance (to the meeting place). Are the witnesses outside the *fylki*, they should be given a public summons (announced at the assembly), that they have to come and bear witness to that at which they were present. If they witness that they were present when he paid all the debt on his part, then he has correctly defended himself against the claim; that is called conclusive testimony. To this no counter-witness must be produced. But if conclusive testimony does not come forward, then he should owe the claim.[13]

Female or male kinsmen or near relatives by marriage cannot bear witness for a man unless they are equally related to both parties.

Two men may receive the testimony from one, if this one is an original witness[14] who was present (at the transaction); then that testimony is fully valid as if they all had been present.

## 60 On counter-witnesses

Now men produce counter-witnesses, then they should add one witness, then those who testified before are false witnesses. If both sides produce equally many witnesses, then those who are last to testify are false witnesses. They can never bear witness in such a case later, and each of them (should) pay a fine of three *merkr* to the king.

8 Witness that the procedure indicated in Ch. 35 has been followed.
9 Witness that someone has been summoned to meet before the assembly.
10 See Chs. 37 and 266.
11 See Chs. 265 and 266.
12 Lit. 'in an alehouse'.
13 Cf. Ch. 116.
14 A witness that was originally present, but is unable to appear for some reason, e.g. illness; then two others may receive his testimony and present it.

## 61 If a man gives a slave his freedom

Now someone leads his slave to church[15] or sets him on a chest[16] and gives him his freedom. Now he gives it free from debts and dues (to his master), then he (the slave) need not give his freedom ale; neither does anyone who is born free.

Then he should himself arrange his business affairs and marriages; still he must remain loyal[17] to his lawful master, just like him who buys his freedom.

Now a man gives his slave or his bondwoman their freedom in return for payment: everyone is free who has been given his freedom, provided that it is given by one who has the right to give it.

Now a slave moves around like a free man for twenty winters or more, and no one complains about his dealings or his business affairs or his marriage, whether he goes outside the *fylki* or stays inside (it), then he is free if he wants to be called free.

A man who receives his freedom from the king need not give his freedom ale; nor does the one who is given his freedom before he has (lived) three Christmas Eves and been brought up free from debt.

Now a slave or a bondwoman pays his/her ransom (for their value as slaves[18]), then (their master) should lead them to church and lay a (Gospel) book on their heads and give them their freedom. Afterwards he still has to work twelve months for his master. If the slave is freed in so far as half of his value or more remains (to be paid), nothing of this goes to the king, even though the master collects the rest by force.[19]

## 62 Concerning manumission

Now a freedman wants to control his business affairs and marriages, then he should give his freedom ale, an ale brewed from three *såld* (of malt) at the least, and invite, with witnesses, his master to the party, but not his opponents in a lawsuit, and place him (i.e. his master) in the high seat and put six *aurar* into the scales the first evening and offer it to him (i.e. his master) as the ransom fee. If he receives it, it is well. But if he gives it back, then it is as if it were paid.

But if the master refuses to come, then the freedman has to produce witnesses to testify that he did invite his master, and leave his high seat vacant, and put six *aurar*[20] into the scales the first evening and carry them to the vacant seat, that

15 In the year 321 the Roman emperor Constantine decided that a slave might be given his freedom in a church in the presence of the bishop and the congregation. This provision was kept in Roman law. The practice of giving slaves their freedom in church in front of the altar is known from Anglo-Saxon law from the years 696 and 1114–18.

16 Probably the slave's own chest, where he could keep his personal belongings.

17 Cf. Ch. 66.

18 See Book I, note 26.

19 The slave was still considered as such, so that his master had the right to punish him corporally.

20 These may have been the second and final instalment of the ransom fee.

should be called the ransom fee. If his master has authorized someone to receive (it), then it is well. But if no one receives (it), then the freedman must keep the money until the next morning and offer it once more at the meal. If no one then receives it, he should have it and keep it until the one to whom it is due comes to seek it. Then the freedom ale procedure has been carried out in full.

## 63 Concerning a freedman's marriage

Now a freedman who has given his freedom ale takes a well-born woman[21] to wife and they separate while still living, then all the children should go with her. But if she dies first, all the children must return to the father and live on his means so long as there are any; and when all is consumed, the children should follow the better kin and the father should return to his master.

Now a freedman who has not given his freedom ale takes a well-born woman to wife; no matter how their marriage may come to an end, all the children should go with her.

Now a freedman marries a freedwoman, and her freedom ale has been given, but not his, then the children inherit from neither. If his freedom ale has been given, but hers not, and her master nevertheless renounces his right of inheritance after her (i.e. holding out to her the prospect of being granted freedom), then their children become entitled to inherit from both of them.

Now a freedman marries a freedwoman, and the master of one of them has consented, but the master of the other has not; he who does not consent, may claim his share if there are goods to distribute, but if there is poverty, he may renounce every claim.

Now a freedman marries a freedwoman and they have both given their freedom ale, then the children are entitled to inherit from both of them. But if they[22] become paupers, then they are (regarded as) ready for the grave: a grave must be dug in the churchyard and they are to be placed within it and left there to die.[23] Their master should take out (of the grave) the one who lives longer and support him or her afterwards.

Now a freedman marries a freedwoman, neither having given the freedom ale; now they beget children, then these enjoy the same personal rights as their father. Then they have to work for man and wife (i.e. do the kind of work incumbent on their parents). If any one of them wants to go away it must leave three *merkr* in its place.

## 64 Concerning a slave and a bondwoman

Now a slave and a bondwoman are given their freedom and live together in marriage, then he should own two thirds[24] of what they acquire, and she one third.

21 I.e. a woman from a householder's kin.
22 I.e. the freed couple, or their children, or both.
23 See Sunde 2006, 131, 134.
24 This concerns co-ownership in marriage.

She may also keep the bride-price which he gave to her while they were still in bondage, whether that price was smaller or bigger.

## 65 Concerning the inheritance of two unfree brothers[25]

Now two brothers have been brought up in bondage in the same man's house and are both brothers and foster-brothers and are released by their master, but continue to live together, sharing the work for their master as well as that for themselves, then each of them is entitled to inherit from the other. Their children do not inherit unless they have given their freedom ale.

## 66 Concerning freedmen's respect and loyalty towards their master[26]

Now a freedman should owe respect and loyalty to his master. He must not use fraud against him or join in any design on his life or goods, and not engage in lawsuits against him unless he has to defend his own case, then he must defend himself against him as against other men. He must not consider himself his equal and not turn point and edge against him, and not side with his enemies, and not bear witness against him, and not enter the service of a man more powerful than his master without permission and not appoint another man's court against him.

If he does anything of this, he will have to return to the same seat (i.e. position) where he sat before, and redeem himself from there with full ransom; he has also forfeited his property.

Two generations, father and son, should remain in dependence on father and son on the other side. If his son does anything of this, he will be liable to such penalty of ransom towards his master as his father paid.

For twenty winters[27] a freedman has the duty to produce witnesses that he has given his freedom ale. But if no one complains of his doings for twenty winters, it shall be considered given, although it has not been given, when he says it has been given.

A freedman may buy inheritance to his children if they (i.e. he and his master) agree; then it is the same as if he had made his status clear (i.e. given his freedom ale). But if his parents are poverty-stricken and (the right to inheritance) has been bought, then their children should work for their parents with their master as long as the parents live, and then they may leave free of debt. If they (the children) will not, each child which wants to leave, must pay for (the parents') maintenance.[28]

25 This chapter and Ch. 114 both concern co-ownership, in which case the master of one of the co-owners inherits from neither of the two. Otherwise the master inherits from freedmen who have not given their freedom ale.

26 See note 17.

27 This rule is connected to the provision that the validity of testimonies is limited to twenty years.

28 Cf. Ch. 63, end.

## 67 If a freedman leaves the *fylki* without his master's permission

Now a freedman leaves the *fylki* without his master's permission and acquires property or articles of trade, then his master should go after him with witnesses. If he will return, then it is well. But if he refuses to return, his master has to produce witnesses against him, that he is his freedman, and take him back as he likes, unbound or bound, and put him in the same seat (i.e. position) as he sat in before.

## 68 If a slave runs away

Now a slave runs away and someone captures him within the *fylki*, but outside the quarter, then the finder should have an *eyrir*. But if he captures him outside the *fylki*, but within our law province, then he should have two *aurar*. Now if he captures him within the realm, but outside our law province, he should have half a *mǫrk*. If he brings the slave home in fetters he should have the finder's reward, otherwise nothing.

## 69 Concerning responsibility for another man's servant

Now someone hires a slave (as a servant) from another man. He who hires him shall be held accountable if he sends him out into impassable rivers or upon impassable ices, or to bears' lairs, or to impassable mountains or seas, or to other dangerous places.

If the slave loses his life in such a place, and his servants (i.e. of him who had hired the slave) are not with him, nor others of his workmen, then he has to give the owner compensation for the servant.

He must send him (the servant) home after half a year. But if, in sending him home, he lets him go alone and he runs away and does not come home to his master, then he who hired him has to give compensation (to the owner) for the servant.

No man must help a servant to run away from his master, unless the man is willing to take the consequences for it himself; every man should send (the servant) back to his master without fear of punishment. Every man must obtain consent from the master if he wants to use his (the latter's) servant as a workman, otherwise the man is accountable in every respect.

Now the hired workman becomes ill or wounded, then he may lie there for seven nights, but after that he who hired him should return him to his master. If the master has left the country, he who hired must bring him to the master's manager. If he who hired him is willing to keep the servant longer there, then the hire should be reduced proportionately; but he gets no compensation for the food that the servant eats while lying there ill.

If the servant runs away from him who has him (i.e. hires him), he has to notify the owner, otherwise he must pay the hire even if he does not have him.

## 70 Concerning workmen[29]

Now someone buys work from a free man, then he should keep everything they agreed on.

But if the householder will not keep the agreement with his workman and dismisses him, then he (the latter) must demand his keep before two witnesses and offer his work which they had agreed on. If the householder does not want this, then he is liable to pay a fine of twelve *aurar*; but the other should have his pay and compensation for the food that has not been eaten.

If a workman refuses to keep the agreement with the householder, then he (the latter) should demand from the workman such work as he promised by shaking hands and offer him his keep before witnesses; if the workman does not accept this, he is liable to pay a fine of twelve *aurar*. Then the householder may demand the same from him as he (the householder) should have paid him; but for food he must demand nothing, because the workman himself renounces it.

If he undertakes a man's work and is not able to do it, then men must value how much his pay should be reduced.

Now the workman becomes ill or is wounded; if he lies (in bed) five nights his pay should not be reduced; but if he lies longer, men must value the loss in work and the food he consumes; otherwise he should be brought to his heir.

Now someone takes a minor into his service, that (agreement) should also be kept. But if he dismisses him and the man goes (begging) from house to house, then he has to pay three *merkr* and take care of him according to agreement.

Such as I have now said each man should be fined who lets his minor go (begging) from house to house.

## 71 Concerning debtors

A debtor should be taken in the assembly, he may first be offered to his kinsmen (to ransom him); he who is the nearest (of his kinsfolk) has priority, if he wants (the debtor), otherwise he to whom the creditor prefers that the debtor is given. No one can take a woman into debt without the consent of her kinsmen. A freedman's children may be taken at any gathering that one prefers.

Everything that men agree to and witnesses know of shall be kept.

He must not force him to work by blows, unless he cannot (otherwise) get his due from him. But after that the debtor has no right to claim compensation either from him (the creditor) or from his wife or from anyone of his household, and likewise they from him.

29 [*AM 146 4to has the following version of this chapter:* Now someone hires a free man, then he should work as they have agreed, if he wants to receive his pay. If he runs away from service, men should value his work, what it is worth in the autumn, then he must pay that much to him who hired him. But if a householder dismisses his workman, but he (the latter) offers the householder his work, then he must have his pay if witnesses know that he worked well and offered him his work.]

If other people beat him, the creditor has the same right to compensation for him as for his overseer;[30] he (the debtor) must himself have the rest of that compensation to which he is entitled by birth and kinship. An equally big compensation must be paid for him (by the violator), as if he had been free of debt.[31]

If a female debtor sleeps with a slave, then the king's representative has no claim (to a fine) from her until she has paid her debt.

If someone sells his debtor as a slave, provided that he does not run away from his debt, then the seller is liable to pay a fine of forty *merkr*, and so is everyone who sells a free man. If a landed man is the seller, he is liable to pay half of the fine to the king and the other half to the men in the *fylki*. If the king's representative is the seller, he must pay a fine of forty *merkr* to the men in the *fylki*.

A well-born man may give his child for a debt if he does so in the assembly or in an alehouse or in a gathering at church, then he may give it for a debt of three *merkr*, but not more; then the arrangement must be kept, the child cannot break it, nor can anyone else.

He should use his debtor as his slave and assign work to him in the same way; he should allow him to work for his (i.e. the slave's) own benefit just as (he allows) his other slaves.

Now he must remain there and work off the debt for which he is bound; if he will not stay there, he may move around half a month within the *fylki* and try to raise money for the debt he has to pay. But if he goes away hiding or leaves the *fylki*, then he is a slave if he to whom money is due, seizes him.

The king has no claim to fines for a debtor when he (the latter) can claim no compensation in his own right.

Now a free and well-born man of age gives himself into debt service, he may be bound for as large a debt as he wishes.

Now the creditor wants his money from his debtor, then it is well if he looks after the matter himself. But if he will not look after it himself, then the creditor should offer him to his kinsmen. Then it is well if they accept to buy him, otherwise he should sell him (the debtor) wherever he likes within the *fylki*, but not for a greater sum than he was held for.

No one must sell a free man as a slave, but if someone is identified and convicted of this, he has to pay a fine of forty *merkr*, and so must the buyer if he knows that the man was free.

If the debtor begets children, then it is well if he has enough money to get his children fostered and cared for. But if he has not enough money, then the creditor should arrange for the fostering, then the debt increases by as much as he pays for the fostering. They are both responsible for providing a place for the child. The debt should be increased until his (the debtor's) full value seems to have been reached. But if he begets many children, his kinsfolk must take care of the

30 I.e. his chief bondsman. See Ch. 198.

31 The violator should pay compensation according to Ch. 200, from this the creditor takes a part according to Ch. 198.

children afterwards, however many they may be. Now he cannot work off his debt and grows old in his service with the creditor and becomes incapable of self-maintenance, then he is his (the creditor's) dependent person. The creditor may remit the debt while the debtor is still able to work, then he returns to his kinsfolk if he becomes a dependent.

If someone sells a free man into a heathen country, then he has to pay a fine of forty *merkr* and have the man returned; otherwise he must pay compensation to his kinsfolk.

Now a debtor is stubborn and refuses to work for his creditor, then the creditor should take the debtor to the assembly and offer his kinsfolk to release him from the debt. If his kinsfolk do not want to release him, then his creditor is free to cut limbs off his body, whether he wants to do so from above or from below.[32]

Now a free man comes into debt service but has got into it wrongly, he should go to the assembly and declare himself free from debt; he does not have to summon any man to this (assembly).

If a man takes another man's servant and forces him to work for himself, then he undertakes responsibility for that servant, and he should pay the other man a compensation[33] if he (the latter) claims it, unless he catches him (the servant) as a runaway.

32 According to the *Frostuþing* Law, Book X, Ch. 26, the cutting shall start with the limbs that have the lowest price.

33 For illegal seizure of another man's goods, according to Ch. 92: one and a half *aurar*.

# V The book on tenancy

## 72 The book on tenancy

Now someone leases land from one who owns it, according to proper contract, then he shall have a legal right to occupy that land for twelve months and pay to the other the rent which they had agreed upon.

Now a day has been set for payment of the rent: if it is not paid on that day, the tenant loses his right to that land. If he pays a part of the rent but not the rest, then what remains should be claimed with witnesses.

Now he refuses to pay, then (the other) should mark the crop and the field with a cross for the rent and forbid him to use what has been cross-marked, after five days; but if he uses (it), he must pay a fine of a ring to the king and still pay the rent.

The tenant may live on the land until moving days the next spring.

He must not let another man have any part of that land for rent, unless he reserved for himself, when he leased the land, that he had the right to transfer some of it to another man in return for rent. If he does transfer (it), then he has no right to the land, neither has he who rents from him; both have to pay a compensation for trespassing on another man's land;[1] he who rented from the tenant must leave that land.

For everything he loses, he (the tenant) who rented to him should give him compensation and (in addition, pay) six *aurar* for breach of contract – in this way everyone must pay who sells unlawfully to another man – unless he has other land equally good to offer him.

## 73 Concerning the upkeep of buildings

Now the tenant should keep in repair all the buildings that were on the land when he came to it; he is not responsible for the wear and tear of time.

If it is part of his contract that he should build a house, he must have built it before he leaves the land.

1 See Ch. 91.

If he builds houses which he has no obligation to build according to agreement, he has to build them for himself (i.e. for his own use). He should offer to the landowner, in front of witnesses, to buy the house if he took the material from that land and if the owner is in the *fylki*, otherwise he must have the house moved away before the moving days. But if he (the owner) is not in the *fylki*, the tenant should offer it to the one who comes to the land. If the house stands there after the moving days, it becomes the property of the landowner, unless the other, before the moving days, has moved it upon a stony ground or to a heap of rocks, where it cannot cause damage to field or meadow; then he may take the house away after the moving days, as soon as he has time for that.

During the moving days, the first nine days of the summer, the tenant may occupy all the buildings. If he has not then managed to have his things ready for moving, he may occupy one half of the buildings for another nine nights, (during that time he should) go on the lower side of the fire[2] and not be required to forward the message arrow. Then he must leave, unless there are hindrances and his new dwelling-place is so (located) that he has to move over mountains or fjords; in that case he should move into boathouses or shieling huts and live there the third period of nine nights; then he must have moved away (if he will remain) guiltless; and he should have water and wood there and fodder (hay) from the farm.

## 74 What a man may take away from the land with impunity

Now he may take away from the land whatever he has the right to take away: that is three cart-loads of fodder from each man's work (on a full farm[3]), we call that horse fodder; one (cart-load) of hay and two of straw, as spring fodder for himself. He may also take away with him all his timber.

## 75 If a man carries more away from the land than he is entitled to

Now the doors should be left standing, three outer doors, even if there were no doors when the tenant came there: doors to living room, storehouse, and kitchen, and all those have to be left which were there before. If he takes any of these doors and removes it, he has to bring it back and pay compensation to the landowner for unlawful use of private property if he has broken it (the door) out (of the frame). But if any part of the threshold or the lintel or the doorframe follows above or on the side, if only a sliver, then that is house damage, and he must pay three *merkr*. But if he breaks bench supports[4] from the house, or bench boards that are morticed together, then he must bring them back and pay three *merkr*.

2 I.e. move to that long side of the house where there was no high seat.

3 I.e. a farm paying nine or ten months' food in yearly rent.

4 Beams on the front of benches along the walls on two sides of a house. The benches were used as seats as well as beds.

(He may take away) loose boards in the barn and the stable, and pile of wood, and bridges he has made. His stacks and houses[5] he should place where they do not cause damage to field or meadow. But if he who succeeds the tenant finds them annoying, he (who moves away) must remove them as soon as the other wants him to.

Floor planks running lengthwise and wainscot and everything which has not been morticed into place or nailed to a beam or girder may be removed. Everything that is removed by causing damage to the house must be paid with a compensation of three *merkr* to him who owns the house, and the building should be restored to its former condition.

He must not dig up stack supports after moving days, he may cut them off above the ground and remove them. But if he digs them up, he must pay compensation to the landowner for trespassing on another man's land.

If a man plants an angelica garden, he may remove (the roots) before the moving days if he wants to. If someone sows winter rye where there is a field and then leaves the land, he shall have nothing of it. But if he digs up a field for the rye within the fence, he should have the value of the seed. If he digs up (ground) for the rye outside the fence, they should have one half each, he who comes to the land and he who sowed, if he has fenced it (the field) in.

The man must not allow others to take anything off the land except two cart-loads of wood and one cart-load of scraped bark, this the tenant may allow, and so may the landowner, even though the tenant does not want to.

If there are hawks nesting in the forest the tenant should have them, unless the other has reserved them for himself.

No one must take another man's hawks, unless he is willing to pay compensation for trespassing on another man's land, and he has to bring the hawks back. But if he takes a hawk bound in its nest, then he is a thief, if the other had declared, in the presence of witnesses, that he had bound it.

He who leased the land is entitled to use illegal products[6] of the farm if its worth does not exceed half a *mǫrk*, when he lets the landowner know; but not if he conceals it from him; and he who developed the products must pay compensation for trespassing on another man's land.

He may use the (resources of the) land to build a ship for his personal needs, one that need not be counted by the number of oar benches.[7] But if he builds a ship (so large) that the oar benches need to be counted, then he builds it for the landowner.

He cannot strip birch bark for sale, unless he needs it to buy black salt[8] for himself.

5 I.e. a dwelling-house, a storehouse and a house with a fireplace for cooking, etc. Cf. the three doors mentioned previously.

6 I.e. the yield, timber, wood, etc., acquired by illegal use of another man's land.

7 Cf. Ch. 301.

8 I.e. dried and burnt seaweed.

He must not prepare more salt than he needs to give his livestock, unless he has to buy birch bark (for his roofs).

He must not boil more tar than he needs for covering his boats.

No one must give a feast on another man's land unless the tenant needs to give an ale feast (fixed by law).[9] But if he does give a feast he has to pay a fine of three *merkr*.

## 76 If he who has rented the land does not want it

Now someone leases another man's land and does not want what he has leased, then the owner should go to the land when there are five nights left to summer solstice and sow the land and use it as if the other had not leased it, but (nevertheless) claim the rent from him who had leased the land.

## 77 If someone goes onto another man's land unlawfully

Now someone goes onto another man's land without having got the legal right thereto by the owner, then the owner should give him a respite of five days to leave, and (the other should) release himself by paying a fine for trespassing on another man's land. If he refuses to leave, the owner should summon him before the assembly for robbery, then the men at the assembly must award to the landowner everything that is on the land except free men, and (to order the robber to) pay a fine to the king for unlawful seizing or holding of property.[10]

If the other will not leave the land, the owner should demand so many men among those present at the assembly that he will be able to drive him away from the land; anyone who is not willing to support (the owner in this) is liable to pay a fine of three *aurar*. The king's representative is obliged to join and gets the fine of a ring for that.

## 78 If someone conveys the same land to two men

Now a man conveys the same land to two men, then he who leased it first should have it. Whenever someone conveys the same thing to two men, he who buys or rents it first should have it. He must set a court of arbitration[11] and produce his witnesses, (to the fact) that he was the first to rent; the one who rents out must let him have another (portion of) land, if he has one, or pay six *aurar* for breach of contract. But if he has only the land he lives on, then the other man should have it, and not he himself.

9 See Ch. 6.
10 I.e. a fine of twelve *aurar*.
11 Such court as is mentioned in Ch. 37.

## 79 If someone wants to cancel a contract

Now someone rents out a (portion of) land but will not let the one have it to whom he rented it, then the renter should summon him as he may prefer: either to the assembly or to the place where the contract was made and produce his witnesses, how he leased the land. If his testimony is found satisfactory, he should then set up a court of arbitration[12] for his leased land as well as for land given in mortgage.[13]

If one of them dies, their contract[14] is terminated, and the money for which no value has been received should be returned.

## 80 Concerning fencing and uncultivated land

Now a man is outlawed on (i.e. while renting) another man's land, then the owner should have the rent, if it was not paid, and all rooted crop.

If there is uncultivated land nearby, then he who owns it, should fence it in and maintain the fence, because no one may serve as a fence post for another. If he will not fence, no one should pay compensation if animals graze there.

## 81 Here relations between neighbours are defined

Now two neighbours live next to each other in a farm and rent the land from the same man. If the land is undivided, then whatever division they arrange between themselves shall hold as long as they live on that land.

If one stays on the land while the other moves away, he who stays must not refuse to make a new division with the one who comes to the land.

If two men live on one farm, neither one of them should have more livestock in the summer than he can feed through the winter without harvesting another man's land. If he has more beasts in the pasture, be it only a lamb, without the other man's permission, he must pay compensation for grazing his cattle in another man's field, compensation for trespass to the landowner, and the value of the grass to the owner. All roads and fence gates shall be as they have been in the past.

If people live together in a neighbourhood, they should drive (their cattle) out of the home pasture when two months have passed of summer, unless they all think that something else is better. If someone sits down (i.e. stays) longer,[15] his neighbour must forbid him to sit there (with his cattle). If he still sits quietly, he must be summoned to the assembly for robbery and remaining quiet,[16] then the men at the assembly have to award a fine of a ring to the king, double compensation for trespass to the landowner, and six *aurar* to his neighbour for stealing grass. The complainant should call upon as many householders and men of the

12 See note 11.
13 Cf. Ch. 283.
14 ON *leigumáli*. The term is disputed in this context. Robberstad 1981, 353–4.
15 I.e. keeps his livestock longer on the farm.
16 I.e. unlawful pasturing.

district as he wants to drive the other's livestock out of his home pasture, everyone who refuses to join is liable to pay a fine of three *aurar*, and the same applies to the case in which he goes down (from the mountain pasture) before the double month.[17]

People are entitled to (use) the aftermath in the autumn, but no one must let (his animals) graze before the rest; he who does has to pay a ring as compensation for stealing grass.

## 82 More on relations between neighbours

A fence is a mediator between neighbours.[18] Now two or more men live in one farm, they should maintain the fence in proportion to the size of their part of the land and as it has been in the past.

They should have repaired the fence by the last of the moving days, and each man is responsible for the fence enclosing his field, until the first night of winter. But if he does not fence (his part of the land), he will be responsible for all damage done to the other (farmers), be it by his own or other men's cattle.

If a cow is a fence breaker or crawls through fences, the neighbours should inspect the fence. If they find it satisfactory, he who owns the fence breaker must pay for all damage caused by this cow.

If livestock breaks out of its pen and causes damage to others, the owner should compensate for the damage according to men's assessment.

Now men live each on his farm in the same neighbourhood and one of them wants a boundary fence built between them, but the other does not; then he who wants it, should summon the other to meet him, in order to determine the length of the fence to be built, and appoint a day, before witnesses, and demand the building of a fence.

If the other refuses to come to (discuss) the fence building, then he (the former) should produce witnesses that he did summon him and allot the length of fence to be built by casting lots in front of witnesses; afterwards he has to fence that part which his lot assigns.

If the other will not fence (his part), and cattle gets inside the fence and grazes in the field and the meadow, no matter who owns that livestock, they who neglected to keep the fence in repair must pay for all damage having been done there.

In the same way the limits of the home pasture shall be dealt with;[19] the fence enclosing the pastureland is properly built if the branches reach up to the mouth (of the workmen); then the cattle may be sent home with warnings[20] afterwards. (The cattle) may be driven home with warnings, and with witnesses, no matter

17 The fifth summer month, i.e. August 14th–September 14th. Magnús Már Lárusson 1967, 131.

18 The same expression is found in chapter 26 of the law of the Gotlanders; cf. *Guta lag*, ed. Ch. Peel 2015, 66.

19 I.e. the parcelling out of fences between pasturelands.

20 I.e. one may ask the owner to look better after his cattle. But cf. Ch. 84.

where it is found. He is then allowed to kill the other's cattle if he finds it in his own pastureland and witnesses know.

One may kill cattle with impunity[21] if it goes through a pasture fence or a boundary fence, if the one whose land it has entered has fenced his part, even if the other has not fenced his.

## 83 He who opened a gate should close it

Now people go through a fence gate, then he who opens the gate is responsible for closing it. If livestock or a horse comes inside and damages the field or the meadow, he who left the gate open must pay for all damage that is done, according as men assess it.

## 84 Concerning shielings and their boundaries

Now for the shielings up on the mountains the boundary marks shall remain as they have been in the past. They must not be moved unless this is done in such a way that no man finds it inconvenient.

The same goes for the use of the mountain pastures. Cattle must not be driven home from there with warnings;[22] for there horn should meet horn and hoof (should meet) hoof.[23]

## 85 Concerning fishing waters

All streams shall run as they have run in the past. No one must lead water off or onto another man's land, if it does not break its way by itself. If someone changes its way, he should lead it back and in addition pay compensation for trespassing on another man's land.[24]

If a stream runs between farms and there are fish in it, then each (farm) owns half of it, out to the middle of the stream, if they have land next to the stream on both sides.

If a stream breaks its way into the land of one of them, then he owns the stream who owned the land it broke into; but the other owns the sandbank which has been laid bare, where the stream ran when it ran straight.

No one must spoil for another man or deny (him the use of) a fishing place which has belonged to him formerly.

Whenever people own a salmon stream together, each should set his fishing gear in his part of the stream, but in such a way that fishes may go up in every part of the stream.

21 I.e. he who kills it does not have to pay compensation.

22 See Ch. 82.

23 I.e. all men's cattle may move freely around, their rights being equal on the mountain pastures.

24 See Ch. 91.

God's gift may go to fell and foreshore, if it wants to. If someone bars the stream, then those who own the land higher up should summon him at the assembly with five days' notice, to tear down what was set up unlawfully. If he refuses to take it out, they must demand the assistance of others to tear it out; every householder who refuses (to join) is liable to pay a compensation of three *aurar*. And the catch goes to those who live higher up the stream.

No one must go to fish in another man's stream unless he wants to fish for him who owns the stream, and he has to pay compensation for trespassing on his land.

## 86 Concerning shielings and parcel of forest land

Whenever men dispute about a shieling pasture and one of them takes the issue to court, then the court should award the pasture to him who produces witnesses thereto, unless the other man has more witnesses.

Now people dispute about a lot in the forest and one of them takes the issue to court, then the court should award the lot to him who produces witnesses thereto, unless the other man has more witnesses.

Whenever people dispute about a shieling pasture, or a lot in the forest, or a boundary line outside the fence, he should win the suit who produces witnesses (to his court). If both have witnesses, he should win the suit who is willing to take an oath (to his claim). If both are willing to swear, or if neither is, the matter in dispute must be divided into halves.

Any man, free and of age, who wants to, may bear witness to boundary lines which people dispute about. He has to pronounce the words "Here is the boundary line", and then it is rightly so.

Now people dispute about a shieling pasture or a lot in the forest, then he should have it (the disputed object) who has possessed it for twenty winters or longer than twenty winters unquestioned and unimpaired, if witnesses know with him.

He who has possessed it, should take the issue to court, but the one who will not grant him that, should summon him to appear at the forest lot and in court with no less than five nights' notice. He must go to that place when the day comes with his judges and all the witnesses he needs; he must let the judges be placed where he says the boundary mark is. The other, who prosecutes him, should appoint half of the members of the court.

The complainant has to produce witnesses that he summoned the other to that place, and then witnesses to testify that the boundary marks are as he says they are; then that is true, unless other and more witnesses are produced against it, in that case the boundary marks are as they testify. If there are equally many on both sides, then they should win who testified first. If there are no witnesses, he should win the suit who is willing to take an oath to it (his claim). If no one wants to swear, or both of them, the matter in dispute must be divided into halves.

This procedure shall always be followed, as I have now said, whenever people disagree about boundary marks; and they must set the court in the forest lot.

When they have set the court, the complainant should produce his witnesses. Any man may bear witness to this, even if he worked on that lot as a slave and, provided he is free at the time, he is to witness. The one who has more or better witnesses should have the lot, although the complainant produced his witnesses first. If both of them possess the land, then he who caused the dispute must appoint the judges.

## 87 Concerning the division of odal-land[25]

Now people want to divide land between themselves, and divide the odal-land.[26] If they all agree they may divide as they like and cast lots[27] at the assembly. Then that division cannot be reversed.

Now people want to divide their odal-land, then the oldest co-owner[28] should summon them and divide the odal-land in the presence of the men of the district; he must summon them so far in advance that they may get people (to provide assistance with the division) while the soil is still bare and unsown.[29] The one who wants to divide the land into the larger holdings should direct the parcelling. They may divide the land by measuring with the eye unless they think it is better to measure with a rope. Boundary stones must be set and placed in the earth where men agree (to have them).

If he who was summoned does not come, the division should nevertheless be undertaken in such a way as I have now told. He (who claimed the division) must produce witness that he has summoned the other to join him in dividing the land with him that day.

Then they have to draw lots, one for each part of the co-ownership. Men should see the owner's mark on each lot and must know what each co-owner is entitled to: house or in land. Others should draw lots for those who do not want to do so themselves.

Then they must go to the assembly and publish their division of the odal; then they have divided their odal according to the law.

If a co-owner is not in the country, he who wants a division should summon the other from the assembly to appear within twelve months (to come) back to join in dividing the land. If he does not come by that time, the other should summon his heir to join him in dividing the land and make the division with him as (if it were made) with the man himself.

25 This chapter mainly deals with division of land between co-owners.

26 The ON term *óðalsskipti* is ambiguous in this context. It may refer generally to land which is the property of one or more persons, or to inherited land, passed on from father to son at least to the sixth generation from the first possessor. The former interpretation is supported by Ch. 91, the latter interpretation by Chs. 270 and 272, and the reference in this chapter to the oldest co-owner.

27 Or: make it known. The word *luti* has also been interpreted as an error for *lýsi*. Meissner 1935, 72.

28 The oldest co-owner is the oldest person in each family of brothers and sisters or in the group of heirs owning parts of the land.

29 Or: unfenced (so Hertzberg 1895, 489; Larson 1935, 98).

No one can refuse the request of another to have the land measured with a rope[30] within three winters, if the land has not been measured; then he who has more land (than the rope allows) should surrender a part, but still keep the lot that fell to him. When the drawing of lots is finished they may discuss the boundaries.

Now one wants to have a division while the other does not, then the former should summon, before witnesses, him who is unwilling, to the home farm, and there the plaintiff must produce his witnesses that he has summoned him to a division of land. The one who wants to divide the land into the larger holdings should direct the parcelling; they may divide the farms into halves, unless they think that some other method of dividing is more appropriate. Afterwards impartial men should make the division formally and have lots cast[31] at the assembly; (each man) should mark his own lot, but impartial men should draw an unmarked lot for anyone who is reluctant to mark his own;[32] then that division must be kept ever after.

## 88 If a man wants to live on his odal-land

Now a man shall be allowed to live on his odal-land rather than a stranger, (that is) on all land close to his homestead within the same yard.[33]

If his co-possessors refuse to sell it to him, he must offer the principal odal owner rent before moving days, such rent that others would have offered without a ridiculous bid; he must not acquire another man's land through a ridiculous bid.

If someone else goes upon the land (to live there), (it is a robbery from the first); the odal owner should forbid the other to go upon it. If people do go upon it, they have to surrender the land and pay compensation for unlawful seizure of property.

If the land does not lie close to his homestead the odal owner should nevertheless have it, if he tills all the land that he had before and it lies in the same district and is not separated by mountains or fjords or impassable streams.

## 89 Concerning boundary stones

Now people disagree about boundary lines within the fence, be it those of the fields or the meadows. The one says that another man has tilled outside the land that he (the latter) owned and has stolen the land, having dug up boundary stones, then those men should be summoned who have the best knowledge of boundary lines between them; if they think that the boundary stones stand in the right places, just as they were put down from the outset, then they should offer their testimony that the boundary stones stand in the right places; then it is well.

30 In order to readjust and rectify the division, if necessary.

31 Or: announced. See note 27.

32 Or: anyone who does not come (to the division).

33 The meaning seems to be that a farmer who has odal-right to the land should be preferred to one who has no such right, if the odal man's farm is contiguous to the one that he wants to lease. Larson 1935, 99–100, note 17.

If the boundary stones have been dug up and not replaced, and the man has tilled beyond them, he must give compensation for the crop and pay a fine for trespass to the landowner.

If he has dug up boundary stones and set them down in other places and moved them on to the land belonging to him whose land meets his own, then he is a land-thief and an outlaw.

## 90 Concerning the highway

The highway and the road to the shieling, and all the cattle-tracks shall be as they have been from times past. Now a highway runs across a man's farm, he may move the road off his farm on the condition that he builds a new road outside the fence, equally good to go in dry and wet weather, then people should follow that road even though it is longer.

The highway must be so broad that a man sitting on a saddled horse should (be able to) set a spear shaft on the ground and move his thumb up to the socket, the spear point must be a span[34] long up from there, the spear must be laid down across the road, it (the road) may not be broader than that. If someone damages a strip of the field or the meadow in greater breadth, he has to pay for the damage.

Now someone blocks the highway[35] for another man, he must pay a fine of three *merkr* to the king, and the same for hand seizure.[36]

Now someone breaks a bridge on the highway, he has to rebuild it and make it as good as it was before and pay three *merkr* to the owner of the bridge.

Now someone blocks the road to the shielings for another man or the cattle-track which has been there from times past, he should pay a fine of a ring to the king, and the other should use the road as before.

## 91 Concerning trespass on another man's land

Now a freedman, if he owns land, should have as compensation for trespass on his land one *eyrir*, acceptable as tax money,[37] within the fence, but his son one *eyrir*; a householder one and a half *aurar*, a freeholder three *aurar*, a landed man six *aurar*, an earl twelve *aurar*, the king three *merkr*. Within the fence each should have as I have now told; they should have half of it outside the fence.

The compensation for trespass is doubled if a prohibition has been imposed and (then is added) a fine to the king for unlawful seizure or holding of property.

All co-owners should have compensation for trespassing on undivided land, they must take it (the compensation) according to the rank of the highest ranking

34 The span between the stretched fingers, perhaps equal to a half ell, i.e. 23.7 cm.
35 Or: the road to the shielings. Cf. the end of the chapter.
36 Lit. 'wresting something out of another's hand', forcible seizure from someone's grasp. Cf. Ch. 143.
37 I.e. money which can be used for tax paying, here (and in Ch. 198) one counted *eyrir*.

man among the co-owners; according to the rank of the king, if he owns part of the land. But if the land has been divided as odal-land[38] each takes full compensation for his share.

Now someone goes into another man's forest without permission and does work there, then he has to pay compensation for trespass. If the owner has witnesses to prove that the man was in his (the owner's) forest, he should summon him to be at home, – the whole day is available for the meeting between them – and claim that compensation as for any other debt that is known,[39] when he has witnesses that the man was in his forest.

If the latter denies (it) and the plaintiff has no witnesses, he should summon him to be at home and from there before the assembly. At the assembly the accused must either swear a three-man oath or pay compensation for trespass.

Whenever someone finds tools or fruits of unauthorized labour in his forest, he may take it away with impunity.

If someone finds a net on his sealing grounds,[40] and a seal (is found) in the net, then he should have the net and the seal, until the owner redeems his net with the fine for trespass. A man may shoot a seal from his boat if he rows straight forward,[41] whether the seal is in the water or on the land, unless it is lying on a sealing ground where a trap has been set up, then he (who kills the seal) catches for him who owns the ground. If someone shoots a seal from land where no trap has been set up, then he who owns the ground should have the seal. But if a trap has been set up, the owner must have both the seal and compensation for trespass. Now someone hits a seal with a harpoon, then he who finds the seal should have it, but he who hit should have his harpoon if it follows.[42]

## 92 Concerning unauthorized use of another man's movable property

Now no one must take another man's ship or horse without the permission of the owner. If he does take it he has to pay a compensation of one and a half *aurar*.

If the owner comes upon someone on his ship or on his horse and claims compensation for unlawful seizure, then it is well if the other is willing to pay. But if he will not, then (the compensation) is doubled, and a fine to the king for unlawful seizure (is added).

Now someone takes another man's ship, (so large that) it needs to be counted by the number of its oar benches, then he who is appointed ship's master has to pay a fine of three *merkr* (to the king), and he must pay a fine of one and a half

38 See Ch. 87.

39 The corresponding sentence in the original may be corrupted. Hertzberg 1895, 721.

40 Places where seals used to lie. Nets for catching seals were laid along the shore, so that the seal got stuck when it tried to get back into the water.

41 I.e. the common route.

42 I.e. if the harpoon is stuck in the seal.

*aurar* for each thwart. Whatever kind of ship is taken, every free man must pay his compensation for unlawful seizure.

A man is entitled to compensation for unlawful use of his horse, whether another man drives it (in a harness) or rides or lays burdens on it; such compensation is also due if he keeps the horse longer than the time it was lent for.

All men are entitled to receive equally much in compensation of this kind, free men as well as slaves.

If a man takes another man's ship, he has to pay compensation, (to be counted) for his slave (as) for himself and for those of minor age. The king must neither claim nor pay compensation for unlawful seizure.

Now a man leaps upon another man's saddled horse, then he should release himself with compensation for unlawful seizure. If he leaps upon another man's horse, which is not saddled, and he rides forward, he has to release himself with compensation for unlawful seizure; but if he does not ride the horse forward he must pay no compensation.

## 93 Concerning lakes and fishing grounds

Everyone shall have the lakes and fishing grounds that he has had from the past.

No one must place traps on (another) man's land; but if he does he has to pay compensation for trespass and give the catch to the landowner.

## 94 Concerning the hunting of bears

Bear and wolf should be outlawed everywhere – no one wants to answer for what they do – except in the case where a bear is enclosed in its lair; then the man should announce before assembled people that the barred lair belongs to him. If other men hunt the bear, they hunt it for him who owned the lair.

Now people go to hunt a bear and come to the lair above the barricade[43] and drive the bear out, then they who drive it out should compensate for damage made if the bear bites other men's livestock. But if the bear runs into the forest, they must pay nothing.

## 95 Concerning deer hunting

Everyone may hunt deer with weapons wherever he can, no matter who owns the forest.[44]

Now men go deer hunting, then every man should go where he owns the forest when he wants to hunt with dogs. He who startles a deer should have it when he

43 A pile of lumber used as a trap.

44 The words "no matter . . . forest" translate ON *hverr sem mǫrk á*. This passage is understood as a parallel to an almost identical passage in Ch. 145. On a possible different translation see Larson (1935, 103) and Meissner (1935, 78).

pursues it, even though another man brings it down. If the deer comes to a place (where it has) to swim, the one who brings it down owns the shoulder; the shoulder must be cut off with the skin, or the owner must pay to have the skin taken off uncut.[45] If the animal leaves the course and other men kill it, then each should have one half of it, the one who brings it down and the one who startled it.

Now someone goes into another man's forest to hunt with dogs, then he hunts for the one who owns the forest.

The (owner of the) dog should have the skin when men kill a deer.

If someone comes upon a seal or fish above the shore's edge, then it belongs to the (owner of the) land. But if the finder carries it away, he has to bring it back and pay compensation for unlawful seizure if it is demanded.

And if someone finds a dead animal on dry land, he should keep what he found himself, whatever kind of animal it may be.

## 96 Concerning damage

No one must do damage to another man's property. If he does damage amounting to half a *mǫrk*, then that is damage work, and so is all damage which men estimate at half a *mǫrk*. If someone cuts the tail off another man's horse and some part of the tail bone at the same time, then that is damage work. If someone hews into the stem of another man's ship, in the prow or at the stern and the damage is estimated at half a *mǫrk*, then that is damage work.

If he pledges himself to take an oath in defence, he has to take a six-man oath, otherwise he will be outlawed. If he confesses to the deed, he must compensate for the damage according to men's estimation.

Now a man does a smaller damage to another man and he confesses to the deed, he must compensate for it according to men's estimation and pay six *aurar* as compensation for unfriendly conduct. If the man denies (it), he must take a three-man oath (of denial); but if the oath fails, he must pay that which has now been said.

## 97 Concerning damages that are to be compensated in half

Now a minor does (some) damage,[46] or cattle injures cattle,[47] that is all of half the value.[48] The man to whom the cattle or the minor belongs may deny (it) with a three-man oath.

Now a horse stands tethered and another horse comes up to him and they start fighting; if the first breaks loose and chases the other over a cliff or to death, then no compensation should be paid for the latter. But if both fall over (and get hurt),

45 I.e. he shall pay in order to keep the whole skin.
46 This stipulation probably also concerns damage made by slaves. Iversen 1997, 51.
47 Or: property.
48 I.e. it shall be compensated to half of its value.

then compensation must be paid for the one that was tethered, because he would have stood quietly if the other had not come up to him.

## 98 Concerning arson[49]

No one must burn another man's house or barn with evil intent. But if he does burn (it) and he is identified and convicted of the deed, then he is outlawed and deprived of all personal rights and is called a fire-wolf, and he has forfeited each penny of his property in land and movables.

If he denies (it), the other (who charges him) should go to his home and summon him before the assembly for arson and to outlawry;[50] then he has to take a six-man oath (of denial) at that assembly; he must have taken it within ten weeks of oath days; the oath leads to outlawry if it fails.

Now someone instigates arson and is identified and convicted of having done this, then he should pay for half of what has been burnt. If he denies (it), he must do so with a three-man oath, if it fails, he has to pay half the damages.

## 99 Concerning responsibility for fire

Every free man of age is responsible for his own fire. Fire belongs to the one who has it in his hands and feeds it afterwards.

Now someone sets fire (to something), but does not do so with evil intent, (he) has to pay full compensation or deny (it) with a three-man oath if he denies (it).

If a minor sets fire (to something) for somebody, half compensation should be paid; but if he denies (it), his master must deny (it) with a three-man oath.

Now a slave sets fire (to something) with evil intent, then the slave is outlawed.[51] But if he denies (it), his master must deny (it) with a three-man oath. This oath leads to outlawry for the slave if it fails.

## 100 Concerning responsibility in wayside shelters and (during) stays there

All men have equal rights in a wayside shelter.[52] Now it is well if they can all be accommodated inside with their luggage. But if they cannot all be inside with their luggage because the room is too small, then they should all carry their luggage outside. Then it is well if there is room for all of them; they should all be inside if there are seats for all. If some of them have been there three nights without need, they will have to go out; otherwise it must be decided by drawing lots who has to leave. Then it is well if they who have been by selected by lot are

49 On this and the following chapter see Iversen 1997, 58.
50 According to Ch. 135 arson is a crime that cannot be compensated for.
51 Cf. Ch. 204. See also Iversen 1997, 57–8.
52 Building such houses was regarded as acts of charity.

willing to leave. But if they are not willing to leave, then they are liable to pay a fine of a ring for robbery (illegal stay) and pay full wergild for those who die outside but were allowed by lot to stay inside.

If a wayside shelter burns while men are staying there, then all who were within are to be held responsible.

## 101 If someone makes use of land that another man holds as a grant

If someone makes use of land that another man holds as a grant from the king, then he who holds the grant should prosecute the other for trespass and have half (of the fine); otherwise the king's representative may claim the whole fine.

## 102 Concerning lawful summons[53] and demand for surety[54]

Whenever people have to give a lawful summons to a man at the assembly, they should do so with half a month's notice (if he is) within the *fylki* but outside the quarter. A month's notice (if he is) outside the *fylki* but within our law district. Two months' notice (if he is) within the country but outside our law district. Twelve months' notice if the man is abroad. The heir has to send him the summons; or the men present at the assembly if the heir is not present there. Every man has the right to a defence.

Now someone demands surety from another man. No one must deny another man surety, (he should) give him surety on the same day. If he refuses to give (it to) him, he is liable to pay a fine of three *merkr*. His estate should serve as surety, if he owns one that is worth three *merkr*. Then he must be held for one month in that surety, if his counterpart demands lawful surety. But if he does not own an estate worth three *merkr*, someone else who owns an estate worth three *merkr* must give surety for him. If he refuses to give him surety, he is liable to pay a fine of three *merkr*.

Now he hits the other away from home and demands surety from him, then he (the latter) should give him surety that he will go home and give him surety afterwards; (he may) declare himself released from the surety when one month has passed.

Now someone demands surety from another man on a day when legal actions are not allowed, then he (the latter) should remain in that surety until litigation days, then the former is the first[55] to bring a legal action on the next litigation days, even though other men have other causes to prosecute against him. But he

53 A summons announced at the assembly (ON *lagastefna*) because the defendant's residence is not known.

54 Surety, which renders ON *tak* here, was a legal aid to assure compliance with a demand, e.g. the seizure of a man's property.

55 Cf. the end of Ch. 47.

should have brought action within the first month in which there are litigation days, the other must not remain in surety longer than that. Anyone who owns a merchant ship on land,[56] if it is large enough to have the oar benches counted,[57] may serve as surety for him.

Now someone demands surety from another man that he (the latter) be present at a certain place, then the latter should name the man who gives him surety; then they have to go where that man is, then it is well if he wants to give surety for him. But if he refuses to do so, he (the accuser) may point to three places within the *fylki*, point forward and not backward.[58] Now he points to a second place, and they fail (to get it) there, then to the third place, and it is not there either. He who demands surety must provide a boat and food and row the sea, shackle the other together with one of his (the former's) own feet and go home with him. Then he must release his own foot and prosecute him as if the other were unbound.

Now he has prosecuted one of his sailors on the ship, then he (the latter) should give him surety for a half month. If he (the defendant) owns a merchant ship that is large enough to have the oar benches counted,[59] then that may serve as surety for him.

56 See Book II, note 30.
57 See note 7.
58 To places where he has already been.
59 See note 57.

# VI The book on inheritance

## 103 Here begins the book on inheritance[1]

This is the first inheritance that a son inherits from his father or a father from his son if one of them dies before the other.

This is the second that a daughter and a son's son inherit, each of them half. The father's father should inherit in the same way unless children (sons) of the deceased stand in the way.[2] She (the daughter) inherits the movables and he (the son) the odal-land.

This is the third that a brother inherits from his brother and siblings having the same father inherit from each other if their mother has been bought by bride-price.

This is the fourth that a mother inherits from her son.

This is the fifth that a father's brother and a brother's son inherit from each other; they both inherit from one man, if it so happens.

This is the sixth that sons of brothers inherit from each other and a brother having the same mother, if there is one; he inherits the movables and they the odal-land.

## 104 Inheritance of nooklings and scrublings

This is the seventh (inheritance) that a nookling and a scrubling and a son of a bondwoman who has not been legitimized inherit from their father, the movables as well as the odal-land.

A nookling is one who is the son of a free woman who has not been bought with bride-price, but to whose bed his father has gone without concealment. A scrubling is one who is the son of a free woman but begotten secretly. And a son of a bondwoman is a son of an unfree woman, (a son) who has been given his freedom before he has (lived) three Christmas Eves. These have full rights of inheritance.[3]

1 On the principles underlying inheritance laws see Vogt 2010, 159–60, 172–4, 177–8, 180.

2 This passage about the paternal grandfather is probably a later interpolation, meaning that a paternal grandfather inherits together with the daughter when there is no son or son's son.

3 Cf. Ch. 58.

This is the eighth that they who come next after first cousins (i.e. agnatic second cousins) inherit from each other.

This is the ninth that the mother's father and a daughter's son inherit.

This is the tenth that the mother's brother and a sister's son inherit from each other.

This is the eleventh that sons of siblings (brothers and sisters) inherit from each other.

This is the twelfth that sons of sisters inherit from each other.

This is the thirteenth which is called the inheritance of the unborn; if a woman is pregnant and the child is alive in her womb before she dies, and two housewives know this with her, then that child inherits the husband's gift (i.e. the gift from the bridegroom, which in effect reverts to the father), but the portion from the bride should go to (her) heir (i.e. her husband, the father of the child).

Now all family inheritances are enumerated. Those who have been enumerated and all other equally related shall inherit before the inheritance may pass on to the king.

## 105 Inheritance among kinsmen

### *(Part I)*

Now no one of those enumerated is there, but there are others, equally close, on the male and the female side.[4] Then those on the male side should inherit. But if those on the female side are closer, they should inherit.

If there is a shift in the order of inheritance,[5] then the one who is closer must have the inheritance.

Now he is counted in one line, but not in the other, then that is as if he were counted in both.

Now no one of those enumerated is there, but there is other kinsfolk equally close, then they should inherit who are equally close to those enumerated before.

A son's daughter inherits first among the women not enumerated.

### *(Part II)*[6]

Now it must be said about those who have not been enumerated, when they should inherit. If there is no one there of those who have been enumerated, then a son's daughter and the father's mother should inherit, if they are there.

If they are not there, and no one of those enumerated, then a father's sister and a brother's daughter should inherit.

4 I.e. in the agnate and the cognate lineage.

5 I.e. that the heir is related in two or more ways and in different degrees to the person who leaves the inheritance.

6 The contents show that this part must be younger than part I.

If they are not there, and no one of those enumerated, then the daughters of brothers inherit.

But if they are not there, and no one of those enumerated, then illegitimate daughters should inherit.

If they are not there, and no one of those enumerated, then those women should inherit whose fathers were the sons of brothers of the one who leaves inheritance.

If they are not there, and no one of those enumerated, then the mother's mother and a daughter's daughter should inherit.

If they are not there, and no one of those enumerated, then the mother's sister and a sister's daughter should inherit.

If they are not there, and no one of those enumerated, then daughters of brothers and sisters of the father and the mother should inherit.

If they are not there, and no one of those enumerated, then the daughters of sisters should inherit.

This is called the rightful order of inheritance, but the kinship of men may take so many forms that no one can establish the full extent of the order of inheritance, but those who need to (establish forms of kinship) will have to do what seems most reasonable.

Now all those have been enumerated who are equally close to those enumerated in the inheritance on the male side. Everyone should inherit according to where he is enumerated, except that a daughter inherits in preference to the father.

## 106 Here a freedman's inheritance is explained

Now the fourteenth is freedman's inheritance. It shall go to the ninth degree (according to canonical counting) before it passes on to the king. When the son of a freedman inherits from his father, one should inherit after the other.[7]

Now the family of the freedman dies out,[8] and there is no one who is entitled to inheritance from him who is deceased in the family of the freedman, then one who belongs to the master's line should inherit to the ninth degree before the inheritance passes on to the king, even though he is in the eighth degree from the deceased freedman.

## 107 Here inheritance by gift is explained

This is the fifteenth which is called inheritance by gift, if a man gives his inheritance away once (i.e. decides who should have it), then he may revoke it and give it away a second time in the assembly and then it shall remain valid.

But if a woman gives her inheritance away, she may revoke it, and also a second time, and (she may) give it away a third time, then the gift shall remain valid.

7 I.e. the son of a freedman may also inherit from his father's brother, and in case one of them dies before the other, the father may inherit from the son or the father's brother from the brother's son.

8 I.e. there is no heir left.

## 108 Inheritance through fosterage

This is the sixteenth which is called fire inheritance, if someone takes another into his house,[9] for good or for ill, and supports him up to fire and pyre,[10] as the old saying goes.

## 109 A housecarl's inheritance

This is the seventeenth which is called a housecarl's inheritance, if someone unfastens his bag in the autumn where he fastened it in the spring.

Now he dies, then his master should keep his property for three winters. If no heir comes forward (by that time), then he owns all of it, if it is worth three *merkr* or less. But if it is more, then he owns half of it, and the king the other half.

## 110 Land inheritance

This is the eighteenth which is called land inheritance, if someone lives on another man's land and dies there; then he (the landowner) should keep his property three winters. If no heir comes forward (by that time), he owns all of it, if it is worth three *merkr* or less; otherwise he owns half of it, and the king the other half.

## 111 Ship's inheritance

This is called the nineteenth which is called ship's inheritance. If someone dies on board a merchant ship on this side[11] of the (North) Sea, no matter in what direction he travels from Norway;[12] then the king owns half of his property, if it is (worth) more than three *merkr*.

But if he dies on the other side of the Sea, then the ship's master owns all of it, if no heir comes forward within three winters. If his (business) partner is on board, then he must keep it and not the ship's master.

Now they lie moored and he dies (on land) in the tent booth, then the landowner should have everything that is not bound in the cargo.

## 112 A partner's inheritance

That is the twentieth which is called a partner's inheritance. If two men share the same purse and one of them dies, then the one who survives should keep (the inheritance) and have it, if it is not (worth) more than three *merkr*, but if it is more,

9 For reasons of old age or disability.

10 This refers to the especially heathen practice of burning the bodies of the dead.

11 On the middle of the sea as a dividing line in questions of inheritance.

12 Or: whether it (the ship) is heading for or away from Norway (so K. Robberstad); from wherever in Norway it has sailed (so R. Meissner).

then he owns half of it and the king the other half, if no heir comes forward within three winters.[13]

## 113 A guest's (stranger's) inheritance

This is the twenty-first which is called guest inheritance; if someone is another man's guest and dies there, then he (the master of the house) should keep his property three winters; if no heir comes forward, (he should) have it, if it is not (worth) more than three *merkr*. But if it is more, then he owns half of it, and the king the other half.

## 114 The lesser inheritance

This is the twenty-second which is called the lesser inheritance.[14] If two men are brought up as slaves in the same household, sharing their work for their master as well as that for themselves, and do not divide it (what they have earned for themselves) before they are free, then each of them inherits from the other, unless their children stand in the way. No other inheritance stands in the way for this, when there is no family inheritance to be considered.

## 115 Concerning seventh day's (funeral) ale feast[15] and the settlement of debt

Now a man is dead; his heir should take place in the high seat, he must summon all the creditors: that they have to come there on the seventh day and receive what is due to them, such as witnesses testify.[16]

Now there is not that much property left, then they should all accept a reduction in the proper ratio. He to whom the most was due must accept the greatest reduction.

He who fails to come to the seventh night's feast may claim with witnesses what is due to him, if there is property left, and he should summon the heirs for testimony. And if there is nothing, he loses what was due to him.

Now minors have property in the estate and the wife her share (portion), then it is well if there is enough property for both. But if it is not, she should surrender her husband's gift and other gifts.

If the property does not suffice for all of them, he must lose most to whom most was due from him (the deceased), this goes for his wife as well as for other

13 According to *Egils saga Skallagrímssonar* (Ch. 64) the inheritance of a foreigner passed on to the king when the person died in the country and left no heir within the same country.

14 See also Ch. 65.

15 The ON Bible translation *Stjórn* says (ed. Astås 2009, I, 357–8), on the basis of Genesis, Ch. 50, that Christians mourn for thirty days after the death of their beloved ones and hold anniversary masses during those days; some hold the third day in highest regard, others the seventh day.

16 Cf. Ch. 38.

creditors; a calculation must be made to this purpose. But if someone had an object taken in pledge, he should have that first.

The wife should rather accept reduction of her bridal gift than that those men (should accept reduction) to whom money was due before he got her; for no one should buy himself a wife with another man's money.

Now she should have her portion, and the minor should have his money.[17] Now there is not that much property, then each one must lose (accept reduction) in proportion to the size of his claim.

If there are sons or daughters, then they should pay the debts, if they have property thereto, (but) no one else (may need to pay) unless he is heir to the property; because the children should meet both good and ill.

Now man and wife have ownership in common and one of them dies, then the debts have to be paid according to the terms of their ownership.

Old men and women (who were supported by the deceased) and children of a bondwoman[18] should be apportioned like other obligations, and their children and property must be taken care of by him who is their nearest heir.

Whether the guardian is a man or a woman, the property should be appraised when it is received. He must not carry the property of a minor out of the *fylki*, unless someone who owns lands there will provide security that the property will be given back where it was received, when the minor attains majority.

Now the appraisal shows that there is full capital for maintenance, four *merkr* for each minor child – it is well if there is more – then she (the widow?) should take that amount, it may neither decrease nor increase, she has to give back just as much as she received.

If the capital for maintenance is not sufficient, the minor should be allowed half a *mǫrk* for subsistence every twelve months until he is twelve winters old, after that he must be regarded as one who works for his living. Interest should be paid on that money which is more than he takes for himself in one year. A minor should receive half a *mǫrk* from the ground rent.

The stipulation of the ground rent must remain as it was assessed the first year, whether (the rent) decreases or increases (after that).

The guardian must not transfer his guardianship to someone else. But if he transfers the guardianship to someone else, then the ward is entitled to claim from any one of them what is due to him.

If the ward owns land worth half a *mǫrk*,[19] then that should be counted as maintenance capital.

If someone gives away the property of a minor, unless it has been taken from him by an act of court, then he must give his own property (as security) instead.

17 The privileged position of the wife and the minors in this respect seems to have been influenced by Roman law, esp. Justinian's *Corpus juris civilis*.

18 See Ch. 104.

19 I.e. land giving half a *mǫrk* in yearly rent.

## 116 Concerning debts

No debt has been paid unless witnesses know. But if the creditor denies (that it is paid), then he (the debtor) has to pay a second time and seek redress with legal claim.[20]

## 117 Concerning the money of minors

Now a householder is deceased, but his wife survives him, and there is no more property than that which is due to her, then she should take care of her poor children.[21] If he has other children, they should go to their father's kinsfolk. But if her children have some property, then the brothers and sisters should consume it first, with the advice of their kinsfolk, and then they should go to their father's kinsfolk.

## 118 Concerning the needy

Now a householder in the district is poverty-stricken, then his minor children should be distributed into three groups, two of these he must keep himself, and she (his wife) the third (and hand it over) to those of her kinsfolk who are the nearest heirs if they have the means for maintenance (of the minors); four *merkr* for each one of the minors, that is maintenance money.

If the kinsman has four *merkr* more than this, he should take care of one minor child, he must take care of so many as he can provide maintenance for; but those who still remain have to go forward to the next heir, if he has the maintenance money. But if he has not, the minors should pass further out in the kin until they find maintenance money.

In this manner also those who follow their father's kinsfolk should be distributed.

## 119 If someone takes possession of unassessed inheritance

Now a man keeps an unappraised inheritance, which has not been assessed at the seventh day's feast; then the minor (heir) should go before the assembly when he has reached full age and present a sworn claim to as much property as he swears (that the inheritance was), and his kinsfolk should advise him, so that he does not swear falsely. Then he must have the property that he has claimed under oath, unless the other (his opponent) produces his witnesses to a different estimate. He must have sworn (to this claim) within the five winters before he is twenty.[22] But if he has not sworn by that time, he cannot win his case.

20 According to the provisions about debts which are not acknowledged, cf. Ch. 38.

21 This is an exception to the rule that the nearest heir must support the needy.

22 A person who was fifteen years old had reached full age.

## 120 Concerning suits for inheritances

Inheritance should be sued for in the *fylki* where the inheritance is left. If he (an heir) produces witnesses in another *fylki* or according to town law, then he has lost his case.

For every dispute that arises between us, townsmen and men of the district,[23] (it is fixed by law) that whatever is done in a town should be judged by town law.[24] Whatever is done contrary to district law or disputed among us men of the district should be judged by district law.

## 121 If a man demands the court's decision to defend something he has no right to

Now a man has taken possession of an inheritance and demands the court's decision,[25] but another man claims to have a legal right to the inheritance, then he should summon the former by correct procedure to be at home and he must claim the inheritance and demand that the other withdraws.

If he will not withdraw from it, the plaintiff should summon him before the assembly for robbery and unlawful possession; if all his witnesses, proofs and evidence are found satisfactory in the case and no counter-witnesses come forward, then the men of the assembly have to award him the inheritance.

The other must pay a fine of three *merkr* to the king for having demanded the court's decision about an inheritance which he had no right to.

Now he still refuses to withdraw from it, then the plaintiff should demand assistance from the men at the assembly so that he has enough people to oust him from the inheritance; everyone who refuses to offer assistance is liable to pay a fine of three *aurar*. Now they come to the place and the other defends himself with point and edge; he is liable to pay a fine of forty *merkr* and everyone who joins him and offers resistance with him three *merkr*. Now there is a fight, then everyone who resists the award is outlawed, but they who (lawfully) claim it should remain protected by the law.

## 122 If a man fails to claim an inheritance

Now a man of full age sits at home on the seventh day or in the morning of the thirtieth day and does not claim his inheritance, then he may never claim that inheritance later.

Now he sits there and is not of age, then he should announce publicly that he is entitled to have the inheritance. Another man may announce it for him. He must have claimed the inheritance within the first five winters after he has reached full

23 Or: townsmen and men of the district alike.

24 Town law (municipal law) was the law which applied to towns, district law applied to the countryside.

25 That he shall not waive the inheritance unless the court passes a sentence to that effect.

age. But if he does not, then he may never claim that inheritance later [*AM 146 4to adds:* Now a man sits within the *fylki* and is of full age and does not claim his inheritance within the first twelve months, then he may never claim that inheritance later], unless he is lawfully excused because of some serious hindrance.

Now he is not within the *fylki* and not in the country, then he must have presented his legal claim within the first twelve months after he has arrived in the *fylki* where the inheritance is left, unless he is lawfully excused because of some serious hindrance.

Men should decide what may be considered lawful hindrance.

## 123 Concerning the division of an inheritance

Now people have an inheritance to divide, then it is well if all who have a share in it come and join in the division of the inheritance.

If some refuse to come, they should be summoned to join in the division. If some still do not appear, the division must be undertaken in front of witnesses and lots be drawn, he (each of those having been summoned, but are not present) should have that share which is indicated by the lot.

If he (anyone) asserts that the division is unfair and says that the other (the keeper) has concealed (part of the) property, then the other should deny (it) with a three-man oath.

## 124 How a man should prove his right to inheritance[26]

Now there are doubts whether a man is entitled to inherit or not; he should summon to the assembly the one who stands between him and the inheritance; then he should produce his witnesses that he summoned him to the assembly. Other witnesses must testify: "We were present there when his mother was bought with bride-price" – and say where that took place – "and bridesmen as well as bridesmaids were present, and the gift which was promised her was given, not less than twelve *aurar*, (which is) a poor man's payment". Now the witnesses of the defendant say this: "We were present as well as you; bride-price was not paid as the law prescribes"; (the defendant) may have one more witness, if so, the other has lost his case.

If no opposing witness comes forward, the men of the assembly must award the inheritance to him.

Whenever a man wants to prove his right to inheritance and produces witnesses, but fails to summon the other who is next to inherit, then that testimony is of no value.

A suit for an inheritance must be concluded where the inheritance was left, or where the odal-land is, or where the deceased had his household.

26 Cf. the beginning of Ch. 51.

## 125 If a man goes to bed with a woman in broad daylight

If a man lives with his concubine for twenty winters or longer than twenty winters and lives with her openly, and there is no separation between them during that time and there is no announcement to the contrary these first twenty winters, then their children are entitled to inherit, and the law regulates their co-ownership.[27]

## 126 Concerning the division of an inheritance (when the person to be inherited is still alive)

No man must divide (another man's) property or his inheritance without the permission of the owner or before men see that he is wasting it.

If a man is in possession of his senses and is capable of managing his household and his business transactions and is able to ride a horse and take part in ale feasts, then he should have the control of his property and no man must divide it. But if someone does divide it, that (division) shall not be valid.

## 127 Concerning the distribution of minors

Now men distribute among themselves (the care of) minors and dependants; no matter how they do it, and draw lots (for them) afterwards, that distribution between them shall hold. These (minors and dependants) have to follow the shares of inheritance.

If a minor owns property, then that (property) is regarded as already acquired, if it has been announced in the assembly that the minors have been distributed.[28]

## 128 If a man gives more to one of his daughters than to another

Now a man gives his daughter in marriage, but some (of his daughters) are unmarried, and they are all his nearest heirs; then he dies before all are married. They who are not married should take as much of the undivided inheritance as the others brought with them from home (as their portion); afterwards they have to share equally what is left.

Whenever a girl is of full age she should herself take care of her property and also accept guardianship (for others).

## 129 Concerning gifts

If a man gives one of his sons more than another, then he (the latter), when they divide the inheritance from their father, should take as much of what is undivided

27 According to the rules at the end of Ch. 53.

28 This second paragraph seems to imply that an heir who had to take care of a minor as part of his inheritance, at the same time took possession of the minor's property. The minor had the opportunity to free himself according to the rule in Ch. 130 (first paragraph).

as was given to him who got more; and afterwards they have to divide equally what is left.

Therefore a gift is better than payment, because everyone owns his gift (what has been given to him) (so long as it is) unpaid; no gift is requited unless just as much has come in return as that which was given away.

Now those gifts shall be enumerated that must remain valid:[29] Granting of freedom to a bondman, unless he (the master) is in danger of death or becoming a beggar, in that case he should take reward for fostering by the other (the freedman),[30] if he (the latter) had not paid for his freedom. Payment for fostering children shall hold. Those gifts shall hold which the king gives to us[31] or we give to him. And all tithe,[32] and freedman's purchase money, six *aurar*. A freeholder may give his son with a bondwoman three *merkr*, but a landed man (may give his son) six *merkr*, a householder twelve *aurar*, son of a freedman six *aurar*. These gifts cannot be taken back unless he who is entitled to inherit, gets less in his share. A nookling and a scrubling may have just as much as the son of a bondwoman.

## 130 Concerning the distribution of wards

If someone is included in the distribution of wards, then he is released from wardship if he sets up a household for himself or declares in the assembly that he wants to go back (into the position of a self-supporting man) into his family and enjoy full personal rights of law, or (if he) marries.

Now a man is given (charge of) a minor whom he is not obliged to provide for, then he should summon home the one who has the obligation to provide for him. His witnesses should say this: "Here is the minor whom you should provide for, but not he who brought him here"; then they must place the responsibility with the other.

Now a minor comes to a man, then the man may do what he prefers: let him go the same way back or to the assembly; the men of the assembly should determine where he is to be brought. But if he takes him the same way back, he must take him to those night-quarters which he came from on his way forward, and he who refuses to receive him (at those night-quarters) is liable to pay a fine of three *aurar*. Whoever refuses to receive him, is responsible for him with three *merkr* if he dies of for want of care.

Now people have minor wards to distribute, and one wants to arrange a distribution, but the other does not, then he (the former) should summon the other to a distribution of wardship.

29 I.e. gifts for which no return service may be demanded.

30 I.e. the freedman must help to support his former master. Larson 1935, 118.

31 Such as land given in reward for a drinking-party (Ch. 270) and other land given by the king (Ch. 292).

32 Here = *ǫfuðtíund* (capital tithe), i.e. one tenth of a man's property, which he had to pay once during his lifetime. Hertzberg 1895, 312.

If the other comes to the distribution, it is well. But if he does not come, the plaintiff should produce his witnesses (to testify) that he had summoned him to that place; afterwards impartial men must distribute the minors between them and then draw lots; he (the summoner) must take his lot with him, and the responsibility for the other lot should rest with the one who did not come.

# VII Summons to an assembly

## 131 Concerning summons to an assembly

Now any man who seems to need it should be entitled to summon an assembly; then everyone has to carry the message stick forward and no one may fail (to do so). It must go to the winter houses and not to the shielings. A message stick to summon an assembly must not stop anywhere when the weather is fit for travelling, except where there is a night-quarter[1] – unless hindered by necessity. If anyone fails to bring the message forward he is liable to pay a fine of three *aurar*. If he (carries it) past two farms, he is (only) responsible for the one he lives in.[2]

The one who carries the message stick should cut three notches into the doorpost or the casing and set the message stick in the lintel above the door.

All householders should go to the assembly when the message comes, except those who work alone,[3] they must attend three assemblies: assembly held on account of a murder,[4] king's assembly and an assembly held for mustering;[5] those who work alone shall be exempted from all other assemblies.

A man is counted as working alone when a man younger than fifteen winters helps him in his work, whether it is his own son or another man's son who joins him at work.

A widow or a disabled householder should go to the assembly only if they want to. But all other householders must go to the assembly when the summons comes to their house, if not, they have to pay a fine for not appearing when summoned.

If someone lets the message stick remain with him so long that it does not come forward as far as it should, because it remained so long with him who ought to carry it (farther), then he is liable to pay a fine.

Even if the message stick comes (too) late to those who have the longest way to go, they should nevertheless set out for the assembly until they meet men from the assembly (on their way home).

1 There seem to have been regular routes for the message stick.

2 Here the ON text is incomplete and unclear.

3 ON *einvirkjar*, i.e. men whose farms were considered not to be complete.

4 Cf. Ch. 151.

5 Cf. Ch. 296.

Now if five men, or more than five, have all been charged with the same offence, the message stick may summon them by name to the assembly, if they have been charged with the offence in the presence of witnesses.

## 132 Concerning twelve-man oaths and six-man oaths

If the king accuses someone of high treason, he may deny the charge with a twelve-man oath. In the same way charges of murder and violation of a peace pledge may be denied.

Six men should be appointed (and placed) on either side of him, all of the same social standing as the accused, and he should have two of them, and his two nearest relatives, he himself (should be) the fifth, and seven which he selects freely.

## 133 Concerning six-man oaths

A six-man oath shall apply in cases of theft, arson, damage to movables, libel carved on a tree, libel by word of mouth and crimes against women, and likewise in cases of a band of villains and for anyone taking revenge on thieves.

Six[6] men should be appointed (and placed) on either side of him, all of the same social standing as the accused; of those he should have two for theft and arson, but one in all other cases that call for six-man oaths.

## 134 Concerning mask oath

Now there is mask oath,[7] three men should be appointed (and placed) on either side of the accused, all of his own social standing, (he) should have all of them (with him), he must himself be the seventh.

## 135 Concerning three-man oaths

Now a three-man oath shall be taken in the following way. The accused himself should swear and another (who) enjoys equal rights, not a cognate nor an agnate nor anyone closely related by marriage. The third should (be) one who can be held to account for pledge and promise, a free man of major age.

All oaths may be lawfully sworn during ten weeks of days on which oaths may be taken. The whole week is counted as such (i.e. being available for oaths) even though oaths may be sworn on one day (only) in that week.

The twelve-man oaths, when failing, are all liable to crime (i.e. cases that cannot be atoned for by money), and (so are) mask oaths and (six-man oaths in cases of) theft and arson. All other six-man oaths, when failing, are liable to outlawry.

6 Probably an error. The right number seems to be three, according to Book IX, Ch. 14 of Magnus the Law-Mender's Law of the Realm (NGL II, 173).

7 Referring to men being masked or disguised.

A three-man oath, when failing, is liable to such fine as is stipulated for the charge which the oath was intended to refute.

A single oath should be taken as soon as the one to whom the oath was promised wants to hear it and has a book[8] to offer him who should swear.

## 136 How oaths are to be taken

Now it is well if they (the litigants) agree to what time the oaths should be taken; otherwise he (who should take the oath) should summon the other, with at least five nights' notice, to (appear at) whatever church he likes within the *fylki*. Now he who is to hear the oath fails to come, then the other must present his witnesses in front of the church door, that he had summoned him to that place, and take the oath before witnesses.

Now they both come, the one who should take the oath and the one who is to hear it, then they must each appoint two men to decide whether the oath has been correctly taken.

Now these men disagree, some say that the oath has been correctly taken, others wrongly; those who are willing to swear (to support their view) shall win. But if both sides are willing to swear, then those who want to help (i.e. are on the same side as he who should take the main oath) are nearest (to win); (he should) present his witnesses in the next assembly, if someone raises objections.

If the oath fails him, his case should be heard in court within the first twelve months, as always (when oaths are not taken). If the case has not been presented by that time, the oath must be regarded as lawfully taken, even though it has not been sworn.

## 137 Concerning slander

No one of us must defame another man to the king or to anyone more powerful than oneself. But if he defames another so that it may cost him his life or property, then he has forfeited his own property by that slander, or his life, if it turns out to be slander. If he denies (it), he has to deny (it) with a six-man oath, if it fails, he is liable to the same penalty as he had intended for the other.[9]

## 138 If someone insults another man

No one must insult another man, neither by word of mouth nor by carving on a tree. But if he is identified and convicted of doing this,[10] then he is liable to outlawry; he has to deny (it) with a six-man oath, it leads to outlawry if it fails.

8 Oaths were sworn on a missal or a gospel-book in church.

9 This reflects the law of retaliation (talion), ultimately derived from Mosaic Law (Exod. 21:24; Lev. 24:20; Deut. 19:21). On the influence of Mosaic Law in general see Tamm 2002, esp. 301–8.

10 It was thought that this might lead to illness or even death for those who were exposed to it.

No one must circulate impossible tales or slander about another. That is an impossible tale if someone tells about another such things that cannot be or happen and have not been true: says that he is a woman every ninth night and has given birth to a child and if he calls him a werewolf; he who says things like this, is an outlaw, if he is proved guilty of this; he may deny (it) with a six-man oath, it leads to outlawry if it fails.

### 139 Concerning damage to weapons

If someone damages another man's weapons, then he must pay a fine of six *aurar* to the other for evil intent and repair the weapons so that they are not in a worse condition than they were before, or else give him compensation for the weapons.

### 140 If someone trades with an outlaw

Now someone trades with an outlaw, then the king should have what that man bought from him (the outlaw). But he who traded is liable to pay a fine of three *merkr*; he must deny with a three-man oath that he knew that the other was an outlaw.

### 141 If the king's representative seizes the property of a householder without legal judgement

Now a landed man or the king's representative seizes the property of a householder before it has been inventoried or awarded (by legal action), then he must bring it back and pay a compensation of forty *merkr*; because everyone is worthy of his possessions before the law.

### 142 If the king's representative[11] rows home to a householder

Now men row a fully manned ship to a householder – or a group of men go to his home – and by force break into his house and take away his movables, then that deed leads to outlawry. If any one of those (perpetrators) wants to remain in the country, he must bring the movables back to the householder, everything he took, and pay a compensation of forty *merkr*, otherwise he will be outlawed.

### 143 Concerning hand seizure

Now someone wrests a thing out of another's hand[12] and the other (i.e. the latter) gets witnesses thereto, then he who robbed is liable to pay a compensation of three

11 These words are misleading here. This chapter deals with robbers.

12 By force, but without using weapons. Cf. Ch. 90.

*merkr*. If he runs away with what he took and the owner runs after him and kills him, then he is outlawed.

## 144 Concerning finds

Everyone who finds something should keep it until the owner comes to seek it with witnesses. Everyone must publish his find, if he wants to follow the correct procedure.

Now people go together on the road and he who goes in front finds something, then they own it in common, he and those who go behind him. Those who go past the thing own nothing of it.

Now people sail on a ship and find something of value, then they have to divide it according to their number.

Every man should be responsible for what he has borrowed and bring it back unharmed.[13]

Everyone owns what he has got by betting, if he bet in front of witnesses; (he) may sue for it as for any other acknowledged debt.[14]

If people row upon others, or sail upon them, they have to make good for all the damage they have caused, unless the others rowed out in front of the prow.

## 145 Concerning jetsam and rights to the common

Every man should have the right to use water and wood in the common.[15] Every man should have such rights in the common as he has had from times past. But if a farm is cleared in the common, then it belongs to the king. If there are field and meadow enclosed by a fence, then he (the settler) should own (the ground) so far from the fence as he may throw his sickle; but beyond (i.e. farther out) is common land.

Everything that drifts ashore into common land is the property of the king.

Now people sail along the shore or towards land from the sea and are shipwrecked, then every man should have that property which he claims to own and has witnesses to, no matter who owns the land where it drifted ashore.[16]

Everything else that drifts ashore from the sea belongs to the king.

## 146 Concerning loading and taking passage in a ship

Now someone loads a merchant ship in his home district and people take passage with him, then he should load the ship in such a way that all those who have taken

13 Cf. also Ch. 49.

14 See Ch. 35.

15 The wording indicates that the common was not supposed to belong to the king. The king's right to own newly farmed land seems to have been a new rule, introduced by the king in order to promote the clearing of new land.

16 Cf. Book V, note 44. On a different translation, see Meissner 1935, 101.

passage can be accommodated. If the ship is overloaded, the ship-owner must carry his cargo ashore but allow passage to those who have booked. If they (still) do not find it seaworthy, then those who booked last should remove their cargo from the ship; each who has to do so is entitled to six *aurar* for breach of contract.

## 147 If a dog or a farm animal injures someone[17]

If a dog or a horse or an ox butts a man, or any other farm animal bites or strikes anyone, then he who has been bitten should claim the animal in front of witnesses; then the owner must bind the animal and hand it over to the one who has been bitten.

But if he refuses to hand it over, he who has been bitten should ask witnesses to note the fact, and the owner must pay to him who was injured and to the king as much as if he had injured (the other) himself.

17 Such cases are also known from Mosaic Law (Exod. 20, 28–30). Tamm 2002, 305.

# VIII Amendments

## 148 Here are the amendments which Magnus the Good[1] authorized at Langøyarsundet,[2] and some that Håkon[3] gave, the foster son of (Steigar-)Tore

Christmas gifts (to the king)[4] shall never be levied from now on.

A man shall have that which is found on his land, even though another digs it up.[5]

### *Concerning a man's ship*

Every man is entitled to use his ship in perfect peace and sail wherever he wants.

### *This concerns land dues*

No man shall pay land dues[6] if he contributes to the levy.

If a man leaves our country and stays in another place, he is entitled to come back whenever he wants to, if he has not joined a band of enemies to our kings.[7]

Now a man is outlawed from here; if someone dies here whom he should inherit from if he were in this country and were not an outlaw, then the heir who is next in line should take over the inheritance.

1 Magnus Olavsson, King of Norway 1035–47.
2 C. 1040, in North-Western Norway, near Kristiansund.
3 Håkon Toresfostre, pretender 1093–4.
4 A tax introduced by King Svein Knutsson, also named Alfivasson (1030–5).
5 Treasures hidden in the earth were earlier claimed by the king, probably because in heathen times they were thought to have belonged to deceased people.
6 Originally a tax paid by Norwegians to the king for licence of sailing to Iceland, later a tax to be paid by every man travelling between Norway and Iceland.
7 This probably refers to the amendments given by Håkon Toresfostre.

# IX Rules for whaling

## 149 Here begins the law of whaling

A freeholder or a man of higher social standing than a freeholder has the right to the whole of a whale longer than eighteen ells,[1] and any other man (has the right) to a whale half as long.

Now a man finds a whale, then he should cut it up in front of witnesses, or leave the backbone, the head and the tail behind; then that shall serve as testimony for him if he has no witnesses.

He must cut the whale in deep water and not carry it up on the green sod. But if he does carry it up, then the landowner has the right to half of the whale, unless the other releases it with compensation for trespassing, if he thinks the whale is worth more. Now a man starts to cut up a whale; if there is then so much grass (in the place) that it may feed a ewe and a lamb there in summer, he should release (the parts) with compensation for trespassing if he brings (the parts) up.

If a whale drifts up on a man's land within the fence, the landowner owns the whale. If the whale drifts up on a man's land outside the fence and is bigger than the finder has the right to keep, then the king owns half of it and the landowner the other half. If a whale drifts into a fiord where an arrow may be shot across it from either shore, then the whale belongs to both shores; but if there is a shoal there and the whale is stopped farther out, (the owner of) the land[2] still owns the whale.

A man may hunt whales wherever he can.

Now a man hunts a whale and the whale is killed on the deep, then the hunter owns the whale whether it is smaller or bigger. If a man shoots at a whale and hits it and drives it up on the shore, then the hunter owns half of it and the landowner the other half. If a man shoots at a whale in a shoal of herring and thus drives God's gift away, then that man is liable to pay a fine of forty *merkr*.

1 8.5–10 m.
2 I.e. the land nearest to the shoal? Larson 1935, 126, note 14.

## 150 Concerning the finder of blubber (whale fat)

Now a man finds a whale which can be expected to come to land and is bigger than he has the right to own the whole of, then the finder should have the finder's blubber. He should cut a mark into the whale and then go to the king's representative and tell him; then he must have the finder's blubber of that whale; he must have the shaft of an arrow: (he must take an) arrow-shaft as long as a man's hand and measure out a square piece and cut this down to the bone, and (then he should have a piece) as long as the mid-ship oar, wrap a bast rope around the oar where the blade begins and cut a piece down to the bone as broad as the length of the bast rope (and) as long as the rudder and as long as the scoop and the bottom board of the stern.[3]

Now a man finds a whale and binds it with a rope; if people then come at night and cut up the whale at night while it is still bound, then each one (who does so) is a thief and liable to pay a fine of forty *merkr*, but fifteen *merkr* if he cut it up by day.

If a man chases a whale into another man's whale cove[4] and blocks (the entrance) with stakes,[5] then the owner of the cove owns the whale, and the other has to pay compensation for trespassing. If a man chases a whale into a cove which is not a whale cove, then the hunter owns half the whale and the owner of the cove the other half.

Now a man finds a whale out on the fishing grounds, he may cut off from it as much as he can and then let the carcass drift, but he may not cut into the cavities of the animal. If a whale drifts up on the shores of the common, the king owns the whale. If people cut it up, then the one who steers the ship is liable to pay a fine of forty *merkr*, but the others who row together with him, three *merkr* each.

3 This seems to presuppose that the rudder had the same length as the scoop and the bottom board of the stern taken together. Hertzberg 1895, 587.

4 I.e. a cove where whales are usually caught.

5 This way of catching whales has been common in some parts of Western Norway up to modern times.

# X Concerning personal rights

## (Concerning personal rights)

[*Here is a lacuna in the main MS. A part of what is missing may be supplied by AM 146 4to:* Eye witnesses shall decide what kind of killing has taken place. He is guilty of killing whom witnesses bear witness against or whose wife says is guilty of killing. The statement that the wife made in the assembly should be supported by the witnesses she met first.

There are three cases in which women must decide what kind of killing it was: if a man is killed in his high seat; if a man is killed within the enclosure of the field and one of the women may catch sight of it from the houses where she has her daily rounds and there is neither a stone altar nor a hill in the way and she may recognize a man from there. ([1]The first (of those houses) is the hall,[2] the second the storehouse,[3] the third the living room[4]); the third (case is) if a man is killed on a journey and one of those women who should decide what kind of killing it was joins him on the journey. There are four women who can decide what kind of killing it was: wife, daughter, sister, mother, etc.

If a man is present at the assembly when the killing is being committed, or at church, or at a drinking-party, or on board a ship fully manned, and there are twenty-seven men, then they may decide whether he is guilty or not.]

## 151 (Concerning witnesses to killing)

. . . [5] who first come to the place, to inspect the wounds.[6] The name that was first sent with the arrows[7] should follow it if (on the dead body) there are wounds

1 The first (outermost) pair of parentheses is in the MS.
2 A dwelling house, a kind of long house which was the main – and for some time the only – building on a farm. Stigum 1969, 676–7.
3 A log house, often built on posts, for storing meat, flour, and cereals, etc. Stigum 1957, 366–7.
4 A log house where people stayed during the day, cooked their meals, and slept. Stigum 1958, 555–88. Cf. also Ch. 75, first paragraph.
5 Here one sheet has been removed from the MS.
6 To see what kinds of weapons have caused the wounds, so that people can know how many killers there were.
7 I.e. the verbal summons to the accused to appear at the assembly.

inflicted by three men, but the names which were attached to the arrows later should be withdrawn. If there is a wound inflicted by one man only, then those names should be withdrawn which were attached to the arrows later.

The wife must send the arrows; but if there is no wife (to do so), then the heir should send the arrow – and have witnesses thereto – on the same day that the other lost his life. (They must) have the assembly in the place where the killing was committed, if she wants to; then they may pass judgement in the case even if no more than twenty-seven householders come to the assembly.

If a judgement is to be passed correctly in the place where the assembly is held, a quarter of the members must come; then they may pass judgement in the case although more men fail to come.

All should forward the arrows on and no one neglect it; whoever neglects it is liable to a fine of twelve *aurar*. But he is liable to pay a double fine who does both: neglecting to forward the arrows and staying at home when the assembly is held.

A widow should have witnesses that she sends the arrows, and she must do so the same day, unless her advisers[8] are so far away that she cannot reach them.

If the arrows come to him who is accused of the killing, and he does not appear at the assembly, then he acknowledges guilt. But if the arrows do not reach him he should be granted a respite until there is a second assembly, there he may present his means of defence. If he has kinsfolk or heirs they should send word to him. If he fails to come and avoids the message he acknowledges guilt, unless he has offered excuses.

## 152 Concerning killing in a group fight and resistance

There is now also (the case, that) if a man is killed in a crowd, then it is well if he is revenged. But if the killer runs away into the woods, then all should run after him and no one hinder it.

But if they fall who hinder the pursuit, then they are outlawed, but their property is not outlawed.[9] If they do not fall, they should nevertheless pay a fine of forty *merkr* to the king for breaking the peace. If the killer is caught in the pursuit, then the hand (of the catcher) must bring him safe to the assembly and from there to his execution.

The kinsfolk of the killed man may keep the killer, if they want to, and bring him to the assembly; otherwise he should be brought to the king's representative; he is liable to pay a fine of forty *merkr* if he refuses to receive him. A landed man should receive him if the king's representative is not there, he too is liable to pay a fine of forty *merkr* if he refuses to receive him.

The king's representative or the landed man has to find an executioner or pay a fine of forty *merkr*.

8 The advisers of a widow were her nearest kinsmen.
9 I.e. it cannot be confiscated.

The householders shall have the money that the king's representative pays as a fine. But the king shall have half of the money the landed man must pay as a fine, and the householders the other half.

## 153 If someone helps an outlaw to flee

Now a killer runs away onto a ship, then anyone may with impunity throw an oar out to him or a scoop or a rudder or a bottom board of the stern, any of those things and not more. But if he does more than this, he helps an outlaw to flee and then he is liable to (pay a fine of) forty *merkr*.

## 154 Concerning killing in a group

It is called a group when at least five men are together. Now four men walk on the road together and one of them becomes a killer there and kills one of his companions, then he is the killer who stands alone in his assertion.[10] If a slave is in company with them, then he is the killer if they choose to accuse him.

## 155 If two men are accused of killing

There is now also (the case) that three men walk on the road together, then one of them kills one of the others; then two are still alive and each accuses the other, then they are both killers. Now one of them goes to the assembly but the other does not, then he is the killer who flees the assembly.

## 156 Concerning the announcement of killing

There is now also (the case) that men meet at a crossroad and one becomes the killer of the other, now if he (the dying one) is able to speak when people come to him, then he is the killer whom he accuses, unless the big testimony[11] helps him. If another man announces that he himself has committed the killing, then they are both killers, even if there is only one wound in the body of the killed man.

When a man announces killing in the proper way, he should go from where the killing was done in whatever direction he wants and report it at the nearest house, unless there are kinsmen of the killed in there, either on the mother's side or on the father's side or near relatives by marriage. But if such people are there, he should go past that house and to the next, unless the same is the case there; then he should go to the third house and there report the killing, no matter what kind of men are inside. He must not give his name as *Ulfr* or *Bjǫrn*[12] unless that is his real name. He must show proofs of his identity and tell where he stayed the night before.

10 I.e. he is accused by the others.

11 I.e. trial by ordeal, esp. by carrying hot iron. Cf. Ch. 24.

12 Lit. 'Wolf' or 'Bear', common male names.

On the arrow assembly witnesses to the report of the killing shall be presented; one man's testimony is sufficient; and he may also present reports from his household.

You may not accuse anyone of planning or attempting killing unless his name followed the arrows and he is charged at the assembly. Two should bear witness that the accused moved around in that district in such a way that he could have been present at the killing, they must bear witness to his night-quarters. Witness to his night-quarters is only needed in case one (person's name) has been sent forward with the arrows and another has announced that he himself has committed the killing.

If the heir of the killed man accuses another man than him (who announced that he committed the killing), the accused may deny the charge with a three-man oath.

He should go to the assembly and request access, lay down his weapons and offer to abide by the law and swear a three-man oath; if it fails, he is outlawed. If they deny him access to the assembly, then they give immunity to him and all his property.

But if he reports (the killing) in another way (than prescribed previously) he acknowledges (himself) to be guilty of murder.

One (man) may present the indictment from the others[13] and from any free man.

## 157 If someone is killed in an alehouse

There is now (the case, that) if a man is killed at a drinking-party while the fire is burning or at daylight, then the men in the alehouse should find his killer or pay full fines for him (the killed man) both to his kinsfolk and also to the king.

Now someone is killed at night after the fire has gone out. If the killing is reported in the morning when people wake up, then he is the killer (who reported that he committed the crime); but if the killing is not reported and one (person) is missing, then he is the killer; he must (otherwise) explain his errand or come back in the morning.

If they are all there, and no one is more likely than any other to be the killer, then the men at the drinking-party should investigate the murder; but the heir (of the killed man) may accuse anyone he wants, and that man may swear a murder oath[14] to defend himself.

If that oath fails him, it leads to outlawry. If he takes the oath correctly, the heir may accuse someone else, (but) a third only in so far as he can prove his guilt.[15] If he cannot prove his guilt he (the heir) should himself be subjected to the same punishment as he intended for the other man.[16]

13 Or: from his household. The ON text has *hinna*, probably an error for *hiúna*.

14 A twelve-man oath. Cf. Ch. 132.

15 If he cannot, he is guilty of making a false accusation.

16 According to the retaliation principle. See Ch. 22 (Book II, note 69).

## 158 If someone is killed on a journey

Now two men who are messmates and partners travel together in search of gain. If one of them is killed, the other should go to the heir and tell (about the crime to) the first man he meets. If the heir accuses him of having killed his messmate, he may deny (it) by carrying hot iron.[17]

## 159 If a woman kills a man

If a man kills a woman, then he is just as much of an outlaw as if he had killed a man.

If a woman kills a man, then she is an outlaw and her kinsfolk should send her out of the country.

Likewise, if a minor becomes a killer, he too should be sent out of the country and his kinsfolk should send him on his way out before five days have passed, but (he may) stay with them five nights apart from cases of necessity. But if he stays longer a fine of forty *merkr* must be paid or (the charge be) denied by a three-man oath.

## 160 Concerning charge against a dead man

There are three cases in which legal action may be brought against a dead man.[18] This is the first case that a man comes across another man having sexual intercourse with a woman for whom he is entitled to killing committed in revenge. These are seven women. The first is a man's wife, the second (is his) sister, the third (his) daughter, the fourth (his) mother, the fifth (his) stepmother, the sixth (his) brother's wife, the seventh (his) son's wife. If a man comes across someone having sexual intercourse with any one of these, he may kill that man, if he wants to, and tell (about the killing to) the one whom he meets first, and likewise (tell him) what was the cause.

He should wait until the heir of the killed (man) has sent out the arrow stick, if he is within the *fylki*, otherwise he has to send the arrows himself.

Now he should go to the assembly and lay down his weapons outside and ask for (preliminary) security and offer to comply with the law and present testimony from the men he met first. If people deny him access to the assembly, then they give immunity to him and to everything he owns. Then he who was killed is an outlaw, but his property is not outlawed; and he who killed shall be immune by the law.

This is the second case, when a man comes across another man in his storehouse and he (the latter) has made himself a load of stolen goods and clothes, then

17 See Ch. 156 and note 11.

18 This action allowed the killer to elicit a decision of the court to the effect of avoiding prosecution. In addition to the three cases listed here there is a fourth case in Ch. 196. These rules justified blood revenge provided it was performed immediately after the action that caused it.

he may kill that man, if he wants to. He should go to his neighbours and show them the wound and have them as witnesses at the arrow assembly.

This is the third case, then, if a man comes across another man in his pen or cow-house and he (the latter) puts ropes on the cattle and wants to lead it away, then he may kill that man, if he wants to. He should also go to his neighbours and show them the wound and then go to the assembly with his witnesses; then he always outlaws the other (i.e. the killed man) in all those cases which I have now enumerated.

## 161 If someone happens to make a bad find

This is also the case, if you find a killed man out in the forest, then the finder should first cover up the corpse and then tell (about the find to) the first man he meets, and go to the heir, if he is in the *fylki*; otherwise he must send a message stick and summon and inform the assembly.

Now whoever remains away from that assembly is guilty of paying a fine of six *aurar*; that is called the greater assembly fine (for not appearing when summoned).

Now he (the finder) fails to do so, then he acknowledges guilt of murder, if the heir wants to indict him.

## 162 If a man asks for assistance against someone else

Now a man asks for assistance against someone else for something,[19] and he kills that man when they come to his house, then they (his companions) should go away from the killer and each of them must pay a ring (as a fine) to the king for their misconduct,[20] but forty *merkr* if they join the killer and go away with him.

Now a man is outlawed at the assembly and his home, his livestock and his property,[21] then the king's representative should give a five nights' summons[22] to all creditors; each should have what is due to him so far as witnesses know the debt, before the king's representative takes (anything). Whatever is rooted in the soil follows the land, but even there the creditors should have what is due to them.

## 163 If a man's slave is accused of killing

Now a man's slave is accused of killing, then his master should deny (it) with such an oath for him as (he would have taken) for himself. And if the oath fails, then

19 E.g. to collect debts. Cf. Ch. 35.
20 I.e. their share in the crime.
21 Outlawed property accrued to the king.
22 A summons with five days' notice.

it leads to outlawry for the master himself. He who cannot defend himself with an oath[23] must dismiss the slave[24] or pay a fine of forty *merkr* when a sentence is passed on him.

## 164 Concerning killing committed in a madman's way

Now a man kills another in a madman's way,[25] a son kills his father, or a father his son, or a brother a brother, or a brother or a sister kills a brother or a sister, or a child kills its mother, or a mother her child; then the killer forfeits the inheritance he was entitled to; he who is the next heir should have that inheritance, and the king should have it rather than he who killed. But he may remain in the country and go to confession and keep what he has.

## 165 If a dog or some (other) animal injures people

Now if a horn or a hoof or a dog causes a man's death, (the owner) should dispose of (the animal).[26] If he feeds it after sentence has been passed, he should pay a compensation of forty *merkr*. But if he denies the charge, he has to deny (it) with a three-man oath; (if it fails,) it leads to (a compensation of) forty *merkr*, and he must pay wergild to the kinsfolk (of the killed man).

## 166 If men watch a fight

Now men fight for life and people watch their fight from the other side of streams or impassable areas but cannot identify them. If one of them has been struck so that his head is cut off, or his brain laid on the ground, or his back is broken, or both hands are cut off, then this one has begun the fight, for he could strike no man afterwards; then the other is immune.

## 167 Concerning killing in a group fight

Men call that killing in a group fight when people attack each other in two groups and fight; those who begin the fight should pay a fine of forty *merkr*, but the others who defend themselves may not (pay anything), when witnesses know (the facts). But if both sides are stubborn and say that the other side began (it), then they should (together) pay wergild to the kinsfolk (of those who are killed) and each group (pay a fine of) forty *merkr* to the king.

23 If, e.g., the accusation is justified.

24 This is the one and only case where the surrendering of slaves is mentioned specifically. Iversen 1997, 59.

25 See Ch. 32.

26 There are corresponding rules in Roman law, ultimately derived from the Bible (Exod. 21:28–36). Jacoby 1986, 172–4; Tamm 2002, 306–7.

## 168 More on killing in a group fight

It is a group when five men are together, or more than five. Now men attack each other and a man is wounded and dies, then they (who attack) should prove one man guilty of the killing or else pay forty *merkr* to the king and wergild to the kinsfolk.

## 169 Concerning unintentional harm[27]

Now two men are hewing the same tree and the axe flies out of the hands of one of them and causes the death of the other. If he is able to speak when people come to him, then he should decide what it is to be called; it shall be unintentional killing only if he wants to.[28] If he is not able to speak, then the heir should decide what it shall be called.

## 170 Concerning the killing of the king's representative

Now someone kills the king's representative; then he should pay a fine of fifteen *merkr*, unless he kills him in front of the king's table while the king's representative is serving the king. Then the killer is an outlaw, and likewise if he kills the king's representative at the assembly when he prosecutes on behalf of the king.

He has to pay a fine for the king's representative according to the money value[29] here in Gulen, with one *eyrir* equalling six ells of wadmal.[30]

## 171 If a man is killed on board a ship

If a man kills another man on board a ship, then it is well if that man is revenged or the killer is pushed overboard. They (the crew) may bring him ashore to the mainland with impunity. But if they take him farther, then each of them is liable to pay a fine of forty *merkr*; then those who want to set him ashore should turn the ship towards the land, but the others, who row out (with him) to sea, are outlawed. But those who hold their oars up are clear of guilt if they report to the first men they meet that they did not want to row the killer (any further).

## 172 If someone throws something at another[31]

If a man throws (something) down[32] from a house or from a ship to a place where he cannot see it, and it causes the death of another man, (then) he should pay wergild for the (man) killed to his kinsfolk, but the king must have nothing of this.

27 On this chapter in general see Bagge 2010, 192–4.

28 The example is taken from the Bible (Deut. 19:5). Tamm 2002, 307.

29 This refers to the relation between coin and pure silver; the six ells *eyrir* had the worth of six ells of wadmal, corresponding to one half of a weighed *eyrir* of pure silver.

30 Wadmal was the standard homespun woollen cloth.

31 Concerning Chapters 172–7 see Bagge 2010, 192–4.

32 Presupposing that this is done inadvertently or unintentionally. The same is supposed to be the case in Chs. 173–6.

## 173 If a man is killed under a ship

Now men drag a ship ashore or shove it out (into the water) and a man is killed under the ship,[33] then they should pay wergild for him, but the king must have nothing of this.

Now people carry ship's timber or draw long logs and it causes the death of one of them; (they) should pay full wergild for him, his own part deducted.[34] The king must have nothing of this.

## 174 Concerning sailing upon someone at sea

When people are out on the fishing grounds, having their fishing-lines over the side of the boat and (other) men sail upon them, then wergild should be paid for them, if it causes the death of any one of them; the king must have nothing of this. But if they have no fishing-line over the side of the boat and they row out in front of the prow of (other) men's boat, then they are half their own killers, then half wergild should be paid for them; the king must have nothing of this.

## 175 Concerning half wergild

Now two men are felling a tree and it falls on one of them, then he is half his own killer. But the other should pay half wergild;[35] the king must have nothing of this.

Now two men go into the forest and a tree falls on one of them, so large that one man cannot move it off or on, [then the heir should decide.[36] The same procedure applies to (working with) a rock.

## 176 If someone lowers himself with a rope

Now a man lowers himself (e.g. down a mountain wall[37]) with a rope and it causes his death, then he has killed himself. But if other men lower him down with a rope, then they are his killers. The king must have nothing for this, but they should pay wergild for him to his kinsfolk.

## 177 Concerning unintentional harm

Now two men go into the forest and one of them falls down over a cliff. Now the other goes to a house[38] and reports the accident; if the heir wants to accuse him,

33 By being squeezed between the ship and the rollers. See Book II, note 30.

34 I.e. the wergild shall be reduced by as much as he shared in the work. Larson 1935, 136.

35 This rule is probably taken from Canon Law of the 11th century, a version attributed to Burchard of Worms. Sunde 2011a, 61.

36 [*Holm perg 31 4to, has the following:* then that tree causes his death. But if the tree is so small that one man can move it off or on, then he may deny (it) with a three-man oath, that it was not his intention, and he would gladly have helped him if he could.]

37 Hertzberg 1895, 594.

38 To see people (Hertzberg 1895, 298). Or: to the (dead man's) house (Larson 1935, 136).

he may deny (it) with a three-man oath. But if he does not report the accident, he should deny (it) with a murder oath.[39]

## 178 Concerning attack on a man's home

Now someone attacks another man's home and breaks into his house and kills him; that is called foul murder.[40] It is foul murder if someone kills a man to whom he has pledged surety; it is also foul murder if someone kills another man who has been given quarter; it is also foul murder if someone throws a man on a stock or a rock or a stump of wood; it is also foul murder if someone burns another to death; it is also foul murder if someone robs a fallen man: strips his clothes off and takes his weapons; it is also foul murder if someone murders a man;[41] it is also foul murder if someone takes revenge for thieves; let him deny (it) with a six-man oath.

And whenever someone commits foul murder, he shall go outlawed and unprotected by the law and (have) forfeited every penny of his property, in land and movables, and never come (back) to the land, either with king or earl, unless he brings true news of war.[42]

## 179 Concerning mutilation[43]

Now a man's hand or foot is cut off, then half wergild shall be paid. But if the limb is still joined (to the body), half [*AM 146 S and UppsUB R 713:* a quarter of the] wergild shall be paid.

But if an eye has been blown out of a man's head, half wergild must be paid.

But if both hand and foot have been cut off, then a man is worse off living than dead, then wergild must be paid as if he were killed.

## 180 Concerning wergild

Now the wergild in Gulen is enumerated. For a freeholder eighteen *merkr* in lawful money shall be paid. The wergild must increase or decrease from that (point of departure) as other legal compensation.[44] According to the wergild which is enumerated in Gulen (all that wergild) must be assessed which should be paid for a hand or a foot and an eye,[45] and likewise the private compensation for a crime.[46]

The thumb shall be as dear as all the other fingers (taken together), for the thumb must be paid a compensation of three *merkr*. But a *mǫrk* for the next (finger), and

39 A twelve-man oath. See Ch. 132.
40 Jørgensen 2014, 68–70.
41 Not making the killing known.
42 See Ch. 312.
43 See Ch. 180.
44 See Ch. 200.
45 See Ch. 179.
46 The size of this compensation is not specified, but it was probably half wergild.

the same for the long finger. But six *aurar* for the next, and two *aurar* for the smallest one.

## 181 Concerning sending messages with arrows[47]

But if a man is killed at the assembly, then his heirs should send forth an arrow and let it come to his booth; there the men at the assembly have to pass judgement in the case. But if other quarrels arise between men (the aggressor) should be summoned to the assembly and witnesses brought to inspect wounds or estimate evil intent.

The (man's) heir shall receive the compensation.

## 182 Concerning inspection of wounds

Now a man is accused of having killed his slave; that killing shall be publicly announced, otherwise he is a murderer. Now he is accused, but denies (it). If he is accused so early that they can examine the dead body, then they should do so. If a mortal wound is found on the body, then he is guilty in the case. But if no such wounds are found on the body, then the charge is false.

If the accusation comes so late that the dead body cannot be examined, then he should deny (it) with a three-man oath; it leads to outlawry if it fails.

If someone kills another man's slave, he must pay such compensation as men assess for the naked slave.[48]

## 183 Concerning wounds

It is now also (the case, that) if a man wounds another in a group and if he offers to submit to the law and lays down his weapons, then he should be bound with fetters. But if the other dies from the wounds, then he must be killed at the feet of the dead man and thus be released from the fetters.

If the other lives longer than a scab is formed on the wound, (then) he should pay him compensation for the wound, and a ring (as a fine) to the king.

Now three men meet and one of them inflicts a wound on one of the others, then men should bear witness for full compensation to the injured man.

## 184 More about wounds

Now two men meet and one inflicts a wound on the other, then he (the injured man) should go with the wound unbound, if he can, and show it on the same day to the first man he meets, and send people to the house of the offender, where

47 See Ch. 151.

48 The master was entitled to protection for his slave, who was part of his master's property. Iversen 1997, 44.

he lives, and summon him to the assembly, to a five-day assembly[49] at the very shortest. That is always correct, even if the other is not at home.

In the same way a bruise shall be dealt with.

Those he met first must bear witness whether they thought the injury looked like a wound or a bruise, and they have to name the offender on the same day. Now they bear witness to compensation for a wound. But if they refuse to testify either for or against (the accused), then each of them is liable to pay a fine of three *aurar*.

The one who is accused should deny (it) with a three-man oath; that oath leads to payment of financial compensation if it fails.

## 185 Concerning the evaluation of wounds

Now if a freedman wounds a man he should pay one ring, (that is) twelve *aurar*.[50] But his son (should pay) two rings. And a householder three rings. A man born to odal-right six rings. A landed man and the king's marshal twelve rings. And an earl twenty-four. And a king two rings less than fifty (i.e. forty-eight).[51]

Now a man wounds another, then he should pay compensation for the wound to the injured. An *eyrir* for touching the other. An *eyrir* for cutting into his flesh. An *eyrir* for the edge striking the leg bone. An *eyrir* for each (bit of) bone being loosened, when it tinkles in the scales.[52] An *eyrir* for each spot which is burnt (in dressing the wound),[53] unless there is dead tissue in the wound. An *eyrir* for lips twitching (in pain). An *eyrir* for every tear in the clothing. An *eyrir* if he sits alone (relieving himself). An *eyrir* if he is rising from bed. An *eyrir* for every cut that has to be made (in dressing the wound), if the cut bleeds. Half a *mǫrk* for a wound in the cavities of the chest or the abdomen; half a *mǫrk* if someone is wounded into the marrow.[54] An *eyrir* in case the weapon comes out.[55] And they have to evaluate scars, external injury, (other) blemishes and any harm.

He who caused the wound must pay the fee for the cure and provide the injured and the physician with food, a month's food of both kinds.[56]

If a man cuts a (bit of) flesh from another, so that it drops to the ground, he has to pay a compensation of six *aurar* and six *aurar* if the man gets a scar on his head. He who is wounded must have witnesses if the other denies having loosened so many bones from the first as he (the latter) says.

49 I.e. an assembly that was summoned with at least five days' notice. Hertzberg 1895, 189–90.
50 The rings were fines to the king. The value of a ring was one and a half *merkr* (= twelve *aurar*).
51 This must refer to a situation when two kings ruled at the same time.
52 When the money (burnt silver) was being paid.
53 Bleeding was usually stopped by putting red-hot iron on the wound, a procedure known in classical medicine.
54 The distinction between (ON) *holsár* and *mergundir* was known from the Salerno school of medicine.
55 I.e. the wound goes through the body.
56 I.e. butter and meal.

All wounds on the breast shall be evaluated. And (wounds) on the back are twice as dear as those on the breast.

Now a man is present and watches people fighting and does not try to separate them nor help either side, then he should pay a sloth-fine[57] to the king, (that) is twelve *aurar*.

## 186 Concerning men's right to personal compensation[58]

No one has the right to claim personal compensation more than three times, be it a man or a woman, if he does not take revenge in the meantime.

## 187 Concerning quarrels in an alehouse

Now men quarrel in an alehouse when men are drunk, then those who have quarrelled should go outside and come back in the morning when men wake up; then men may pass judgement in their dispute there as if at the assembly, if they know the law.

A man's bench-mates should bear witness with him, or messmates, or men who sat close to him, or drinking-mates, if the others are not present. What they witness must stand, and no counter-witness[59] may be brought forward against them.

But there every man has a right to personal compensation twice as large as at his home.

Now they may settle the matter there, if they know the law, or refer the case to the assembly.

Now the king's representative or a landed man say that they have quarrelled inappropriately,[60] and they all deny (it). Then each of them should take a (Gospel)-book into their hands and swear that they were all drinking peacefully. He who swears is innocent, but whoever fails in the oath should pay a fine of a ring to the king. And everyone else who is accused of inappropriate quarrelling[61] should deny (it) with a three-man oath; but if the oath fails for them it leads to a fine of fifteen *merkr* for each of them. Now a quarter[62] of the men in the alehouse leave and refuse to swear, then all men in the alehouse are liable to pay the fine. But if fewer men (than a quarter) leave, then they who leave are guilty, they must pay a fine of a ring to the king; but the others should defend themselves with oaths.

## 188 Concerning quarrels among men

Whenever someone watches men quarrelling and he is called upon to bear witness, then he should witness either for or against, or else pay a fine of three *aurar* to the king, if he is called upon (to witness).

57 A fine for having shown indifference.
58 On this chapter see Sunde 2007, 316–20.
59 Cf. Ch. 60.
60 Implying that the king had a right to claim fines.
61 This must refer to intruders wanting to make trouble.
62 Cf. Chs. 151 and 35.

## 189 Concerning premeditated harm

Now a man inflicts a premeditated blow on another man (while they are) in a group. If he who inflicted the blow is killed, he falls as an outlaw and unprotected by the law. But if he runs away into the forest, then all men should run after him and no one hinder it. But if he falls who hinders the pursuit, then he falls as an outlaw, but his property is not outlawed.

A man may put a (spear) shaft, or a ski [*AM 146 4to:* shield] or his foot once in front of one who is running after (the evildoer), if he wants to, and thus impede his running. But if he does more than that, then he is liable to pay a fine of forty *merkr* to the king for having tried to help an outlaw.

If the outlaw is caught in the pursuit, then the hand (of him who catches) protects him (on his way) to the assembly and from there to his execution.[63]

If he escapes into the forest, he may offer to submit to the law from there, then he should have those parts of his property that are not listed and seized.[64] But if the king's representative arrives before the man has offered to submit to the law, then he should have all that has been listed and seized.

Now he should redeem himself from outlawry, then he must pay the other the usual compensation[65] according to his social standing. And then the injured man should take another such compensation from the hundred.[66] He (the outlaw) is to be restored to his rights, but only so that he who was injured should have all that he was entitled to before the king's representative takes anything.[67]

## 190 If a man beats a woman

Now if a man beats a woman, or a woman (beats) a man, then such compensation shall be paid as the injured person is entitled to, and a ring to the king.

But if women fight, then no one is entitled to compensation except the women themselves.

A minor may neither claim nor pay any compensation before he is twelve winters old; then he is a man of half personal right in both respects[68] until he is fifteen winters old.

## 191 Concerning threatening behaviour

Now a man rushes towards another, but is caught, then he should pay a ring to the king.

63 Cf. Ch. 152.
64 I.e. not confiscated. Cf. Ch. 141.
65 As opposed to double compensation. Hertzberg 1895, 519.
66 The fine of 120 *aurar* (= fifteen *merkr*) was what the evildoer had to pay to be allowed to stay in the country.
67 Cf. also Ch. 200.
68 I.e. with regard both to claiming and paying compensation.

But if he brandishes his weapon against someone or swings the butt (of an axe) towards the man and the other asks witnesses to note the hostile behaviour of his enemy, then he (the aggressor) should pay half a wergild to the one he threatened.

## 192 Concerning throws

If a man throws (something) at another and hurts him; that is called a wound if he has any[69] kind of weapon in his hand, but otherwise (it is) a bruise.

## 193 Concerning shots

If a man shoots with a bolt[70] at another and hurts him, then that is called a wound.

## 194 Concerning wounds

If a man strikes at another and hits him with the handle or the shaft, then that is called a wound. Likewise if the spear hits him with the flat side (of the spear-head).

## 195 This concerns gross insult for which full personal compensation is due[71]

If a man thrusts at another with a stake or a pole or an axe handle or a spear-shaft, then he should pay him half compensation, but full compensation[72] if he falls down. If a man pushes another so (hard) that he staggers, then he should pay full compensation even if the other only falls down to his knees. If a man pushes another into a fire, then he must pay him full compensation and a ring to the king, and likewise (must be dealt) with every (case requiring) full compensation.

If a man pushes another overboard, or off the gangway, or into deep water from a steep undersea bank, then he has to pay him full compensation, unless he pushed him overboard on the outer side of a moored ship, for that he may take up arms.[73]

If a man pulls another man by the beard with evil intent, then he must pay the other full compensation. If a man pulls another man by the hair and jerks him forward, then he must pay half compensation. But if he does both this and pushes him aside, then it is called hair pulling, and he should pay him full compensation for that.

Now if men throw aside their weapons and seize each other by the hair, then it is called squabble between friends, no man is entitled to compensation for that.

69 The corresponding ON MS. form *ecki* usually means 'no', but it cannot have that meaning in this context. Hertzberg 1895, 159.

70 A blunt, heavy arrow shot from a crossbow.

71 On the general content of this chapter see Sunde 2011a, 60.

72 See Ch. 200.

73 I.e. kill him.

## 196 Concerning defamatory words

There are words that are called words of defamation,[74] one (such case) is if a man says about another that he has given birth to a child. This is the second (case), if a man says it is proven that another man has been engaged in unlawful sexual intercourse. This is the third (case), if he compares him to a mare or calls him a bitch or a whore or compares him to any female animal. Then he should pay him full compensation for that. Then he (i.e. the person defamed) may also kill that man as an outlaw in revenge for those words which I have now enumerated, if he has asked witnesses to take notice of them.

People may repent their words and take them back if they want to, (and) say that they do not know of worse things about him than about any good man.

These are also words of defamation, if someone calls a free man a slave or calls him a troll or a sorcerer. This is also defamation against a woman if someone accuses her of adultery and calls her a whore, when she does not give cause thereto.

## 197 Concerning the right to personal compensation

Now a man has the same claim to compensation for his daughter or for his sister as for himself, if a man sleeps with her, and likewise for all those women to whom he is the heir, and for any woman whom he has in his household,[75] if she has no heir here in this country.

## 198 Concerning sexual intercourse and the right to personal compensation

If a well-born woman sleeps with a slave, then she has to go to the king's courtyard[76] and (she may) release herself from there with three *merkr*.

Every man should take six *aurar* for his freedwoman.

For a woman in bondage for debt[77] a man should take such compensation as for his best bondwoman, the heir (takes) what exceeds that payment according to her social standing.

If a freedwoman sleeps with a slave, then she must go to the farm of her master.

A householder should have one and a half *aurar* (in compensation) for his best bondwoman, but half as much for each of the others; if he has only one, then she should be (counted) his best.

74 Insulting remarks for which full compensation has to be paid.

75 The words 'any . . . household' (*kono er hann hever i griði með ser*) probably refer to a *griðkona*, a female counterpart to the *griðmaðr* mentioned in Ch. 255. Frimannslund 1975, 108.

76 To do hard labour.

77 A woman working to pay off her debt.

A freedman should have one *eyrir* in current coin[78] for his best bondwoman. His son should have one *eyrir* for his best; the freeholder should have three *aurar*; the landed man six *aurar* for his best bondwoman. His best bondwomen are two: the housemaid and the housekeeper, and two slaves: the servant and the overseer.

Every man has the same right to compensation for sexual intercourse on the part of his slaves as (on the part) of his bondwoman.

Compensation shall be paid according to the right of the king's representative if someone mistreats a king's slave working in the king's courtyard.

A slave enjoys the protection of a ring[79] when he accompanies his master to the assembly or to church or to an alehouse when he is ordered to go; for in those three places every man's right to compensation (in case of insult) is doubled. A slave should take for himself one twelfth of the usual compensation[80] paid to his master if the slave enjoys the protection of a ring[81] in those three places. His master should be responsible for the slave's words and deeds if he accompanies his master at his consent to a place where many men come together.

## 199 Concerning cases involving forty *merkr*

Now someone rapes a woman and he is identified and convicted of this, then he is outlawed, or else he must pay a fine of forty *merkr* and double compensation to the woman.

If she accuses him of this, then she has to do so on the same day; then he may deny (it) with a three-man oath; if that oath fails it leads to what has already been said.

## 200 Concerning men's[82] right to personal compensation

Now a freedman takes six *aurar* in usual compensation[83] (for personal injury). But his son a *mǫrk* in usual compensation. A householder twelve *aurar* in usual compensation. A freeholder three *merkr* in usual compensation. A landed man and the king's marshal six *merkr* in usual compensation. An earl and a bishop twelve *merkr* in usual compensation. The son of a landed man should have the same right to compensation as a freeholder if he is not endowed with land.[84]

Whenever a man is mistreated or beaten the king should have fifteen *merkr* for it.

Every man who suffers a blow should take a second compensation out of the hundred[85] before the king's representative takes anything.

78 See Book V, note 37.
79 ON *baugr*, a fine to the king if the slave is insulted.
80 See note 65.
81 See note 79.
82 Slaves are not included here. Iversen 1997, 46.
83 See note 65.
84 See Ch. 206.
85 I.e. the 120 *aurar* (= fifteen *merkr*) that was the fine to the king. See Ch. 189.

Now all men shall take compensation after their fathers,[86] except those for whom something else is stipulated. The page should take the same right as a freeholder to the usual compensation. A bishop's son[87] and an earl's son and a son of the king's marshal and a son of a page and a son of a priest and a son of a king's representative should take compensation according to their family standing, if they do not get the same title as their fathers got.

Icelanders have the same rights as freeholders when they are (in Norway) on trading journeys[88] until they have been here three winters and have taken residence here; then they should have such rights as men witness that they are entitled to.

All other foreigners who come to this country have householders' right unless men bear witness to something else.

## 201 Concerning a man's right to personal compensation with respect to his betrothed woman

Now a man shall have as compensation for his betrothed woman, if someone sleeps with her, as much money as he would need to ransom her from the hands of an enemy,[89] no matter how big compensation her heir can claim for her.

## 202 This concerns accusations

Now if the king's representative accuses a man of having harboured an outlaw, one who was outlawed in the assembly district where the accused lives, then he should deny (it) with a three-man oath; but the oath leads to a fine of forty *merkr* if it fails.

Now if the king's representative accuses a man of having harboured an outlaw, one who was outlawed at the *Gulaþing* assembly or out at sea in naval service, and he says it was not known to him that he was an outlaw, then he should deny (it) with a three-man oath, and likewise if the man has been outlawed in another assembly district; the oath leads to a fine of forty *merkr* if it fails.

Now the king's representative accuses a man of having given food to an outlaw in the woods, but he denies (it), then he should deny (it) with a three-man oath; it leads to a fine of three *merkr* if it fails.

Now the king's representative accuses a man of having had contact with an outlaw at the assembly or at church or in an alehouse, but he denies (it); then he

86 I.e. the same rights as their fathers.

87 In the decrees issued by Nicholas Breakspear in Nidaros 1152 there was no general rule prescribing celibacy for clerics. But priests were not allowed to marry widows and married clerics could not be ordained to priests without promising to live in celibacy. A man who was married to a widow or divorced could not be ordained to priest, neither could a man who had remarried. But cf. Book I, Ch. 15.

88 This was already part of the agreement between Saint Olav and the Icelanders.

89 This was stipulated to three *merkr* according to Ch. 51 (end).

must deny (it) with a three-man oath; if that oath fails, he has to pay a fine of a ring to the king.

Now a man has been killed in a group or in a crowd, or wounded or beaten there, then the property of the offender may be seized; no man may sustain him before he has offered to submit to the law. But if someone does sustain him, then he is liable to pay a fine of forty *merkr*; but if he is in contact with him, and it is convincingly proven with witnesses, then he is liable to pay a ring to the king.

To all those who watch this deed he is no unknown outlaw; to the others, who did not watch, he is; they have no responsibility until judgement is passed in the case.

## 203 How long a wife may give food to her husband

A wife may give food to her husband with impunity for five nights after sentence has been passed on him. But if he sits there longer without having been invited,[90] then she should go to her neighbours and tell that he sits there uninvited, then she cannot be blamed.

## 204 If a slave beats a free man

If a slave beats a free man, then his master should come to terms with the one who was beaten or outlaw the slave; the king must have nothing for this.

## 205 Concerning throws

Now a man throws (something) at a man and it hits another, then it is called a goose's crime; then he should pay a compensation of six *aurar* to the one he hits.

## 206 Concerning lands held as a grant

If a man has had land granted him by the king and it is taken from him, then he shall nevertheless have the same right to atonement as a landed man, and likewise his son until he is forty.

## 207 Concerning accusations

Now a man accuses another of preventing the pursuit of an outlaw, the other replies "I pursue him just as you do", then the woods shall bear witness (as to whether he escapes). If the outlaw reaches the woods, then he (who helped him)

90 I.e. sponging on his wife.

may release himself from outlawry[91] with forty *merkr*, although the other (whom they were pursuing) may release himself with fifteen *merkr*.

## 208 Concerning fights

Now two men fight and there are no witnesses and each accuses the other, then each of them should pay the king the amount of his own compensation.

## 209 If a man holds another

Now a man holds another under an axe[92] and he dies from it, then the one who held him should pay half a wergild for him to his kinsfolk. But the king must have nothing for this. Now a man accuses another of having held him under an axe, then the other should deny (it) with a three-man oath.

If a man holds another under an axe and the other is wounded by it, then he should pay half compensation for the wound to the other. If a man holds another under an axe and the other gets a (serious) injury from it, then he must pay half compensation to the other.

## 210 If a man tortures another

Now a man accuses another of having tortured him, then he should deny (it) with a three-man oath; it leads to forty *merkr* to the king if it fails, and to full compensation to the complainant.

## 211 Concerning black blows

If a man claims to have been beaten but is neither blue nor blood-stained and there are no witnesses, then he has lied about himself. For that no one has a right to compensation; that is called a black blow.

But if a man accuses another man of this, then he should deny (it) with a three-man oath. If that oath fails he must pay due compensation to the former and forty *merkr* to the king.

## 212 Concerning a full fight

If a man beats another, three blows or more, that is called a full fight, then he has a right to compensation for each blow up to the number of three; but the king (should have) forty *merkr*.

91 An outlaw might sometimes release himself with fifteen *merkr* to the king and sometimes with forty *merkr*.

92 Thereby assisting a murderer.

## 213 Concerning confiscations

Now the king's representative makes an inventory of a man's property or confiscates it in other cases than those three that have been enumerated[93] for this, then the king's representative is liable to pay a fine of forty *merkr*; and likewise a landed man if he enters a (free) man's home and confiscates something. Every man who assists them in this is liable to pay a fine of three *merkr*.

## 214 If a man is accused of reducing the king's fines[94]

Now the king's representative accuses a man of having withheld fine due to the king and another of having been injured; but they deny (it). Then the king's representative should summon both to the assembly. Then each of them must swear for himself at the assembly with a three-man oath that they have not come to an agreement in the case.

If that oath fails for them, then it leads to a fine of fifteen *merkr* for each. If one takes the oath, but the other does not, then he who takes the oath is guiltless, but the other, for whom the oath fails, is guilty.

But if the king's representative summons one of them, but not the other, then it is as if he had done nothing in the case.

## 215 Concerning compensation for wounds

All have equal rights to compensation for wounds, a free man as well as a slave. If someone wounds another man's slave, then he should pay for his food[95] while he is lying wounded, and full compensation to his master for (loss of) work, and the physician's fee.

## 216 If a man incites another to attack him

Whenever a man does not consider himself injured, then no fine is due to the king.

Now a man incites another to attack him as one baits a bear, or challenges him to duel on a holm,[96] if the other then injures him, he has no right to compensation, provided that the other has taken witnesses to it, and likewise if he blames him for having received compensation before.

93 These three cases are not found in the *Gulaþing* Law now. On confiscations see also Ch. 141.

94 When the opposite sides reached an agreement in a case where a fine was due to the king, the king might lose his share.

95 Cf. Ch. 185. See also Iversen 1997, 44, 46.

96 A duel taking place within a delimited area (often on a small island, hence the name 'holm') according to a fixed ritual. Bø 1961. It is mentioned in several Icelandic sagas, esp. *Egils saga Skallagrímssonar*, in an account which has been characterized as fiction by K. Helle (2001, 28), but accepted as trustworthy by A. I. Riisøy (2019, 18). This kind of duel was forbidden shortly after the year 1000, but as Ch. 216 indicates, fights of a similar nature may probably have taken place later.

If a man takes something of value from another and demands confirmation of it (as his) from the court, and the thing belongs to him from whom it was taken, then the man has that thing by robbery, then he should pay a fine of a ring to the king, but the owner must have his thing when there are witnesses to the ownership.

## 217 If dogs bite people's livestock

Now dogs bite people's livestock, then he who owns the dog should pay half compensation (for the injury)[97] the first time the dog bites, but full (compensation) each time in later cases.

If the owner disposes of the dog as soon as it has bitten, no compensation is to be paid. But should it happen that he or his household throws food to the dog afterwards, then he should pay half compensation the next time (the dog bites), but full (compensation) each time in later cases.

## 218 Here the head ring (the main part of the wergild) is explained

This is the first ring, which is called head ring.[98] It amounts to ten *merkr* – that is thirty-two cows[99] – if he who is killed was born to odal-right. From this (level) wergild increases or decreases as other rights of compensation.[100]

The father should take that compensation if no son is alive. But if both are alive the father must have three *merkr*. If he is not able to fight he must have twelve *aurar* from the killer. But if the killer is outlawed, that compensation shall not be claimed.

When the killer dies his heir receives the axe.[101]

## 219 Brother's ring

This is the second ring, which is called brother's ring. It amounts to five *merkr*, that is sixteen cows.

The third is first cousin's ring (father's brother's son's ring). It amounts to four *merkr*, that is half an *eyrir* less than (the value of) thirteen cows.

## 220 More on the brother's ring

The son of the killed man should take that ring in which there are ten *merkr*. Brother's ring must be taken by a brother, if there is one; otherwise by the son of

97 I.e. one half of the value of the beasts.

98 Here is the second system for assessing the wergild. See Ch. 180.

99 The value of a cow was two and a half *aurar*, cf. Ch. 223; cf. also Ch. 303, where a slaughtered cow (without head, skin, and feet) has the value of two *aurar*. The money mentioned in Ch. 218 is to be understood as burnt silver.

100 See Chs. 200–1.

101 I.e. he has to pay the wergild.

the killed man. But if there is neither son nor father of the killed man, then the brother takes the whole compensation. The first cousin on the father's side (should take the compensation), if he is the nearest (kinsman).

But if there is no such man as I have now enumerated, then the heir of the killed man has the whole compensation after him.

## 221 Gifts to women

In gifts to women[102] there is a *mǫrk*. Four women should share it if they exist; the mother of the killed man, his daughter and his sister and his wife should take two *aurar* each, if they are all living.

But whenever the women are wanting, then the son of the killed man should take (their share instead). If all the women are wanting, then the killer should take that *mǫrk* and give it as a compensation to the son of the killed man. If one of the women is wanting, then the son of the killed man should take the two *aurar*; but half a *mǫrk* if two are wanting; the (whole) *mǫrk* if they are all wanting. Now all the rings have been enumerated.

## 222 Concerning wergild to the kinsmen[103]

Now the killer should pay the head ring to the son of the killed man. The killer's brother, if he exists, must pay the brother's ring to the brother of the killed man; otherwise the killer himself must pay it. Now the first cousin of the killer, if he exists, should pay the first cousin's ring to the killed man's first cousin on the father's side; otherwise the killer himself must pay it.

He who receives the compensation counts as the son of the killed man, whether it is the father or the brother or however he is related to the killed man. Now the rings are defined.

## 223 Concerning conditions and means of payment

Now the means of payment shall be listed. As regards a cow, she has to be worth two and a half *aurar*. If (compensation) should be paid with a cow, then it has to be done with a cow not older than eight winters [*AM 146 4to adds:* and not younger than five winters] unless the other is willing to receive her. It should be paid with cows that are unharmed in horns and tail, in eyes and teats and in all her feet.

Grain[104] should be paid, and oxen and cows of calf-bearing age, to pay wergild and rings. Pay the wergild with gold or burnt silver, if these things are available.

102 These gifts come as additions to the ring compensation. The three rings and the women's gift add up to a total of twenty *merkr*.

103 See Jørgensen 2014, 71.

104 The ON text has *korn* ('grain'), which Hertzberg (1895, 361) suggests may be an error for *þióra* ('bulls').

Pay with horses, but not with mares; a stallion, but not a gelded horse, a horse that has a protruding rectum or a whitish sheath or weak urinating organs or is wall-eyed[105] or has other flaws in a bargain. Pay with sheep and not with goats. Pay with odal-land but not purchased land. Pay with a ship, unless it is rebuilt or so old that the grummets which were first made are worn off; not ships whose prows have been broken, and not ships patched with thin boards, unless this was so done while the ship was still raised on supports.[106]

No object must be paid as compensation when it is worth less than an *eyrir*, unless someone should have (i.e. is due) a smaller compensation, then he should receive such an object, unless the compensation rises[107] to an *eyrir*, and (the other) must have peace pledge in return.

He may pay with weapons that are used, are whole and hard and unbroken, he may not offer those with which the deceased was killed. (He may) not pay a sword in wergild unless it is adorned with gold or silver. Pay with wadmal[108] and every kind of new linen cloth, and every kind of new and uncut cloth, unless the other wants to receive new, cut cloth. Pay with clothes for men, but not for women; new clothes, but not old. Pay with cloaks of fur (of black sheep) and finer cloth, new and uncut. Pay with slaves[109] who have been brought up at home, anyone not younger than fifteen winters, unless the other accepts (a younger slave). Bond-women must not be paid in wergild.

Now is enumerated in what kind of articles wergild may be paid.

## 224 (Concerning additional compensation)[110]

Now the additional compensation shall be enumerated. In the first group of receivers are the killed man's paternal uncle, his brother's son and his mother's father and his daughter's son, they should each have a *mǫrk* from the killer if a freeholder is killed.

In the second group of receivers are the son of the killed man's paternal uncle, the son of his brother's daughter, his mother's brother, his sister's son and the sons of his father's sister or his mother's brother, each of them should have six *aurar* from the killer if a freeholder is killed.

In the third group of receivers are the son of the killed man's maternal aunt, the son of his paternal uncle's son, a son of his father's paternal uncle, his mother's maternal uncle, and the son of his sister's daughter. They should (each) have half a *mǫrk* from the killer if a freeholder is killed.

105 See Matthiessen 1962, 126–7.
106 I.e. when it was being built.
107 Or: unless the one who pays may increase the compensation. Larson 1935, 152.
108 See note 30.
109 Iversen 1997, 43.
110 Compensation paid to a circle of kinsmen beyond the closest relatives (the closest relatives were called the 'ring men', ON *baugamenn*, mentioned in Chs. 218–22). This compensation was divided into three groups of receivers. Each such group of receivers was called an *uppnám*.

But because every man should pay half as much for the doings of his hands[111] as he will receive for a man in the same degree of kinship, then he should pay two *aurar* to the son of the killed man, and so must each of the men in this (third) group of payers. But in the middle (i.e. second) group of payers they should each pay three *aurar* to the son of the killed man. But in the first group of payers each of them should pay half a *mǫrk* to the son of the killed man.

Now all the men of the groups of receivers and payers have been enumerated; and now I will explain how cross payments[112] shall be determined.

## 225 Concerning wergild for a kinsman

Now the killer's paternal uncle should pay half a *mǫrk* to the son of the killed man, but eight *ertogar* to his brother, and five *ertogar* and three *penningar* to the killed man's paternal uncle, and the same amount to the killed man's brother's son and likewise to his maternal grandfather and to his daughter's son. All who are in the same group of receivers shall have equally big compensation.

The killer's paternal uncle should pay four and two-thirds *penningar* and an *eyrir* to the killed man's maternal uncle. He must pay the same amount to the killed man's sister's son, and to the son of his paternal uncle, and to the son of his brother's daughter and to sons of his father's sister or his mother's brother; in this way they should all pay who are in the same group as the father's brother.

The killer's paternal uncle should pay four *penningar* and two *ertogar* to the son of the killed man's maternal aunt, and so must each in that group of payers. In this way they should (also) pay to a sister's daughter's son, and to the child of a paternal uncle's son and to his mother's maternal uncle.

## 226 More about wergild for a kinsman

Now the killer's paternal uncle's son should pay three *aurar* to the son of the killed man, but five *ertogar* and three weighed *penningar* to his brother, but four and two-thirds *penningar* and an *eyrir* to the killed man's paternal uncle, the same amount to the killed man's brother's son and likewise to his maternal grandfather and to his daughter's son. All who are in the same group of receivers shall have equally big compensation.

The killer's paternal uncle's son should pay to the killed man's paternal uncle's son three *penningar* and two *ertogar*, the same amount to the son of the killed man's brother's daughter, to his maternal uncle, and to his sister's son, and to a son of his father's sister or his mother's brother. In this way each of them should pay who are in the same group of payers as the father's brother's sons.

111 I.e. killing.

112 Compensation that has to be paid from one of the killer's groups of payers to the killed man's kinsfolk in the two other different *uppnám*. This compensation is determined in the immediately following chapters. Hertzberg 1895, 751.

The killer's paternal uncle's son should pay eight and two-thirds *penningar* and an *ertog* to the son of the killed man's paternal aunt [*according to AM 315 f:* the main MS. has only sister's son], and so should each in that group of payers. So they must (also) pay to the child of the killed man's paternal uncle's son, and to the son of his father's paternal uncle, and to his mother's maternal uncle, and to the son of his sister's daughter. In this way they should pay who are in the same group of payers as the father's brother's sons.

## 227 More about wergild for a kinsman

Now the killer's maternal aunt's son should pay two *aurar* to the son of the killed man. And so must the son of the daughter of the killer's sister, and the child of his paternal uncle's son, and his mother's maternal uncle. But each of these four (should pay) four *ertogar* to the killed man's brother. But to the killed man's paternal uncle three *penningar* less than an *eyrir*. The same to the son of the killed man's brother and to his maternal grandfather and to his daughter's son.

Such wergild has (also) the killer's maternal aunt's son, and his sister's daughter's son and the child of his paternal uncle's son, his mother's maternal uncle (to pay); each of them should pay eighteen *penningar* to the killed man's maternal uncle. In this way they should (also) pay to the son of the killed man's sister and likewise each of them to the son of the killed man's paternal uncle. Such wergild must (also) the son of the killed man's brother's daughter have from each of them.

The son of the killer's maternal aunt should pay twelve *penningar* to the son of the killed man's maternal aunt. Equally much he should pay to the son of the killed man's sister's daughter, and to the child of his paternal uncle's son, and to his mother's maternal uncle. The son of the (killer's) sister's daughter must pay the same amount as the son of his maternal aunt. The child of the killer's paternal uncle's son and his mother's maternal uncle the same. Each of those who are in the last group of payers should pay twelve *penningar* [*AM 315 f adds:* to each of those in the last group of receivers].

Now I have enumerated all the men in the groups of receivers and payers. Every man should pay every other man such as I have now told. But as the degree of kinship decreases beyond the last group, the wergild is reduced by one third according to a calculation.

## 228 Concerning the men in the groups of receivers[113]

All those in the first group who receive a *mǫrk* from the killer should have one third less from the killer's brother; that makes five *aurar* and an *ertog*.

But all those in the middle group who receive six *aurar* from the killer should have one third less from the killer's brother; that makes half a *mǫrk*.

113 Cf. Ch. 224.

But all those men in the last group who receive half a *mǫrk* from the killer should have one third less from the killer's brother; that makes an *ertog* less than three *aurar*.

## 229 Here additional compensation is explained

Now the killer, in paying the additional compensation, should consider his father's brother and his brother's son and pay compensation for them (if they are wanting), although they have never existed; but they should themselves pay such compensation if they exist.

## 230 More about additional compensation

A brother's son should go with the father's brother with respect to the stipulation of compensation. They should receive one compensation together, and likewise pay one as long as the father's brother is living; but one third less after the father's brother has passed away.

## 231 More about additional compensation

Now there are all the wives who have sons to receive the compensation, and sisters who are capable of bearing children; they should all have equal shares in the additional compensation until they reach the age of forty. But if one or more of these are wanting the compensation reverts to the sister's son.

## 232 More about additional compensation[114,115]

Now the killed man's father's brother should have three *penningar* and five *ertogar* from the killer's father's brother. The son of the killed man's brother should have three *penningar* and five *ertogar* from the son of the killer's brother. The son of the killed man's daughter should have three *penningar* and five *ertogar* from the son of the killer's daughter, and likewise the killed man's mother's father (should have) from the killer's mother's father three *penningar* and five *ertogar*.

## 233 Concerning the men in the groups of payers[116]

Now (the men of the) the middle group of payers should pay to the first group of receivers five *penningar* and an *eyrir*. In the last group of payers each should pay eighteen *penningar* to the middle group of receivers.

114 Chs. 232–4 deal with cases that are also treated in Chs. 225–7, but the provisions are different. Chs. 230–1 and 232–5 may have been two parts of a different list of amounts paid in compensation (ON *saktal*).

115 Cf. also Ch. 225, first paragraph.

116 Cf. Ch. 226, first paragraph and Ch. 227, second paragraph.

## 234 More about the same

Now the son of the daughter of the killer's brother should pay seven *penningar* and an *ertog* to the son of the daughter of the killed man's brother, and likewise everyone in that group of payers.[117]

The son of the sister of the killer's mother should pay twelve *penningar* to the son of the sister of the killed man's mother, and likewise everyone in that group of payers.

From the last group of payers (the compensation) is reduced by a third as soon as the kinship becomes more remote. A kinsman on the male side should receive one third more than an equally related kinsman on the female side.

## 235 Concerning the men in the groups of receivers

He who is the nearest kinsman on the male side from the last group of receivers should have a compensation of eight *ertogar*; that makes twenty-six and two-thirds ells of wadmal.[118]

But (the nearest) kinsman on the female side must have three and a third *penningar* and five *ertogar* from the same compensation; that makes exactly seventeen and two-thirds ells. The same the man in the second degree of kinship on the male side must have, counted from the last group of receivers.

But on the female side they should have four and two-thirds *penningar* and an *eyrir* in that compensation; that makes exactly eleven and a half ells. That is (also) what the man must have who is in the third degree of kinship on the male side, counted from the last group of receivers.

But on the female side they should have three *penningar* and two *ertogar* in that compensation; that makes seven and two-thirds ells. That is (also) what the man must have who is in the fourth degree of kinship on the male side, counted from the last group of receivers.

But on the female side they should have eight and two-thirds *penningar* and an *ertog* in that compensation; that makes exactly five ells. That is (also) what the man must take who is in the fifth degree of kinship on the male side, counted from the last group of receivers.

But on the female side they should have half a *penningr* less than an *ertog*; that makes three and a quarter ells. That is (also) what the man must take who is in the sixth degree of kinship on the male side, counted from the last group of receivers.[119]

But on the female side they should have thirteen *penningar* in that compensation, that is exactly two ells. That is (also) what the man must take who is in

117 This compensation goes better with the third group, cf. Ch. 226, last paragraph.

118 See note 30.

119 It is possible that the list of amounts paid in compensation (ON *saktal*) originally (?) ended here, with the sixth cousin. Cf. also Ch. 24.

the seventh degree of kinship on the male side, counted from the last group of receivers.

But on the female side they should have one and a third ells in that compensation; that makes eight and two-thirds *penningar*. That is (also) what the man must have who is in the eighth degree of kinship on the male side, counted from the last group of receivers.

But on the female side they should have five and two-thirds *penningar* in that compensation, that is one fifth less than a full ell. That is (also) what the man must have who is in the ninth degree of kinship on the male side, counted from the last group of receivers.

But on the female side they should have three and a fifth *penningar* in that compensation. That is (also) what the man must have who is in the tenth degree of kinship on the male side, counted from the last group of receivers.

But on the female side they should have two and two-fifteenths *penningar* in that compensation. That is also what the man must take who is in the eleventh degree of kinship on the male side, counted from the last group of receivers.

But on the female side they should have one and a third *penningar* in that compensation. That is (also) what the man must take who is in the twelfth degree of kinship on the male side, counted from the last group of receivers.

But on the female side they should have one *penningr* in that compensation. That is (also) what the man must take who is in the thirteenth degree of kinship on the male side, counted from the last group of receivers. But on the female side they should have two-thirds of a *penningr* in that compensation. Then they are in the fifteenth degree of kinship to the killed man.[120]

## 236 Concerning persons entitled to an additional portion of the wergild[121]

Now there are three men who are (called) increasers of the wergild; that is the son of a bondwoman and a brother who is the son of a bondwoman and a brother born of the same mother.[122] The son of a bondwoman should have twelve *aurar* from the killer and a *mǫrk* from the killer's brother, and so must each of the three men entitled to such additions. But all who descend from them should take half as big compensation as another man in the same degree of kinship.

## 237 Concerning wergild for a kinsman

A man should have three *aurar* for his mother's brother, son of a bondwoman; and so must each of them (have) for the other. A man should have the same amount

120 Provisions for the fourteenth degree of kinship are missing.

121 I.e. more distant members of the kin who did not originally have a share in the wergild.

122 But having a different father, implying that the two are half-brothers.

for his mother's brother, (but only if he is) born of the same mother[123] and each of them for the other. Six *aurar* for his father's brother born of a bondwoman and the same amount for his father's brother born of the same mother, and each of them for the other, from the killer.

But one third less (each of them should have) from the killer's brother than from the killer himself, and one third less from the killer's father's brother than from his brother. In that way each must have his compensation; those I have now enumerated are all called increasers of the wergild.

All sons of sisters' sisters should have one compensation, however many they are, and pay compensation in the same way. Those men should have compensation together who are sons of (the killer's) father's sister or mother's brother. All mother's brothers must have one compensation; in the same way they should pay if they are born of the same father and born in wedlock.

Whenever a man is an heir of an increaser of the wergild, then the compensation shall be reduced to the half.

Whenever a compensation is paid to the father, then it is (also) paid to the son.

## 238 Concerning dishonourable killing[124]

Now dishonourable killing[125] shall be explained. If someone cuts another into the cheek or into the beard, then an *eyrir* must be paid for each molar. But if the man throws the corpse into a fire or into a stream, he should pay twelve *aurar*; the same for each wound which is inflicted on the corpse.

Likewise if a man lies in ambush for another where the other finds himself in a dangerous place on the other side or at either end of a bridge, so that he has to go either to point and edge or down into the dangerous place, for that twelve *aurar* should be paid.

If a man carries the head away from the body when he has cut it off, that is called over-robbery;[126] three *merkr* must be paid for that.

If a man throws the corpse into the water so deep that a man must wet his head in order to bring the head of the corpse out of the water, then the killer should pay a compensation of three *merkr*.

Full wergild shall be paid to the heir when a man inflicts a blow on another with evil intent, and likewise for all dishonourable killings.

## 239 Concerning wergild

These are two near kinsmen by marriage: if a man is married to another man's daughter (and if either is killed) they should have twelve *aurar* from the killer, each for the other.

123 See note 122.

124 Judging from the subject matter this chapter should have followed Chapter 239.

125 Killing requiring additional compensation because it was committed under aggravating circumstances.

126 A robbery which was considered too bad to require the usual compensation. Larson (1935, 159) translates "insulting arrogance" (following Hertzberg 1895, 485).

If a man is married to a sister of another, then each of them should have six *aurar* for the other from the killer. But if each of them is married to a sister of the other, then they should have, each of them for the other, twelve *aurar* from the killer.

Now a stepfather and a stepson, each of them for the other, must have twelve *aurar* from the killer.

Now there are sworn brothers,[127] each of them for the other, must have twelve *aurar* from the killer.

Now two foster brothers have been brought up together, both having sucked the same breast, then each for the other should have twelve *aurar* from the killer.

Now there is the mother's father of a man's mother, each of them for the other (he and the son of the daughter's daughter) should have twelve ten ells-*aurar*[128] from the killer if a freeholder is killed.

## 240 Concerning dishonourable killing[129]

This is the first (case of) dishonourable killing if a man is killed with the blunt side or end of a weapon and beaten with two blows.[130] That makes two (cases of) dishonourable killing.

This is the third (case of) dishonourable killing if a man is hit by a barbed arrow or a barbed spear, so that (the arrowhead) has to be cut out.

This is the fourth, if the wounds are more than seven.

This is the fifth, if a man has been struck dead without blood coming out.

This is the sixth, if the corpse is robbed.

This is the seventh, if a man is killed when relieving himself.

This is the eighth, if a man is thrown into a fire.

This is the ninth, if a man is pushed down from a cliff.

This is the tenth, if a man is pushed into water.

This is the eleventh, if the corpse is not buried, so that it becomes the prey of ravens and carrion beasts.

This is the twelfth, that the killing is not properly reported,[131] and it is still not (counted as) murder.

This is the thirteenth, if settlement is offered at the next assembly so loudly that the offer may be heard across the assembly circle,[132] in that case he has boasted of the killing.

This is the fourteenth, if a settlement has not been offered within twelve months, then it has been offered (too) late.

127 I.e. men having sworn a pact committing the one who lives longer to avenge the other.
128 I.e. one *eyrir* having the value of ten ells of wadmal.
129 See also Ch. 238.
130 With the shaft of the weapon or with the butt of the axe.
131 See Ch. 156.
132 This shows that the site of the assembly was marked, probably with stones.

But three *merkr* shall be paid in each of those cases which I have now enumerated.

## 241 When the wergild is increased

But if the head is cut off and set up on a fence post or at a crossroads with the mouth wedged open with a stick, or the corpse is turned to lie face down and the head placed between the feet, then the wergild is doubled.

## 242 More about wergild

Now twelve *aurar* should be paid if a man cuts the hand or the foot off a dead man, or tears the scalp off his head, or cuts in such a way that the brain falls out, or such that he wounds his sex organs or cuts into his rectum, and likewise if he cuts a bone off his head, and for all mutilations except fingers or toes.

An *eyrir* (should be paid) for every finger and for every toe, until they are all (cut) off, then it is half a *mǫrk* for each (limb).

For an attack on one's home[133] (the compensation) is forty *merkr*, half of which goes to the king if a man is killed.

But six *aurar* if it is within the fence, and another six if the head is carried away.

## 243 Concerning wergild rings[134]

Now the wergild for a freeholder shall be enumerated. Six *merkr* of twelve-ells *aurar*[135] shall (be paid) in the main ring, and four in the brother's ring, and two and a half *merkr* in the first cousin's ring. Two payments for peace pledge must go with every wergild ring. Each payment for peace pledge must be one and a fifth *aurar*. The payments for peace pledge shall be distributed among the men who share the ring payments.[136]

## 244 Concerning wergild rings and peace pledges

Now the killer pays a ring to the son of the killed man and peace pledge to the killed man's brother and another to the son of the killed man's paternal uncle.

Now the brother of the killer pays one ring to the brother of the killed man and peace pledge to the son of the killed man and another to the son of the killed man's paternal uncle.

133 See Chs. 142 and 178.

134 Chs. 243–52 give the third list of amounts of compensation in the *Gulaþing* Law.

135 One *eyrir* having the value of twelve ells of wadmal. Cf. also note 30.

136 This chapter uses some words – ON *tryggvakaup*, 'payment of peace pledge' and *baugamenn*, 'men who share the ring payments' – which are reminiscent of the wording in the *Frostuþing* Law. Robberstad (1981, 382) suggests that this list of compensation may have come from the district of Sunnmøre before it was added to the *Gulaþing*.

Now the son of the killer's paternal uncle pays one ring to the son of the killed man's paternal uncle and peace pledge to the son of the killed man and another to his brother, (in addition they have to pay) as the price for the settlement,[137] if all the kinsmen reach a settlement at the same time and likewise when the men of the ring payment reach a settlement. But (the payment) for the redemption from outlawry is three *merkr.*[138]

## 245 Concerning (women's) gifts

Now the killer and his mother and his daughter and his wife should present gifts, one and a fifth *aurar* to each, to the wife, the mother and the daughter of the killed man; that makes twelve gifts.

The sister of the killer must give half a gift to the sister of the killed man, half a gift to his wife and (half a gift) to his daughter and half a gift to his mother; that makes two gifts.

The killer, his mother, his wife and his daughter must each give half a gift to the sister of the killed man; that makes two full gifts. That makes altogether sixteen gifts.

With rings and with payment for peace pledge and the payment for redemption from outlawry and with gifts to the women, that makes two and two-fifths *aurar* and twenty *merkr*.

## 246 Concerning additional compensation[139]

There are six men who receive twelve *aurar* each in compensation. The first one is the father's brother, the second a brother's son, the third a brother from the same mother,[140] the fourth the son of a bondwoman, the fifth a daughter's son, the sixth the mother's father.

## 247 More about additional compensation[141]

There are three men who receive nine *aurar* each in compensation. The first one is the mother's brother, the second a sister's son, the third a brother born of a bondwoman. The sons of the father's sister and the mother's brother receive six *aurar*.

137 This price must be twelve *aurar* (or one ring). See Ch. 245 (the end).

138 Here this is a payment to the kinsfolk.

139 This chapter enumerates the first circle of receivers.

140 But a different father.

141 This chapter enumerates the second and third circles of receivers. In Ch. 224 the circles are ordered somewhat differently and reach further into the extended family.

## 248 More about additional compensation

The father's brother, born of a bondwoman, receives a *mǫrk* in compensation. The daughter of the killed man, born of a bondwoman, has a son by a well-born man, that son receives a *mǫrk*.

## 249 Concerning wergild rings

Each of the ring men[142] should pay half as much as he will receive, and a fifth (of this half) in addition. But all the receivers get two thirds from the killer and one third from his brother.

## 250 Concerning ring men and cross payments[143]

The six first ring men receive four *ertogar* from the first cross payment made by those who are in the same degree of kinship to the killer as they are to the killed man.

In the second cross payment each of them receives an *eyrir* from those who are in same degree of kinship to the killer as those who share in the nine *aurar* compensation are to the killed man.

In the third cross payment each of them receives two *ertogar* from those who are in the same degree of kinship to the killer as those who share in the six *aurar* compensation are to the killed man.

## 251 More about the same

The men who share in the nine *aurar* compensation each receives an *eyrir* in the first cross payment from those who are in the same degree of kinship to the killer as those who share in the twelve *aurar* compensation are to the killed man.

From the second cross payment each of them receives an *eyrir* in current coin[144] from those who are in the same degree of kinship to the killer as they are to the killed man.

From the third cross payment each of them receives half an *eyrir* from those who are in the same degree of kinship to the killer as those who share in the six *aurar* compensation are to the killed man.

142 A ring man is a kinsman belonging to one of the circles of receivers of wergild, circles extending up to and including first cousins, counted from the insulted person. See note 112; Hertzberg 1895, 92.

143 See note 112.

144 It had the value of three quarters of a weighed *eyrir*. See Ch. 91. Cf. Book V, note 37.

## 252 More about additional compensation

The men who share in the six *aurar* compensation each receives in the first cross payment two *ertogar* from those who are in the same degree of kinship to the killer as those who share in the compensation of twelve *aurar* are to the killed man.

In the second cross payment each of them receives half an *eyrir* from those who are in the same degree of kinship to the killer as those who share in the nine *aurar* compensation are to the killed man.

In the third cross payment each of them receives an *ertog* from those who are in the same degree of kinship to the killer as they are to the killed man.

# XI The book on theft

## 253 Here begins the book on theft

Now the next thing is that none of us who want to stay in our king's realm must steal from any man.

But if someone steals an *ertog* or more than an *ertog*, then he is outlawed and may by killed. If he denies (it), he should deny (it) with a six-man oath.

If someone steals anything of smaller value, then they should make him run the gauntlet and throw stones or turf at him and let it remain at that. But if he denies he must deny with a three-man oath; if the oath fails he must run the gauntlet.

He has to run the gauntlet from the place where he is (proved) guilty.[1] The course shall be as long as nine bows carried by a full-grown man, and they must pelt him with stones and with turf and he is outlawed if he falls (on the course). But if he comes safely through, he goes free.[2]

If someone steals the carcass of a four-footed animal, then he is outlawed, even if he steals but a lamb one night old.

If a man comes across another man who carries stolen goods in his hands, he (the former) should bind the stolen goods on his (the latter's) back, if there are witnesses present, and bring him to the assembly area where he committed the theft and hand him over to the king's representative, if he wishes (to do so). But if the king's representative refuses to receive the thief, then he is liable to pay a fine of fifteen *merkr*. The amount to be paid by the king's representative shall all go to the householders. Then he should take the thief to the landed man, and if he refuses to receive the thief, then he is liable to pay a fine of fifteen *merkr*, the king shall have one half of that money and the householders the other half. The householders should pay no fines to the king's representative or to the landed man before they (the householders) have brought their claims to the court.

Now the man who caught the thief has to summon an assembly and bring the thief to the assembly with the stolen goods bound on his back, and produce witnesses that he who bound them owns the goods and declared that they were stolen.

1 I.e. where the stealing was done.
2 I.e. he has paid the penalty.

And (he should also produce) witness that he bound those goods on him (the thief); then the men of the assembly should judge in the case.

If they deem him to be unlawfully bound, then the one who bound him is liable to pay a fine of fifteen *merkr* to the king. But if they deem him rightfully bound, then the king's representative should provide an executioner for him; he is liable to pay a fine of forty *merkr* if he refuses to do so. Then the householders must provide an executioner to him for his[3] own money. But if he manages to escape alive the householders should pay forty *merkr*.

If they let him leave the assembly unsentenced they are liable to pay a fine of fifteen *merkr* to the king.

## 254 If a man claims to have a warranty-man

Now a man finds his goods, lost by theft, in the possession of another man who claims to have a warranty-man and says that he has bought the goods, then the accuser should demand bail for him and surety for the goods that he claims as his own and set a day (for the calling of witnesses). On that day he must produce witness that the goods are his property and that he neither gave them away nor paid (fines) with them nor sold them; then he may keep them. He has two choices: either leave with his goods or examine his opponent's claim to them. Now if he (the warranty-man) fails him, then the accused is a thief.

Now a man accuses another of stealing, then he (the former) has two choices: either summon him to be at home and from there to the assembly, or go to the assembly and report the theft there. Then (in the latter case) the men of the assembly should give him a home summons (to appear) at the next assembly if he is in the same *fylki*, or give a public summons[4] at the assembly to appear before the assembly if he is outside the *fylki*; and thus (they should proceed) in every case, and the assembly must set a date for the hearing.

If he fails to appear he admits guilt, unless witnesses can testify to preventing circumstances. Now he appears at the assembly himself, then he should defend himself with an oath there; if that oath fails (him), then he is outlawed.

## 255 Concerning the searching of houses

Now if goods are stolen from a man and he sees footprints leading away from the house, then he should go to the men of the neighbourhood and report his loss and ask for assistance to pursuit and follow the footprints to the (other) man's home. Then they have to sit outside the fence and send one man to the house and state their errand and demand permission to search the house. If he accepts this and

3 I.e. the king's representative's (so Larson 1935, 165), or (less likely) the thief's (Meissner 1935, 146).

4 See Ch. 59.

goes to fetch his neighbours, then the others may enter the house, wearing their kirtles only, and without a belt.[5]

If he refuses to allow the search, then he admits being guilty of theft.

Now if they find the stolen goods between two partition walls, where it cannot have been put in secretly,[6] then the householder is (to be regarded as) the thief if he is at home; but his son of major age if the householder is not at home; but if neither of these is at home, then it is the free male servant[7] if he is at home. If they are not there, then it is the housewife; a daughter of major age if there is no housewife. But if none of them is there the overseer is (to be regarded as) the thief.

The thief is a man if the stolen goods are found (concealed) in a man's clothes, but a woman if they are found in a woman's clothes.

If the stolen goods are found concealed in a bed, then the one who made the bed is the thief.

If the stolen goods are found hidden under lock and key, then the one who carries the key is the thief.

If the stolen goods are found hidden outside in a barn, in a place where they cannot be reached from the outside except by breaking in, then he who filled that barn is the thief. Likewise if it is in a pile of wood.

Now the household people get hold of a steak (by stealing), then the housewife, if she is at home is (to be regarded as) the thief if she eats together with them, even though the others stole (it).

But if she abstains, then the overseer is the thief.

When stolen goods have been placed in the house by strangers, then the householder has a right to deny, and his oaths[8] shall be valid.

## 256 Concerning theft

If a man finds his goods in another man's possession and takes his goods and says this: "I do not in any way reduce the king's right",[9] and he has witnesses present, then the other man is guilty of the charge; but the former, who takes his goods back, is not guilty. But if he hides the thief while taking his goods, then he is liable to pay a fine of fifteen *merkr* to the king.

Now the king's representative or landed man says that they have reached a settlement, the one from whom something was stolen and the one who stole it, thus having reduced the king's right, then each of them should clear himself with a three-man oath. But if those oaths fail, then each of them is liable to pay a fine of fifteen *merkr*; one of them (is guilty), if (the oath) fails for him.

5 This procedure is known from Roman law. Tamm 2002, 307–8.

6 Into an innocent man's house in order to create suspicion. Hertzberg 1895, 110.

7 ON *griðmaðr*, i.e. a free man admitted into the family, sharing in its rights and activities. Frimannslund 1975, 108. On *griðkona* cf. Ch. 197.

8 Cf. Ch. 253.

9 Cf. Ch. 214.

Now a man finds his stolen property but does not find the thief, then he should bring eyewitnesses when he takes his property back and let them know that the thief was not there when he took it (back).

## 257 Concerning accusations

Now a man accuses another of theft and a third one for having received stolen property; (if) he denies (it) he should refute it with a three-man oath, but if the oath fails it leads to outlawry.

## 258 More about theft

A man accuses another of theft but the theft has not been reported: then the accused may deny the guilt with a three-man oath; it leads to outlawry for him if it fails.

## 259 More about theft

If a well-born woman steals she should be driven out of the country and into another kingdom.

If a minor steals, then compensation must be paid for his misdeed.

If a slave[10] of native birth steals, then they should cut his head off, or his master may clear him with a six-man oath. If an alien slave steals, or the son of an alien slave, then they have to flog him, or his master must have him flogged within five days. But if that is not done, the king's representative may seize the slave. Then the king's representative should have him flogged within five days. If he fails to do so, the master should have his slave back and flog him thoroughly. Likewise with alien bondwomen. But if their master wishes to deny (it) for them, he should deny (it) with a three-man oath. If that oath fails their master must flog them and restore the stolen goods, all that is intact and half of what has been damaged; and likewise for a minor.

[If a man's freedwoman steals, or a native bondwoman,[11] they should cut off one of her ears. [If she steals once more[12] they should cut off her other ear. [If she steals a third time[13] they should cut off her nose, then she is called "stumpy and stubby" [and may steal so long as she wants.[14,15]

10 In this case the slave himself is criminally liable, not his master. Iversen 1997, 52.

11 [*UppsUB R 713:* If a bondwoman, born of a bondwoman, steals for (the value of) an *eyrir* for the first time].

12 [*UppsUB R 713:* If she steals for (the value of) an *eyrir* a second time].

13 [*UppsUB R 713:* If she steals for (the value of) an *eyrir* a third time].

14 [*UppsUB R 713:* If she continues to steal that much, she will be treated according to the laws of the country.]

15 This rule is probably taken from Byzantine law. Sunde 2011a, 61.

## 260 Concerning an outlawed thief

Now a man is outlawed for theft, then the man from whom he stole should receive threefold compensation for his (lost) property out of the property of the outlaw and (out of) the stolen goods.

## 261 If a free man and a slave steal together

Now they commit a theft together, a free man and a slave, then the free man is the thief and the slave shall not be considered a thief; for a man steals alone if he joins another man's slave in a theft.

## 262 If a slave is accused of stealing

Now a man accuses another man's slave, a native, of stealing, then the householder should offer him for examination, unless he is willing to take an oath for the slave.

The other should keep the slave half a month for examination and then return him sound in leg and limb and (he must) not torture him, either with fire or with iron or with water. If he is tortured to plead guilty of theft, then he says so in fear unless he presents true signs of evidence, then he is guilty.

If he accuses a free man of stealing, then the slave should be held in custody until the former has cleared himself or is found guilty. But if he clears himself, then the slave must be killed.

## 263 If a man steals hawks

Now a man takes a hawk that is bound in its nest and hides the bird, then he is a thief if the owner reports the theft.

If a man steals mown grass from another man's land, then he is a thief; he may refute the charge with a three-man oath, it leads to outlawry (if it fails); and likewise in the case of hawks.

## 264 Concerning boundary stones

Now a man buys land from the king's representative, then he is a thief if he does not buy it at the assembly.[16]

But if a man sells land held as a grant from the king, then he makes a thief of himself, but not of the buyer.

If a man removes boundary stones from where they stand and sets them down in some other place by moving them on to the lot of one who owns adjacent land, then he is a thief.

16 I.e. in public.

# XII The redemption of odal-land

## 265 Here begins (the book on) redemption of odal-land

The replies[1] determine (the process concerning) redemptions of odal-land. Every man is entitled to have the ownership to his land defended by a judicial decision.

If a man wants to redeem his odal, he should go to the other's[2] house in the autumn when the yard is fenced in[3] and winter begins, and call upon him before two witnesses to surrender the land he wants to redeem. He must have done so before Christmas Eve, in the presence of two witnesses, wherever he finds him.[4] He need not give him a home summons.

The other is free to give the answer he prefers: He may reply like this: "You ask me to surrender the land which you own nothing of. I have received that land to have and to hold, and I shall defend it with law and trial in court". I may give a second answer, that "I have sold the land". And I may give a third answer: "You will never get that land unless you wrest it from me when I am dead".

## 266 The first reply

But if I answer that I will defend it with law and trial in court, then the plaintiff should summon the defendant, when he (the latter) has a permanent residence, to be at home in his high seat on the day which the plaintiff selects, between Christmas and Lent. The whole day is (available) for the meeting, when the sun is up. But if he (the plaintiff) does not find him at his home, he must appoint a day for him, suited in proportion to the distance to his home.

Then he should go and get himself witnesses, men who are born to odal-right. No one may refuse to be witness to a claim;[5] if he does, he will have to pay a fine of three *aurar* to the king's representative.[6] Then the plaintiff should go with

1 Given by the defence in court. The proceedings varied according to the answers of the defendant.
2 I.e. the one who is in possession of the land in question.
3 This passage has been disputed. Robberstad 1981, 383–4.
4 See note 2.
5 Cf. Ch. 37.
6 A landed man or (usually) the king's representative.

his witnesses to the house of the other, whom he has summoned to be home, and come there on the appointed day and present his claim to his land and his odal.

The defendant should reply as he replied to the earlier demand, that "you are asking land to which you have no right; I own that land, and I will defend it with law and trial in court, and I ask you to await the decision of a court".

Any free man has the right to request the decision of a court, if the householder is not at home. If there are no free men at home, his housewife should request the decision of a court. He must make this request from inside his house, but if the plaintiff runs out intending to use trickery, the defendant has to run after him and offer him to make his request outside in the yard. If the plaintiff leaves the yard before having been invited to accept a judicial decision, then the one whom he had made a demand on, makes him liable to pay a compensation of six *aurar*.

The plaintiff must see to it, when summoning someone home, that the first judgement is not passed on a holy day. If that is the case, the suit is worthless for the claimant.

Now the court has been established after a five-day notice, and the judgement should be passed on a weekday; likewise the claim should be set forth on a weekday. They have to select impartial men for this court. All free men are eligible to sit in the court.

They may not have near kinsmen with them in court; agnates and cognates and near kinsmen by marriage will have to withdraw. If they have been appointed to the court they should be removed in the presence of witnesses, and the counterpart should appoint impartial men in their place.

That court shall be set outside the door of the defendant's house. The plaintiff should set his court and turn it towards the main entrance, but the defendant (should turn his court) away (from the door); and they must place the judges so far from the door that both water and wood may be carried in and a cart may be run between the court and the door.

Now the court is set there. (The plaintiff) should enumerate his ancestors on the father's side, the five on the father's side who have owned (the land), and in addition the sixth, who owned it as his personal property.

Then the plaintiff should present his witnesses; first those whom he had for the notice. If they are deemed satisfactory, he must next present those (that he had) when he summoned the other home. If they are satisfactory, he has to present the witnesses to his claim, two men born to odal-right.

Now witnesses to his claim have been presented and his conduct of the case (has been found) correct, then he should produce witnesses to his (right to the) odal, three redemption witnesses who were at least twenty winters old when their fathers died, and other witnesses who may confirm their testimony, they must have been at least fifteen winters old when their fathers died. Witness to odal-right must be born by men who are born to odal-right, men who have odal-land within the *fylki* where the land is which he wants to redeem.

Now witness to his odal-right has been given, and the judges award the land to him. But the defendant replies that "you own nothing in it, because your witnesses have borne false witness; I have other and more witnesses, and they will bear true witness".

Then the defendant should call counter-witnesses, four redemption witnesses and even more witnesses for (further) confirmation. He should override the judgement by having called counter-witnesses, and (he should) appoint a new hearing. There must be five nights between the court sessions, unless the fifth day falls on a holy day, then the court session must be moved to a weekday, and (the court must) be set at the same place in front of the door of the defendant's house.

Now the court is set, then the defendant must present all those witnesses whom he called before the former court, four redemption witnesses and more witnesses for (further) confirmation. The defendant's evidence is satisfactory when there is one redemption witness more and more witnesses for confirmation. Then those who testified first are false witnesses unless both sides have the same number, in that case those who witnessed last are worthless.

Then the plaintiff and the defendant should appoint a place for the court meeting (to be held) on the boundary (midway) between them, count the miles[7] and the quarters (of miles) and suit the time (for the meeting) in proportion to the distance to (the place) where they will set the court.

Men call that court of arbitration;[8] they[9] should either submit a pledge or one of the sides should drop his case. If they want a court (composed) of twelve thanes, six from each side, then they have to pay two *aurar* each, that makes twelve *aurar* (from each side), to be placed in the hands of a disinterested person, and they must call impartial men to witness that they pledge, men outside the group of judges.

They who set the court, the plaintiff and the defendant, should refer the decision made by pledge to the Quarter assembly. When they come to the assembly, they should produce those witnesses to whom they appealed when they made the pledge. Then the assembly men have to decide who is closer to the truth. Then it is well if the assembly men agree, then those who bet on the other side have lost the pledge. They are false witnesses and have lost their case.

If the assembly men do not agree, they must refer the decision made by pledge to the *fylkis* assembly. Then it is well if all agree to this. But if they do not – one (side) wants to appeal to the court, but the other (side) will not –, then the former, although he does not succeed in forcing the appeal, has to call men from outside the district, (men) who do not belong to the assembly area, to witness the denial of legal right which the assembly men have done to him. Then he may still report this to the *fylkis* assembly.

But when he arrives there he must report the deprivation of right that he suffered at the Quarter assembly. "Here are those whom I called to witness the facts";

7 ON *rastir* (pl. of *rǫst*, lit. 'rest, or the distance between resting places', c. 8–10 km, c. 24,000 feet).

8 See Sunde 2006, 122–4.

9 I.e. the two parties among the judges in the court.

and he must bring forward these witnesses. Then the assembly men have to pass judgement in the case.

Then it is well if they all agree in one decision. But if they do not, (and) one wants the case referred to the ultimate court of law,[10] but the other is satisfied with the judgement at the *fylkis* assembly; then the one who wants to appeal should leave the assembly and have men with him. If he is able to gain the support of a quarter of the assembly men at the *fylkis* assembly, then he succeeds in forcing his appeal. But if a smaller number of men supports him, then he has to accept the judgement of the *fylkis* assembly.

Now they have referred the case to the ultimate court of law. There those who are on the one side and have lost the pledge and their case, then the others should take their pledge from the keeper,[11] two *aurar* from each of those who lost the pledge. Each of them must pay a fine of three *aurar* to the king's representative, and thus pay for their misjudgement. The witnesses of the losing party are false witnesses; each of them have to pay three *merkr* to the king's representative and never more bear witness in odal-cases.

Now the man who sued to redeem the land has conducted his suit according to the law, then he should bring money to (pay for) the land in Mid-Lent, on the Saturday when, on the following morning, there are three weeks left of Lent. He has to put the money on the stone where field and meadow meet, and he must speak like this, that "(I ask you to) be here on this land on Thursday of Easter week[12] and receive that price for the land which men find appropriate as legal payment. I shall come here with impartial men, and you shall have the equal number (of men) on your side, they shall appraise the land according to the rules (which apply) when men redeem their odal-land". That money must be half in gold and silver, and half in a native slave[13] not older than forty nor younger than fifteen winters.

In this way a man shall redeem his odal. Now the (process of) redemption has been explained.

## 267 The second defence

But he is free to reply in a different way to the initial demand, "that I have sold that land and I am not the proper man to defend that land, but it is still my odal". Then the plaintiff should ask to whom I have sold that land, and I shall name the buyer, the man to whom I have sold the land, the one within our law province, if I care to do so.

10 ON *lǫgrétta*, the highest judicial authority in the law province, probably identical with the whole body of delegates to the assembly. Hertzberg 1895, 423–4; Bagge 2010, 200–1.

11 I.e. the disinterested person mentioned earlier.

12 I.e. Thursday after Easter.

13 Slaves were considered to be just as much part of their master's property as livestock. Iversen 1997, 41.

No one must convey land to a landed man. But if I reply that I have sold the land to a landed man, then I must take up the defence myself; for no householder shall convey land to a landed man.

Now I have told to whom I have sold the land, but he refuses to believe it and summons me home and comes to my house with witnesses and claims the land from me. I reply the same as I did to the demand that "I own nothing in that land", but still I submit to the decision of the court; for every man shall accept the decision of the court when he meets a formal demand.

Then he appoints a day for the hearing, and when the court is properly set, I shall produce witness to what I replied to the initial demand and other witnesses (to show) how he presented the claim to me and that I denied (the possession of) the land and said that I had sold it. Then I shall break up the court for him and let the judges stand up and not listen to his witnesses.

But if I let the court sit and listen to his witnesses and they are found satisfactory, then I bind myself to await three court meetings.[14] If he is awarded the land that he sued for with those judgements, then I shall convey to him as much of mine in place of it as I have failed to defend successfully (since) I have called for a judgement to defend another man's land.

Now he goes with his witnesses to seek the one whom I said was my buyer and asks him if he has bought that land "which is my odal and I have begun to redeem". Then he is free to reply as he likes.

But if he replies that "he has lied to you, I own nothing in that land", then the plaintiff should call his witnesses to it and go back to the quarter where the land lies that he is (trying) to redeem.

Then he must summon an assembly and go there with his witnesses, in the first place those he had when he gave the notice, when he who had been notified denied possession of the land, saying that he had sold it; secondly those whom he had when the other said that he had not bought the land.

Then he has to produce his three witnesses to his odal-right and all (those other) witnesses, as if he should have called them to the court. The ones who denied possession of the land are permitted to produce no counter-witnesses. The plaintiff must ask the assembly men to appoint a court to assess his witnesses. If they are found satisfactory the assembly men should award the land to him and confirm the decision by raising their weapons[15] that he may defend his land with law and trial, and that he shall have it without payment when the man has presented such a bad defence.

## 268 The third reply

But if he replies like this to the initial demand, that "you never get that land from me unless you wrest it from me when I am dead", then the plaintiff should

14 I.e. court proceedings according to the rules laid down in Ch. 266.

15 By lifting up their weapons (ON *vápnatak*) men showed their approval of an act, a proposal, or a decision. Decisions taken in this way had the highest sanction.

summon the other to be at home and go to his house with witnesses to the claim and he should claim the land. But if the plaintiff does not succeed in getting the other to submit to a judgement, he asks him to be at home in the morning of the next day.

Then he should come there with witnesses to his claim, other (witnesses) than those whom he had before. It is well if he can get both. If he cannot get other (witnesses) he should have one of his original witnesses and another of those whom he had before, and he should claim the land once more.

If the other still does not submit to a judgement the plaintiff must ask him to be at home while he (the former) rows along the shore's edge or walks outside the fence.

Then he has to go back to the man's house once more and present his claim for the third time, and he must get a new witness and another (witness) of those whom he had before; because he must use four witnesses to three claims if he is to arrange it correctly.

If the defendant still refuses to accept the decision of a court he is liable to pay a fine of eighteen *aurar* to the king's representative.

Then the plaintiff should summon him before the assembly for robbery and lawless dealings. He must go to the assembly and produce his witnesses and all pieces of evidence which he had in his lawsuit, that he gave him notice to surrender the land and how he summoned the defendant to be at home to hear the three claims and how the defendant was not willing to find him worthy of a judgement.

Now those testimonies are found satisfactory and his conduct of the case has been in accordance with the law, then he should produce his witnesses to his odal-right and all his means of evidence, just as he should have presented them to the court. Then the other cannot produce any counter-witnesses, but the assembly men must award the land to the plaintiff.

But the other replies as before, says that he shall never get it. The land must be sued for at the assembly if the man does not accept the decision of the court.

## 269 Concerning appeal to an organ of arbitration

But if he had called for the decision of a court but was unwilling to have that court held, then the other should set the court and place his judges before the defendant's door. When the plaintiff has set half of the court, he calls on the other to the court, but he is still unwilling to appoint his counter-judges.

If he appoints some (men), but not all, then he has not a complete court, then he is a defaulter[16] and off the case. But the plaintiff should nevertheless produce his witnesses and pieces of evidence and the defendant should not produce any counter-witnesses, neither can he refer his case to some other place or offer a pledge. Then the plaintiff's judges should award the land to him.

16 One who shirks his duty to attend a case until it has been settled. See also Ch. 37.

But if the defendant does not appoint anyone on his side and refuses to hold a court, then the plaintiff must produce witnesses and pieces of evidence to his judges, just as he would (have done) if the court had been complete. Now the testimonies have been given and his judges award the land to him and he calls witnesses thereto, listeners who stand outside the court.

Then the plaintiff should summon an assembly and go to the assembly and let his listening witnesses tell how he has sued for the land (and) assure the assembly men of his correct procedure; and (the assembly men) must award the land to him.

Then the plaintiff should go to the land on the Saturday when three weeks are left of Lent and bring money to the land and say this to the other from whom he is redeeming the land that he (the latter) has to be on the land Thursday in Easter week and bring impartial men with him. "And I will bring others on my part to assess the land by legal valuation. And when the land has been assessed, then I will pay you such price as the men stipulate".

He should then go to the land with impartial men on Thursday in Easter week. Then it is well if the other man comes there. But if he does not appear, impartial men should assess the land and afterwards he has to show them the worth of the land (in money) and put the money in his purse and keep it as a loan until the other who shall have it comes to get it.

Now the other opposes and defends his possession with point and edge, then the plaintiff should demand assistance from the assembly men to remove his stubborn opponent from the land; whoever refuses to join him is liable to pay a fine of three *aurar*. Everyone who joins in the resistance is liable to pay a fine of three *merkr*, but their leader forty *merkr*. But if they fall, those who resist, then they fall as outlaws, but the others who attack them are without guilt.

Now they have removed the stubborn opponent from the land, and he who is entitled to the land shall have it.

## 270 Concerning odal-land

Now the lands which are to be regarded as odal shall be enumerated. That is the first, land that has passed from man to man. The second is land that has been acquired as wergild. The third is land that has been received in foster inheritance.[17] The fourth is land received as a mark of honour. The fifth is land received from the king as reward for hospitality. The sixth is reward for fosterage of children, whoever gives it. The seventh is land received in exchange for odal-land.

These shall be regarded as odal-land, and likewise all odal-land parcelled out[18] between brothers and kinsmen. All other lands shall follow the movables.

17 Cf. Ch. 108.
18 This refers to land consolidation. See Ch. 87.

## 271 If land comes under the king

Now if land comes under the king, then we should redeem it from one of his representatives, the one who has the right to prosecute in the *fylki* where the land lies. If the king has no representative in that *fylki* we should redeem it from the representative who is nearest, and it must be redeemed before the reigns of three kings have passed. If it has not been redeemed by that time, the land shall remain as it is. But even if there are three kings at the same time in the country their lives still count as one reign.

Now the king wants to redeem land from us, then his representative should redeem it in such a way as any one of us does from others. He should also have redeemed it before the reigns of three kings have passed, or else the land shall remain as it is. He must not redeem it while the king is in the *fylki* where the land lies.

## 272 If land lies unredeemed for twenty winters[19]

Now land lies unredeemed for twenty winters and no terms of redemption have been published, then it must be redeemed for its full value. But publication (of the terms) is useless unless both buyer and seller agree to it. He (the seller) should produce his witnesses (to the bargain) at the assembly if the other disagrees.

He should redeem the land with the help of odal witnesses. They who were witnesses to the bargain are the right odal witnesses for him if they are alive, whatever their descent may be. But if they are not available, then he should redeem his land with the right kind of odal witnesses.

## 273 How land should be redeemed

If a man is a minor he should redeem his land within the first twelve months after he has reached his majority. But if he does not claim at that time he shall never have the right to renew his claim later.

## 274 How land should be redeemed from a woman[20]

Now such land comes under a woman which men have a right to redeem from her, then they should redeem it from her if their kinship is so close that they are either cognates or agnates. Then they must give her notice of (redemption of) the land before two witnesses in the autumn before Christmas Eve and summon her to come on Thursday in Easter week to receive such payment as the law prescribes.

19 This and the following chapter both deal with the right of redeeming land sold on lease (ON *stefnujǫrð*) and mortgaged land (ON *málajǫrð*).

20 I.e. from a woman who enjoyed inferior odal-rights, even though she belonged to a family line having odal-rights. Ch. 285 deals with the same subject matter.

They should have summoned her not later than Saturday when three (weeks) are left of Lent, and summon her to that land which they want to redeem from her.

Then they should go to the land, they who are to redeem as well as she who is to receive the payment. Then he (the claimant) has to produce witness how he gave her notice to (the redemption of) that land and how he had summoned her and her guardian. Then, if that witness has been found satisfactory men should estimate (the worth of) his testimony and decide whether or not he has a right to redeem the land.

If that testimony is found satisfactory they should appraise the land at its full value, and they should appraise it both inside and outside the fence.

When they have appraised the land, then the plaintiff should offer one fifth less in payment than the land is worth or appraised (to be worth); he must pay half of it in gold and silver and the other half in slaves[21] and livestock. Then he shall keep his odal with care, but she (shall keep) the money.

## 275 Concerning a sole heiress[22]

Now a woman becomes the sole heiress to both odal and movables; no man may redeem it from her.

These are the women who are odal women (thus) having a right to odal: a daughter, a sister, a father's sister, a brother's daughter and a son's daughter.

There are two sole heiresses: a daughter and a sister, they should pay (wergild-) rings and receive rings just as men do, and they have the right to redeem land just as men have.

Now they are heiresses of their father. Then one has a daughter and another has a son. Then the son should redeem (land) from his kinswomen, as he is entitled to by law. But if the situation is reversed, she having sons,[23] and he[24] having daughters, then the sons should redeem (land) from the daughters by the same payment as the father of the daughters gave when he redeemed (land) from the mother to the sons. And then the (title to the) land shall remain quiet as it is. Then the land has come under the rule of the distaff[25] three times.

## 276 How a man may sell his odal-land[26]

Now a man wants to sell odal-land, then he should go to the assembly in the autumn and offer it for sale to the other odal men.[27] Then they must come to the

21 See note 13.

22 Lit. a "circle" woman, i.e. a woman who is entitled to pay or receive part of the wergild. Hertzberg 1895, 93.

23 Emended; the MS. has sg. *sun*. Cf. Meissner 1935, 162.

24 Emended; the MS. has pl. *þeir*. Cf. Meissner 1935, 162.

25 I.e. to a woman.

26 The third paragraph and the rest of this chapter deal with *stefnujǫrð* (see note 19) and are probably later additions.

27 I.e. those who share the odal with him.

place on Thursday in Easter week and pay as much money as other men outside the kin are willing to pay for the land. His son should have the first right to buy.

Now a man outside the kin wants to buy, and the one who has the first right to buy doubts that the other is willing to pay so much (as has been said), then both buyer and seller have to swear that "this is the way I want to sell"[28] and "this is the way I want to buy".[29] If he (the other odal man) does not want to buy at that price, then the owner may sell, giving full warranty, to whomever he likes.

Now he wants to sell land for a term of fifteen winters, then that agreement shall be valid; but it may be set aside in one case: If the land was offered (to the odal men), then the bargain may be annulled if the land is not already sold;[30] then the seller is liable to pay a compensation.[31] Then he (the owner) should ask him (the buyer outside the kin) to increase his offer, that he may have the land for the time he bought it.

If he is not willing to increase his offer, then the owner should ask the odal men to buy the land, and if they refuse to do so, he must sell to the highest bidder.

Now the land remains (in the buyer's possession) until the end of the term, then he (who wants to redeem it) should give the other notice in the autumn and do one more thing at the same time: summon him to (appear on) the land on Thursday in Easter week, if he (the latter) is willing to accept such price as witnesses know that he paid to him (the seller, when the land was sold). Then it is well if they agree to this, that he (the seller) summons the other to come the land and to receive the payment.

But if the other denies this, then the plaintiff (the seller) should produce his witnesses how he gave the other notice (of redemption) and how he summoned him to come to receive the payment. If that is satisfactorily testified, then he should produce his witnesses how much money the tenant has in the land; then he must offer him the sum to which witnesses have testified for him; then the plaintiff has to take care of the land, but the other (should have) his money, then he has redeemed his land properly according to the law.

Now the land remains (in the buyer's possession) beyond the term, and remains thus for twenty winters, and they have not published the terms, then it has become (the holder's) odal-land;[32] then he (the holder) may deny (the seller's and the seller's family's) odal-rights and call it his land. Then he should defend that land with a court judgement; the redeemer must sue for it with odal witnesses. Those who were witnesses to the bargain may serve as odal witnesses. That land shall be redeemed at full price, if the terms have not been announced during those twenty winters. The announcement is fully valid when both buyer and seller agree to it.

28 I.e. "this is the price I demand".

29 I.e. "I accept this price".

30 I.e. the buyer has not received the land.

31 Probably six *aurar* to the buyer when he does not receive the land.

32 The meaning of these last words is not entirely clear. A probable interpretation is that the land in question is no longer held on lease, so that odal-rights apply from now on.

## 277 If a man buys land that has not been offered for sale[33]

Now a man buys land that has not been offered for sale, then the odal men may annul the bargain. Now they give him notice of surrender in the autumn, then they may do two things at one time, if they want to: give him notice to surrender the land and summon him to be on the land Thursday in Easter week. The owner of the odal may also summon him afterwards, but not later than Mid-Lent, on that Saturday after which three weeks are left of Lent.

Now he wants to defend his bargain with a court of arbitration; then they should hold the court on the land to which the other has summoned him. The plaintiff must produce his witnesses to show how he summoned the defendant to receive such payment as witnesses know of together with him. If the testimony is found satisfactory they have to award the land to him (the plaintiff), and to the other (the defendant) such sum of money as witnesses know that he paid to him (the seller).

If he (the defendant) says that the land had been publicly offered (to the odal men) and produces witnesses to testify that the land was offered legally, then he shall have the land that he bought.

Now if the other fails to come to the court, then he (the plaintiff) shall offer the money. And if the defendant has authorized someone else, in the presence of witnesses, then the plaintiff must pay the money to him, or keep the money and not let him (the defendant) get it before the latter sues for it.

## 278 If a man buys land to be conveyed by *skeyting*[34]

Now a man buys land to be conveyed by *skeyting* and gets the conveyance, then his (the seller's) co-possessors, if they are within the *fylki* and want to redeem the land, should have redeemed it within the first twelve months, otherwise the buyer shall keep it.

## 279 More about the same

Now a man buys land to be conveyed by *skeyting* and the seller refuses to convey it, then the man should go to the assembly and let bear witness that he had bought the land to be thus conveyed, and he should ask for a raising of weapons, that the assembly men convey the land to him by the show of weapons, then the conveyance is as valid as if the other had conveyed it, if he (the buyer) had taken the sod in the right way.[35]

33 This chapter deals with odal-land.

34 This term refers to the symbolic act used in transferring land: The donor put a piece of sod from the land into the new owner's lap. Hamre 1971, esp. 160–1.

35 See Ch. 292.

## 280 Concerning redemption of land[36]

Now a man buys land and the (former) owner wants to redeem it on any day that he likes, then he should give the buyer notice half a month before Thursday in Easter week, (so) that he (the buyer) may have the use of the (purchase) money that (same) summer. If he redeems the land after the moving days, then the tenant should have both his (purchase) money and the rent.

## 281 If a man wants to redeem his odal

Now a man wants to redeem his odal, and the one who is in possession of the land is outside our law district or abroad, then the plaintiff should go to find him and summon him, before witnesses, to come to the land; and then he should go to the land and set his court there and claim the land from him, just as if the other man were present; and he should produce his odal witnesses and all his other witnesses, as if the other man were present.

## 282 Concerning the division of odal-rights between brothers

Now two brothers are to divide odal-rights between them, then the odal shall pass to that branch of the family which the (drawing of) lots indicate both with respect to the right of redemption and to actual possession;[37] it shall be offered to the other branch only in case the first becomes impoverished or dies out. The latter branch does not lose its odal-rights (to the land which passed to the other branch) until a man in either branch may marry the daughter of one in the other.[38]

## 283 If a man wants to redeem land that has been mortgaged

Now a man wants to redeem land that he has mortgaged,[39] then he should give the holder notice half a month before Thursday in Easter week; and he must go to the land and set half of his court against that of the other man and produce his witnesses there, how much money the other has in the land. He should then pay that amount, unless the other bears witness to a larger amount.

If he redeems it in this way he shall have the land at his disposal.

If he redeems it later, but still before the plough is set into the ground, and there is no fraud,[40] then he is entitled to the rent, but the other (the tenant) has the right to occupy the land.

36 This chapter deals with *málajǫrð* as opposed to *stefnujǫrð*, cf. Chs. 276 and 283.

37 I.e. the right to occupy and run the property (ON *ábúð*).

38 On kinship as an obstacle to marriage cf. Ch. 24. This provision is the background for the rule in Ch. 266 requiring that five ancestors be enumerated.

39 For a debt. See Ch. 280 and note 19.

40 To set the plough into the ground before proper time was regarded as a kind of fraud.

If he redeems it later still, the other (the tenant) shall have both the land and the money without rent for that year.

## 284 If a man wants to redeem land sold on lease

Now a man wants to redeem land that he has sold on lease,[41] then he should give the other notice in the autumn, with two witnesses; he may do one more thing at the same time: summon the other to receive his money on Thursday in Easter week on the land in question.

Now they (both) arrive, then the suitor should set his court and produce his witnesses, how much money the other has in the land. Then he must pay that amount, unless the other produces witness (to the effect) that the sum is larger. He (the redeemer) must then have witnesses who know at what time he has the right to redeem his land.[42]

## 285 How to redeem land from women

In the same way land[43] should be redeemed from kinswomen to whom one is so closely related that the odal-right cannot be denied.

But she may answer that "it is not our odal, it is acquired by our kinsfolk, and the land should follow the movables, but not the odal". Then the man should produce his witnesses before the court where he seeks to redeem the land (to the effect that) the land shall be regarded as odal and not as movables. She must also produce her witnesses there, if she has any.

## 286 Concerning land that has been sold on lease

Now a man wants to redeem land sold on lease[44] or land (that he has) mortgaged and the possessor is outside our law district or abroad, then he should redeem it from his agent.[45] If there is no agent he must redeem it from the man's heir instead.

Now a man (a tenant) sells (to another) land held on lease before the end of the term, then he (the owner) may redeem it from whomever he likes: from the one to whom he sold the land or from the one who has come into possession. Likewise land that is in mortgage (should be dealt with).

If he who has bought land held on lease or land that is in mortgage is outside our law-district or abroad, and there is neither his agent nor his heir in our law

41 Cf. Chs. 272 and 276.

42 So Robberstad 1981, 389. Larson (1935, 184) translates the last sentence: "in that case he (the occupier) shall have witnesses present at the moot where he (the owner) has the land that he wishes to redeem". Meissner (1935, 167) translates: "Then he (the owner) shall have witnesses when he arrives on the appointed day, when he has to redeem his land". (My translation from German, ES.)

43 I.e. odal-land. Cf. Ch. 274.

44 See note 41.

45 The one who takes care of the land while the owner is not present.

district, then he who wants to redeem (the land) should go to the assembly and issue a summons to the one who bought it to come back on an appointed day. If he (the latter) fails to come on the appointed day, he (the former) should go to the assembly and produce his witnesses to show what was agreed between them, and he has to offer the (redemption) money there. But if the other has not authorized someone to receive it, then he (the former) must have the money and keep it until the other comes to get it.

## 287 Concerning odal-land

Now a man wants to sell his odal-land, then he or his agent should go to the assembly in the autumn and offer his fellow odal men[46] to buy the land, ask them to come there on Thursday in Easter week and buy the land on such terms as other men offer. He must do this in the assembly area where the land lies.

Now they both come there on Thursday in Easter week but disagree about the price, then the one who wants to sell should swear to it that he has been offered the price he has set and that the offer is not a fraudulent one. The other should also swear that "I will buy for the price that has now been set". Then his co-possessor shall have the land if he wishes; otherwise the owner may sell to whomever he likes.

Now the one who wants to buy arrives but the one who offered the land does not come, then he (the buyer) shall have the land at a price set by impartial men, whether the other (the owner) is willing or not.

But if neither comes, then it is as if the land were not offered for sale.

But when the co-possessors come there on Thursday in Easter week, then the (earlier) buyer has no legal right to the land.

## 288 Concerning land that is sold on lease[47]

Now a man wants to sell land on lease or give it in mortgage, then he should first offer it before witnesses to those who are the nearest in the odal; to his son he should only offer it if the son wants him to.[48]

## 289 If a man buys land that has not been publicly offered for sale

Now a man buys land that has not been publicly offered (for sale), and there is a co-possessor[49] in the *fylki*, then he (who wants to redeem the land) should have

46 See note 27.

47 This chapter concerns cases where land is offered to each odal man separately instead of – or in addition to – offering it at the assembly.

48 So Robberstad (1981, 261). Or: "He need not offer it to his son, unless he wishes to do so" (Larson 1935, 186). Meissner (1935, 168) translates: "to his son only if he wants to". (My translation from German, ES.)

49 See note 27.

redeemed (it) within the first twelve months. But if he is outside the *fylki*, then he must have redeemed (it) within twelve months after his return to the *fylki*. But if it is not redeemed in the way that I have now told, then he will never be allowed to reopen his case later.

## 290 Concerning the right to redeem land

Now a widow has the right[50] to redeem land that has been sold, then she should find a man, whomever she likes, to publish this fact at the assembly during the following twelve months and have (the land) redeemed within the first twelve months after she is remarried.

But if she refuses to marry, then she may choose any man she wants to manage her lawsuit, but not a man more powerful than he who had bought the land.

## 291 More about the right to redeem land

Now a girl has the right to redeem land, then she should get a man when she is fifteen winters old to publish at the assembly that the land which she has the right to redeem is sold, and she must have (the land) redeemed within the first twelve months after she is married.

But if a girl and a widow fail to proceed as I have now told, then they will never be allowed to reopen their cases later.

## 292 Concerning conveyance of land

Now a man buys land in the presence of a group of men, then the assembly men should convey the land to him. He has to summon the other (the seller) to be at home and from there to be summoned to the assembly and he must produce his witnesses at the assembly to show that he had correctly summoned him to be at home and from there to the assembly.

He should take sod as the law prescribes. He must take it at the four corners of the hearth and from under the high seat and where the field and the meadow meet and where the grove meets the pasture land, and he must produce witnesses at the assembly that he has taken sod in the proper way, and other witnesses which were present when they concluded the bargain.

If this is satisfactorily testified, then the assembly men should convey the land to him with the raising of weapons.

Whenever the buyer and the seller agree that the sod has been correctly taken, the bargain shall be valid, and likewise the conveyance (whether it is made) at a church, in an alehouse or on a fully manned ship (which is large enough to be counted after the number of seats), the conveyance shall be as valid as if it were made at the assembly. Whenever the king conveys land, it shall hold.

50 According to odal-right or special agreement.

## 293 If a man who has sold his land becomes impoverished

Now if a man who has sold his land on lease becomes impoverished, then he should summon the buyer to come to the land that he has bought, giving notice half a month in advance. He should go to the place on the day appointed for the redemption and produce his witnesses that poverty has broken their contract.[51] A co-possessor may have the land if he wants to, otherwise the one who bought it.

## 294 Concerning reduction by a fifth

Now there are two brothers and one dies before their father and one son lives after the deceased, then this son should redeem from his father's brother that part of the odal-land which his father would have had a right to after his father at a reduction by one fifth. But he shall not redeem it before his father's father has passed away.

51 I.e. that the seller was supposed to redeem the land on the appointed day at the end of the term.

# XIII The book on the naval levy

## 295 Here begins the book on the naval levy

The king has the right of command and prohibition[1] and to determine our duties in the naval service. We shall not refuse to serve in the naval levy (even) as far as to the land's end[2] when he requires it because he needs it and we benefit from it.

Now all men must serve in the levy in equal proportions as the king has promised us.

## 296 Concerning the count of men

When the naval levy has been called out people should keep track of the counting of men; no one must deny another man counting for a (more) correct distribution.

He should demand a muster from the men of his warship district. Then it is well if they all come to the mustering and to the oath taking. If some fail to come to the muster, then those who do come must enumerate as many as they want to on the part of those who do not come; then those others have to do service for that number if they have been informed of it.[3]

In the counting every man should include himself and all those of his household who are liable for contribution to the levy, and those of his freedmen who have not given their freedom ales.

The freedman should make his own contribution if he can afford it; otherwise his master should do it.

Every man must count along with himself all those of his children who have lived three Christmas Eves.[4]

Now a man escapes counting and runs from *fylki* to *fylki* or from quarter to quarter and performs his duty neither here nor there; whoever is identified and convicted of this is an outlaw.

1 Cf. Ch. 313.

2 Especially the mouth of the Göta River, the border between Norway and Sweden in the South-East.

3 I.e. if they have been summoned to the assembly. Cf. Ch. 131.

4 Svein Knutsson (Alfivasson, King of Norway 1030–36) prescribed that only children who had lived more than five Christmas Eves should be counted.

If a man helps anyone of his household to evade the oath, if he has a slave, then the slave should be seized by the king's representative; but if he has more slaves, the king's representative should have the one he wants. If he has no slave he is liable to pay a fine of three *merkr* for every (member) of his household whom he helped to evade the oath.

## 297 More about the muster

When full mobilization is ordered every seventh man should be equipped for service.[5] But if we have better terms (of muster),[6] then all men shall benefit from it.

In proportion to our number of men we must provide as many ships from each *fylki*[7] as we have agreed on with our king.

## 298 Concerning the men who are exempted from contribution to the levy

Now it shall be said what men there are from whom we must not claim contribution to the levy.

The bishop should pay no dues to the levy for himself or for his priest or for his deacon. The mass-priest must pay no dues, nor should his wife or his cleric.[8]

But if they have more people in the household dues should be paid for them.

The king's representative cannot serve for himself or for his wife or for his slave.

For leprous people no dues shall be paid.

For a slave no contribution must be paid if he is in poor health, then he should be taken to the assembly and offered; if no one is willing to take him and he is younger than forty years, no contribution shall be paid for him.

The men to whom we jointly give their freedom here in *Gulaþing*[9] shall not contribute to the levy, nor shall those to whom we as *fylkis* men give their freedom.

5 King Svein prescribed that every seventh man of those who were older than five years should be called into service, and the number of oar benches in each warship should be determined in proportion to the number of men.

6 I.e. that there were so many men available in the warship district that fewer men than every seventh man were needed to man the ship completely.

7 According to some ON sources (*Fagrskinna* and *Heimskringla*) King Håkon the Good (King of Norway c. 930–c. 961) established the levy and determined the number of ships to be provided from each *fylki* and the size of each ship, measured by the number of oar benches. On the number of ships cf. Ch. 315.

8 A deacon (Lat. *diaconus*) was a church servant who had received a lower degree of consecration than that of a priest. – In the year 1152 Nicholas Breakspear (later known as Pope Adrian IV) decreed that bishop, priests, and other church officials should be exempted from military service, but they were obliged to see the king for deliberations before impending attacks from heathens. More precise rules to the same effect were given later.

9 Cf. Chs. 4 and 5. The wording shows that this provision dates back to King Olav Haraldsson, which means that it must be older than 1163.

No contribution must be made for people who are forced by poverty back on their family (for support), and not for grave-goers[10] unless they are claimed because of debt.

Now the number of children in a family increases, no contribution to the levy must be claimed (for them) until a new muster has been made.

If a member of your household dies, one for whom you are liable to contribute to the levy, contribution should be paid for him until the next muster is made.

Now a man takes a wife or buys a slave out of the muster list of another man; if he buys him before the oaths have been sworn he should add (that person) to his own list. But if he buys him later[11] he must deposit the next payment[12] and then (in a new muster) enter them on his own list.

Now a man sits for three winters paying no contribution to the levy[13] and is nowhere counted in any muster group, then he is an outlaw. Now he is counted but pays no contribution to the levy, then the king's representative should fine him for neglecting the levy to such an amount as the counting shows.[14]

Whenever there is a general muster the levy districts shall be formed from the land's end[15] forward, so that those who live near each other shall compose a separate group. No one can pass ahead of another unless they all agree to it.

No man may deny another man a new muster. All householders should come to the mustering assembly.

If you want to be enrolled in another eighth or in another quarter[16] you have to state your request at the assembly.

But if they deny you a new count (of men who have to serve in the levy) and refuse an adjustment (of the contribution), then you should charge the reduction (of the number of men counted) to their account, and do it on oath.

Now a man moves his household into another *fylki* or into another quarter, he should not dispose of his ship or buy himself another (ship), and he should enrol where he likes. If he is enrolled where a new ship is being built he must contribute as any other man.

Now a man leaves his levy district and moves into another law district, then he should leave behind (what is needed) for the next contribution.

If a man leaves the country, contribution to the levy should be paid for him three winters. But if that is neglected a fine must be claimed from him when he comes home.

10 See Ch. 63.
11 I.e. after the oaths were sworn.
12 When the oaths are sworn the contribution for the year has been assessed. The one who buys a slave should leave to the seller what is needed as contribution for the slave that year.
13 This seems to presuppose that contribution to the levy should be paid every year.
14 The size of this fine is not specified, but it may have amounted to six *aurar* according to Magnus the Law-Mender's Law of the Realm.
15 See note 2.
16 Subdivisions of a *fylki*, see Ch. 3. The subdivision into quarters was limited to the four central *fylki* in Western Norway, namely *Hǫrðafylki*, *Sygnafylki*, *Firðafylki*, and *Rygjafylki*.

If a man moves with his household from our law district into another *fylki*, he must pay the next contribution where he was before; afterwards he has to pay the contribution in the place to which he moves.

## 299 Concerning the command of a ship

The man who is appointed thereto by the king should command the ship. But if he refuses (to do so) he is liable to pay a fine of six *merkr*.

But if another man takes the rudder from him,[17] then he is liable to pay a fine of six *merkr*.

Now the ship's master should appoint oarsmen to sail with him; they are all bound to sail or pay a fine of three *merkr*.

Now it is well if there are enough unmarried men available. But if there are not enough of them, then those householders who have farmhands should go, if there is a sufficient number of such men. But if there is not a sufficient number, then men who have no helpers should go: one should go and two should stay at home to care for the livestock, if the crew is then sufficient; otherwise two must go and one stay at home.

## 300 Concerning the cook

Those who have slaves in the warship district should provide the cook, and they have to draw lots among them (to assign the duty). Cooks shall have the same wages as sailors. The householder who provides the cook must stay at home, unless the ship is not fully manned. The householders (who have farmhands) are obliged to go to the muster, but the unmarried men (need appear) only if the ship's master wants them to.[18] The ship's master should summon all the men who are to man the ship or launch it. But whoever fails to appear has to pay a fine of three *aurar*.

Every sailor should receive wages, one *eyrir* per month and two *aurar* for two months.

The householders should pay two months' rates of each kind[19] for each oar bench, and a tent cover and an oar.

## 301 If a man does not go to his half room

Now they release the ship from its moorings and a man fails to appear at his half room, then they should raise up his oar and take witnesses that he is liable to pay a fine of three *merkr*.

17 I.e. takes the ship's master's place.

18 I.e. it was left to the ship's master's decision whether or not more men were needed to make the ship ready.

19 I.e. meal and butter.

A widow should let her food and all her other contribution be brought onto the ship if she has no oarsman, and she must give it to the ship's master.

They are not ready for sailing when five oar benches or more are vacant on a twenty-bencher.[20]

A landed man or a king's representative who governs at least an eighth[21] should provide five oarsmen.

If they are not ready for sailing they should offer their crew to another ship. If that does not accept them they are free of guilt if they remain at home but bring the food to the king's representative, that he may receive it on behalf of the king.

Now when they come home, they summon people to a (new) count of men, and if they do not then find enough men they should cut the keel and thus shorten their ship according to their number of men, but they must not make it so short that it is impossible to count the number of benches. If they are too few to man a thirteen-bencher[22] they should go to the assembly and offer to join the service with other men. But if they do not do so they have to make their ship ready for sailing the next spring with food and crew.

If a man contributes to the levy in another place than that to which he is required, then it is as if he has not contributed.

If a man goes with another ship than the one to which he is supposed to go, then he must do both: do the levy and pay the fine (for neglect).

## 302 If a man leaves the ship without permission from the ship's master

Now you turn the stem southward along the coast, and a man deserts from the ship while it is sailing southward, and the king is out at sea to defend the country, then he is an outlaw; he may redeem himself with forty *merkr*.

But if the ship's master deserts, he is an outlaw in any case.

The levy must not be kept out at sea longer than that a man has half a month's rate of each kind of food[23] left.

Now the ship's master allows a man to leave the ship, then he (the ship's master) is responsible for the whole ship. But whoever leaves (the ship) later shall go with impunity.[24]

20 ON *tvítugsessa*, a ship with twenty pairs of oars, hence twenty thwarts (benches), which means that forty oarsmen were required.

21 This word shows that Ch. 301 must be ancient law passed on from the time before the districts of *Egðafylki* and *Sunnmørafylki* were included in the *Gulaþing*.

22 ON *þrettánsessa*; this shows that a ship which should be measured by counting the number of thwarts (benches) had to be at least a thirteen-bencher.

23 See note 19.

24 I.e. he shall not incur such penalty as is mentioned in the first paragraph of this chapter.

## 303 If men run out of food

Now they return northward and run out of food, then they should call other ships to witness and show them their food, that they have no more food than one month's rate of each kind for two squads,[25] then they may slaughter two head of cattle from a householder with impunity, and they should pay two *aurar*[26] for a cow and the same (amount) for a three-year-old ox, and two and a half *aurar* for a full-grown[27] ox; and they should leave the head, the hide and the feet behind; then they are free of guilt if they slaughter in that way. But if they take away the head or the feet or the hide, then they are liable to punishment.

If they slaughter cattle from a householder where others have slaughtered before, but neither the head nor the feet of the slaughtered cattle are presented, then they slaughter with impunity if they pay for the cattle.

Now they slaughter otherwise than here is said, then the ship's master is liable to pay a fine of forty *merkr* and each sailor three *merkr*.

Now they are accused of having slaughtered otherwise than is said, then the ship's master should deny for as many men as he likes with a three-man oath. But if he is unwilling to deny for them, then each should deny for himself with a three-man oath.

Now a man leaves the ship before it has come to the rollers and no one has allowed him (to leave), then he is liable to pay a fine of three *merkr*.

## 304 How the ship should be drawn ashore

Now the ship comes home to the rollers,[28] then people should draw it ashore and hide the tackle; so many men must be called from each levy district that the ship can be hauled up.

If some fail to come and the ship nevertheless is hauled up, [each of them is liable to pay a fine of three *aurar*.[29] But if the ship cannot be hauled up, then those who failed to come are wholly responsible for the ship, if the message came to their houses.

Whenever the ship's master sends a message stick all are bound to carry it forward, whether they belong to that warship district or not. Whoever fails to pass the message stick on is liable to pay a fine of three *aurar*.

Now people come five nights too early or five nights too late, then no one must pay (compensation to) the other. But if there is a greater difference in time, then those who have to pay compensation should pay the others as the reckoning shows.[30]

25 ON *sveitir*; the *sveit* was a military unit of unknown (but probably fairly small) size.

26 According to Ch. 223 the price of a living cow was two and a half *aurar*. Here the price is lower because the hide is not included.

27 Emended; the MS. has *þrítíðung*, 'three years old'.

28 Cf. Ch. 47.

29 [*AM 315 f fol.*: they are liable to pay . . . if the message came to their houses.]

30 This last paragraph deals with compensation (of food) to those who met in time and had to wait more than five days until the ship could be hauled up, because the others came so late.

## 305 On taking care of the sail

The sail must not be torn into more than two parts. But if they tear it into more, then they are liable to pay a fine of three *merkr*.

The one who is given it by lot and lives near the sea should take care of the sail. Now they store the sail in a church;[31] if the church burns down, then the men have to bear responsibility for the sail unless someone else set the church on fire deliberately.

Now they must have a place to set up (the ship), just as they have had from times past. But if the ground is wanting, then the king's land shall provide the site if the king owns land within that quarter. But if he has not, they have to buy a site wherever they want, according to assessment.

## 306 Concerning shipbuilding[32]

Now the ship decays from age and they have to build a new one, then they should build it wherever they want to build it, but they may not spoil field or meadow. Now the king's land has to provide (a construction site) if there is such land. But if there is none they may use whatever forest they like; but if they are to build several ships, they may not spoil one man's forest.

Now they divide the timber among them. Those who have been drawn by lot to supply the keel or the stems, strakes[33] or hooding ends,[34] should pay half a *mǫrk* if that is lacking; for the gunwales near the prow or the crossbeams in the prow, for each missing plank, three *aurar* must be paid and the plank be supplied even if it is (supplied) later. Three *aurar* must be paid for each rib that reaches athwart the ship; an *eyrir* for each piece of knee timber[35] and another *eyrir* even if only a cleat is missing; three *aurar* for a mast and the same for a sailyard and the same for all timber, even if it is to be used on the inside of the ship.

An *eyrir* must be paid for each missing plank, an *eyrir* even if only an ell is missing, the plank should be supplied even if it is later; an *eyrir* for each nail and rove; an *eyrir* for each bucket[36] of tar, an *eyrir* for each strip of oakum, an *eyrir* even if only an ell is missing; an *eyrir* for every meal;[37] an *eyrir* for every *penningr* given in pay to the craftsmen. Now craftsmen should be summoned, all those who are within the quarter until the number is sufficient. Every prow builder is liable to pay a fine of six *merkr* if he neglects to come.

31 In the old stone churches of Moster and Kinsarvik (in Western Norway) there is a hole in the western wall through which the sail could be taken.

32 In translating terms related to ships and shipbuilding I have mainly followed O. Crumlin-Pedersen (1997, 206–8, 2002, 317, 348–50).

33 ON *húfr*, here referring to two of the most important planks of the ship's side: the one to which the upper end of the ribs was fastened, and the one on which the oars rest.

34 ON *halsar*, the converging sides of the ship at the foot of the prow.

35 A piece of timber shaped as a knee, serving as a rib to which the mooring line was fastened.

36 A bucket (ON *spann*) usually contained 4.05 litres in Western Norway.

37 I.e. food to the workers.

Now they have laid the keel on the building berth and begun building, if one of them runs away from the work, the prow builder or deal hewer, then such a prow builder or deal hewer is an outlaw, since he hinders the king in his defence of the country.

The shipwrights should be paid for their work: a prow builder two six-ell-*aurar*[38] on workdays between two Sundays; and a deal hewer an *eyrir*.

They must neither burn nor break a ship before the prows are nailed to the keel of the new ship. But if they burn or break it before, then it is illegal breaking,[39] they have to pay a fine of three *merkr* for each grummet.

## 307 Concerning the building of boat-houses

Now a boat-house shall be built over the ship, then the ship's master should summon men and set a time limit, giving the men convenient time to build the boat-house. But if they refuse to build it, then they are liable to pay a fine of three *merkr* to the king.

Now they distribute the duty to find the materials; then there is a fine of three *aurar* for every post (not supplied) and the same for every cross beam and for every rafter, they should be supplied even if it is later; three *aurar* for every turf lath;[40] three *aurar* for every bargeboard;[41] an *eyrir* for every roof board[42] and the same for every bundle of birch bark, an *eyrir* for every (piece of) turf; (all of this has to be) supplied it even if it is later.

## 308 Concerning summons for sail making

Now the ship's master should set a day for making a sail for the ship. If it has not been done by that time, then all those who have to supply it are liable to pay a fine of three *merkr*. If some do their duty but others do not, (the latter should pay) a fine of an *eyrir* for every ell (of sailcloth), an *eyrir* for every bolt-rope, an *eyrir* even if only an ell is wanting; an *eyrir* for every ball of cord; an *eyrir* for every strap (in the tack); an *eyrir* for every eyelet (in the tack). The length of ropes shall be determined by the number of hides needed; an *eyrir* for each hide which is not supplied, it must be supplied even though it is later.

If something is missing the king's representative or the landed man should supply what is wanting so far as he has lands from the king, and he should claim the fine from the delinquent afterwards.

38 I.e. an *eyrir* being valued at six ells of wadmal.

39 Which means that they have failed in their duties to the levy.

40 ON *torfvǫlr*, a strip of wood along the eaves of the roof to hold in place the turf that covered the roof.

41 ON *vindskeið*, a board nailed to the slanting gable sides of a roof.

42 ON *tróða*, a board laid under the birch bark in a turfed roof.

## 309 Concerning inspection of weapons

Whenever inspection of weapons is to be held, the king's representative or the landed man should give notice in the autumn and carry out the inspection in the spring. All free men of major age must come to that inspection, otherwise each of them is liable to pay a fine of three *aurar*.

Now men have to show their weapons as prescribed by the law.[43] A man should have a broad-axe or a sword, a spear and a shield spanned at worst by three iron claps, and the handle fastened with iron nails. Now there is a fine of three *aurar* for each of these folk weapons (if wanting).

The householders should supply two dozen arrows and a bow for each thwart; they have to pay a fine of an *eyrir* for each arrowhead missing and three *aurar* for the bow.

## 310 Whether a ship is considered seaworthy or not

Now the king sends his men into a *fylki* to inspect his men's vessels, and they or the ship's master deem a ship to be unseaworthy, but the men of the warship district call it seaworthy; then they should summon men from another warship district; they have to declare on oath whether it is seaworthy or not. But if they refuse to swear, then the others should launch their ship and test their vessel; let it lie in water[44] for five nights, then they should bail it out.

Now if one man can manage the bailing all the way out to the fairway, then the ship is seaworthy.

An anchor shall follow the ship, but if it is wanting, then the men of the warship district are liable to pay a fine of three *merkr*. But the ship's master should supply the rudder and the tiller.[45]

## 311 Concerning the watch at the beacons

Now if a hostile army is expected, then men should keep watch at the beacons.[46] Then the king's representative or the landed man should send forth the message stick, and whoever fails to come is liable to pay a fine of three *merkr*. And those who have been appointed by lot to keep watch and fail to go (to the beacon), they are to be held responsible for the beacon.

They have to keep watch and see to it that they do not fall asleep while on duty. But if a man falls asleep he must pay a fine of twelve *aurar*, but if an army comes in the meantime and the beacons are not lit, then he is an outlaw.

43 According to *Fagrskinna* (Ch. 12) King Håkon the Good (c. 920–c. 961) laid down that every free man capable of bearing arms should have a shield, a spear, and a slashing weapon.

44 For tightening.

45 The handle of the rudder.

46 The beacons, ON *vitar*, were special fires which were lit as warning signals that a hostile fleet or an enemy was in sight or had arrived. According to *Fagrskinna* and *Heimskringla* King Håkon the Good (see note 43) ordered such beacons to be built on high mountains all along the coast. They remained in use for several centuries, the last time was in the year 1814.

He should light the beacon at the sight of five ships or more than five. But if he fails to light the beacon and the ships turn out to be hostile, then he is an outlaw.

Now he lights the beacon at the sight of fewer ships, thus causing the men to assemble for war, he is liable to pay a fine of forty *merkr*.

The one who is nearest to the easternmost beacon should be liable to pay a fine of forty *merkr*, but each of the others three *merkr*.

## 312 Concerning the dispatch of arrows

Now a man who was already outlawed from here comes to our country and reports true news of war, then he may stay in the country although he was an outlaw [*AM 146, 4to:* turned into a villain] before.

Now a man reports war news that is not true, then he is an outlaw although he has already been allowed to stay in the country.

Now an inhabitant of the country reports true news of war, then he should have a *mǫrk* from each *fylki* and three *merkr* from our king.

If a man reports news of war, then he must send a message stick with an arrow of iron at the land's end;[47] it has to be carried forward from every landed man to the other and should be sent on a fully manned ship, and it should be carried forward by day and by night and should travel the fairway. They are outlawed if they fail to carry the arrow forward.

Now a wooden arrow should be sent into the fjords away from the fairway, and it should be carried forward before witnesses, and each man must bring it to the other; and whoever fails in this is liable to pay a fine of three *merkr*.

Now the arrow comes to a place where a single woman lives; then she should provide a ship and crew and provisions, if she can afford it. But if she cannot, they must send the arrow past her.

But all those men to whom the arrow comes have a five days' respite to come to the ship. But if someone stays quietly at home, then he is an outlaw, for at such a time both a freeman and a slave have to go.[48] Every man should provide food for himself and his companions.[49]

Now they meet a hostile army and fight and a slave kills an enemy, then he is a free man though he was a slave before.

Now if an army attacks our country and our king fears that people will fail him and he wants to take some of us as hostages, then we have no right to deny (him this). Whoever denies (it) is guilty of high treason.

Now people have been given as hostages, then he (the king) should keep the hostages until the hostile fleet has been out of sight from land for five nights, then he should send them back to their homes.

47 See note 2; cf. also Hertzberg 1895, 381.

48 According to a provision made by Nicholas Breakspear 1152 Canon Law instructs both free men and slaves to fight heathens; bishops and abbots should join in the military campaign, or churches and monasteries should support.

49 This paragraph shows that it was possible to summon men to an assembly for a large region. Sunde 2011a, 57–8.

If the king charges a man with high treason, then he must deny with a twelve-man oath, that oath leads to outlawry if it fails.

## 313 If men sail in defiance of a prohibition[50]

Now men sail despite a prohibition,[51] then the ship's master is liable to pay a fine of forty *merkr*, but each sailor three *merkr*.

There shall be one ship's master on each ship, the one who sleeps nearest the gunwales on the starboard side; he should be charged, but all have to pay according to how much they own in the ship that sailed despite a ban.

There shall be no prohibition against the transport of corn or food between the *fylki*. But if it is prohibited, then all men in the *fylki* are liable to pay a fine of forty *merkr*; half of which goes to the king, and the other half to the men of the law-district.

## 314 Concerning thwart fines

Now a man builds a longship[52] in his district and does not announce where he wants to sail. Then the king's representative or landed man should go to him and ask where he wants to sail.

If he refuses to tell they should demand surety from him to the amount of forty *merkr*. If he refuses to give surety they should cut out a board, five ells in length, from either side of the keel.

But if they fail do so, then the householders have to do it and remove the sail, if there is one, and thus prevent their sailing. If they fail to do so and the ship becomes a warship, then they should pay a fine of a *mǫrk* for each thwart, but three *merkr* for the rudder strap; that is called thwart fines.

But if they bring their own food, then the men of the district should pay the fine for those who live there.

Now they leave and break the peace and raid in the same bay, then they are villains. But if they raid somewhere else, then they are outlaws, but not villains.

Now they leave without breaking the peace, then they are outlaws and villains and have forfeited every penny of their property, no matter where they raid.

Now they raid and the one who is plundered has no force to pursue them, then he may cut a message stick with an arrow and send forward, if he wants to. Every man should go where the arrow directs him, to pursue the enemy.

Now they set out to pursue the plunderers, then all those who are present must join; but if some refuse, then their property may be confiscated and the man be killed if the others want to, then they may divide his property among them.

50 This chapter and the following one are not parts of the instructions for the levy.

51 The king had a right to ban travels abroad and transport of goods from one part of the country to another.

52 I.e. a warship.

Now they come to the place where the man is who sent the arrow forward; if he has sent it with reason, then it is good. But if he has sent it without reason, no enemy having come to his house, then they may confiscate his property and kill him if they like and divide his property among them. If he has sent the arrow forward with good reason, they should go with him as far as he wants. Now if they come upon a band of raiding men and need to redden point or edge in order to regain their property, then those who take the booty shall have it and divide it among them. But if they have no need for this, then the goods shall belong to him who owned them before.

Now they (the plunderers) seize a merchant ship and break up the cargo and bring it back into the district and reconcile themselves with the king. Then those who were plundered follow after them and swear to it that it was their property, then they (the plunderers) should restore everything, unless they nullify the oaths by carrying hot iron.

Now they have raided and sail along the coast and a man buys something of value from them, then the man who owned the article before should have it and recover it with two witnesses. But he who bought (something) from the vikings must pay a fine of three *merkr* to the king. But if the owner cannot produce witness against the one who has bought goods that were wrongfully acquired, then he should summon him to the assembly; the assembly men should award the property to him or demand a three-man oath. Now that oath may be taken like every other oath within ten weeks of oath days; but it is possible to swear in any week in which there is one day when oath taking is allowed. Then the one (who demands the oath) should summon the other, five nights in advance, to (appear at) whatever church he wishes within the quarter.

He should take the oath in front of witnesses, two men must be appointed to hear the oath; they should (also) be the judges of the oath. And if they disagree, some deem it correctly taken, others improperly; then they shall have it their way who are willing to swear (in support of their view). But if both sides are willing to swear, then those who want to help[53] shall have the best right to swear the oath. But if the oath fails, it means that he (for whom the oath fails) should surrender his property to the claimant and pay three *merkr* to the king.

Now we have committed to writing (our laws concerning) the defence of the country but we do not know whether the statement is right or wrong.[54] But if it is wrong, we shall follow the legal regulations about our defence duties which we have had before and which Atle[55] explained to the men in Gulen, unless the king wants to grant us other plans and we all agree to them.

53 I.e. to support the sued part.

54 This sentence shows that the section on the levy has been written separately and after the other sections.

55 Atle seems to have been a lawspeaker in the *Gulaþing* law province. He may have been the same Atle who was mentioned as the spokesman of the freeholders in the dispute with King Magnus (Olavsson) the Good (King of Norway 1035–47) in 1040 or 1041, which was ended by the agreement in Langøysundet (in NW Norway, near Kristiansund).

## 315 How many ships[56] from each *fylki*

The men from *Vik*[57] should provide sixty twenty-benchers[58] and in addition a ship[59] from Grenland (Lower Telemark). The men from *Egðafylki* should provide sixteen twenty-five-benchers. The men from *Rygjafylki* should provide twenty-four twenty-five-benchers. And the men from *Hǫrðafylki* the same. The men from *Sygnafylki* sixteen twenty-five-benchers. The men from *Firðafylki* twenty twenty-five-benchers. The men from Sunnmøre sixteen twenty-five benchers. The men from Romsdalen ten twenty-benchers. The men from Nordmøre twenty twenty-benchers. The men from Trøndelag eighty twenty-benchers. The men from Namdalen nine twenty-benchers. The men from Hålogaland thirteen twenty-benchers and one thirty-bencher, seven in the southern part and six in the northern part, because they have to keep the watch[60] eastward.

56 According to Ch. 297 the number of ships was determined in a special agreement between the king and the people, probably the men meeting at the general assembly (ON *lǫgþing*). This chapter shows that the *Gulaþing* law province provided bigger ships than the other law districts (namely twenty-five-benchers v. twenty-benchers). The towns should also provide warships. The number of warship districts is known from other sources, esp. through king Magnus the Law-Mender's testament from the year 1277.

57 The *Borgarþing* law province, i.e. the coastal districts of SE Norway bordering on the Oslofjord.

58 See note 20.

59 The expression of the MS., (ON) *grøna skip*, is ambiguous with respect to number (sg. or pl.). Robberstad (1981, 284, 400) reads this as plural, meaning 'the ships from Grenland'. But Meissner (1935, 185), Larson (1935, 200), and Seip and Sandvik (1956, 8b) understand it as 'a ship from Grenland'.

60 Probably in the easternmost part of Finnmark where the fortress of Vardøyhus was built.

# XIV A later system of wergild

## 316 Here begins the new scale of compensations which Bjarne Mårsson[1] drew up about (the dividing of) six *merkr* gold[2]

This is what he shall have who is the son of the killed man and receives wergild, if (a compensation of) six *merkr* of gold is imposed for the one who has been killed and those six *merkr* include compensation and rings[3] and all money paid as compensation. Then the son of the killed man receives twelve *merkr*, weighed. And the brother of the deceased six *merkr*, weighed. And his father's brother, if he is living, eight *ertogar* and four *merkr*, weighed. And if his father's brother is deceased but his sons, first cousins of the killed man, are living, then they shall have four *ertogar* and twenty *aurar*, weighed. And if his father's brother is living but has no children, then he shall have one *ertog* and thirteen *aurar*, weighed.

And if he has daughters and no sons and they (the daughters) are younger than forty when the compensation is paid, then the father's brother takes a *mǫrk*, weighed, on behalf of his daughters' sons. And if he has no children except an illegitimate son, then he (this son) shall have that *mǫrk* which his daughters' sons would (normally) receive.

But if all (these) are living, a daughter's legitimate sons and an illegitimate son and legitimate sons, then the illegitimate son is counted with his brothers in stipulation of the compensation[4] and in addition to their share of the fines he receives one *ertog* less than five *aurar*. But if they (the daughters) die childless, then this sum, one *ertog* less than five *aurar*, reverts to the one who receives the wergild.

1 Bjarne Mårsson is mentioned in the *Sverris saga* as a chieftain in Hålogaland (Northern Norway) in 1198 and 1199. He was one of the adversaries of King Sverre and was later one of the royal lawspeakers from the *Frostuþing* law province meeting at the national convention in Bergen in 1223. On the general contents of this chapter see Sunde 2007, 307, note 6, and 311, note 25.

2 In case the entire wergild is six *merkr* gold. This scale provides compensation as far (in the degrees of kinship) as up to and including fifth cousins. It does not take into account the canonical rule from the year 1215 stating that the degree of kinship legally relevant only included one's kinsfolk up to and including third cousins.

3 I.e. compensation to the three circles of receivers. See Chs. 243–52.

4 I.e. he receives compensation just as the others.

And if the father of the killed man is living and his son receives the wergild, then he (the father) shall have three *merkr*, weighed. But if he is not living this compensation reverts to the one who receives the wergild.

And if the father's brother of the same mother is living and a brother of the same mother, then this brother of the same mother receives twelve *aurar*, and the father's brother of the same mother six *aurar*. And if neither of them can be found or one of them is wanting, then his (or their) share in the compensation reverts to the one who receives the wergild. What these men receive amounts to a total of two *aurar* and twenty-seven *merkr*.

And if the man who was killed had a stepson or a stepfather, then the one who receives the wergild has to pay twelve *aurar*, weighed, to each one of them out of the total just given. And if there are kinsmen by marriage such that each one is married to the sister of the other, then the one who receives the wergild must pay them twelve *aurar*. But if their kinship rests on one marriage only, he must pay six *aurar*.

And if the killed man is outlived by both his mother's father and his daughter's son, then they shall receive of the wergild two *aurar* less than four *merkr*, (that makes) fifteen *aurar* to each of them. But if one of them is wanting or both, then this compensation reverts to the one who receives the wergild. And if the killed man is outlived by both his mother's brother and a sister's son, then each of them receives twelve *aurar*.

And if the killed man is outlived by a son of a paternal uncle's son and by a son of his father's paternal uncle, then they receive twenty-two *aurar*, eleven *aurar* each. But if one of them is wanting, or both, then this compensation reverts to the one who receives the wergild. And if the killed man is outlived by a father's sister and she has sons, then they receive one *ertog* and nine *aurar*. And if the killed man is outlived by a mother's brother and he has sons, then these sons receive one *ertog* less than nine *aurar*, weighed, and the sons of his sisters a *mǫrk*. And if the killed man is outlived by a son of his brother's daughter, then he receives thirteen *aurar*. And the men who are nearest in kinship to the sons of the killed man's brothers shall also receive thirteen *aurar*.

And if women who are children of the killed man's brothers outlive him and they have sons, then their sons receive one *ertog* and six *aurar*. But if women who outlive the killed man are children of his sisters or his brothers, and they have sons, then their sons receive five *aurar*.

And the men who are in the fourth degree of kinship on the male side and those who are in the third degree on the female side, counted from brothers and sisters, receive one *ertog* and five *aurar*.

And the man in the fifth degree on the male side and the man in the fourth degree on the female side, they receive ten *ertogar* each.

And those who are in the sixth degree on the male side and the fifth degree on the female side, they receive two *aurar* each. And the man in the sixth degree on the female side (each receives) four *ertogar*.

Everyone shall receive as much of the compensation from the one who is in the same degree of kinship (to the killer) as the compensation (he has to) pay to one in the same degree of kinship (to the killed man). Whenever compensation is paid to the father it is also paid to his son, except when the killed man's paternal uncle and his sons, and the sons of his father's brother, (are living), then each of them receives his own compensation, and likewise the killer's paternal uncles and their sons have to pay with him the same amount as those receive who are in the same degree of kinship to the killed man. But as soon as the paternal uncle has passed away his sons receive a single compensation and have to pay in the same way.

But whenever daughters outlive the one who should receive or pay wergild and they (the daughters) have sons, then these sons must pay or receive compensation according to calculation.

And whoever withholds money he has to pay in wergild or claims larger compensation than he is entitled to and this leads to difficulties,[5] then he is called a violator of a peace pledge.

## 317 How five *merkr* of gold shall be divided

This is what he shall have who is known as the son of the killed man and receives wergild, if (a compensation of) five *merkr* of gold is imposed for the one who is killed and those five *merkr* include compensation and rings[6] and all money paid as compensation, then the son of the killed man receives ten *merkr*, weighed. And the brother of the killed man five *merkr*, weighed. And his father's brother, if he is living, and his sons, (receive) one *eyrir* and three and a half *merkr* and six and a third *penningar*. And if a father's brother has passed away but his sons are living, first cousins of the killed man, then they receive seven *penningar* and eighteen *aurar*. And if a father's brother is living but has no children, then he receives six and a half *penningar* and eleven *aurar*.

And if he has daughters but no sons and they (the daughters) are younger than forty when the wergild is paid, then the father's brother takes one *ertog* less than seven *aurar* on behalf of his daughters' sons. And if he has no children except an illegitimate son he receives that amount, one *ertog* less than seven *aurar*, which the sons of daughters would normally receive.

But if all (these) are living, a daughter's legitimate sons and an illegitimate son and legitimate sons, then the illegitimate son is counted with his brothers in stipulation of the compensation,[7] and in addition to their compensation he receives six and a half *penningar* less than half a *mǫrk*, weighed. And if they (the daughters) die childless this compensation reverts to the one who receives the wergild.

And if the father of the killed man is living and his son receives the wergild, then he (the father) shall have twenty *aurar*. But if he is not living, then this compensation reverts to the one who receives the wergild.

5 I.e. in case no agreement is reached and someone takes revenge.

6 See note 3.

7 See note 4.

And if a father's brother of the same mother is living and a brother of the same mother, then this brother of the same mother receives ten *aurar*, and the father's brother of the same mother, five *aurar*. And if neither of them can be found, or one of them is wanting, then this compensation reverts to the one who receives the wergild. What these men receive altogether amounts to a total of one *ertog* less than twenty-two and a half *merkr*.

And if the man who was killed had a stepson or a stepfather, then the one who receives the wergild has to pay ten *aurar*, weighed, to each of them out of the total just given. And if there are such kinsmen by marriage that each is married to the sister of the other, then the one who receives the wergild must pay ten *aurar* to each of them. But if their kinship rests on one marriage only, he must pay five *aurar*.

And if the killed man is outlived by both his mother's father and his daughter's son, then they receive one *eyrir* and three *merkr*, weighed, of the wergild, (that makes) twelve and a half *aurar* to each of them. But if one of them is wanting, or both, then this compensation reverts to the one who receives the wergild. And if the killed man is outlived by both a mother's brother and a sister's son, then each of them receives ten *aurar*.

Now, if the killed man is outlived by a son of a paternal uncle's son and by a son of his father's paternal uncle, then they receive one *ertog* and eighteen *aurar*, half an *ertog* and nine *aurar* each. And if one of them is wanting, or both, then this compensation reverts to the one who receives the wergild. And if the killed man is outlived by a father's sister and she has sons, then they receive three *penningar* and seven and a half *aurar*. And if the killed man is outlived by a mother's brother and he has sons, then these sons receive six and a half *penningar* less than seven and a half *aurar*; and the sons of his sisters one *ertog* less than seven *aurar*. And if the killed man is outlived by a son of his brother's daughter, then he receives half an *ertog* and ten *aurar*. And the men who are nearest in kinship to the killed man's brothers' sons also receive half an *ertog* and ten *aurar*.

And if women who are daughters of the killed man's brothers outlive him and they have sons, then these sons receive three *penningar* and five *aurar*. But if the women who outlive the killed man are children of brothers and sisters and they have sons, then these sons receive half an *ertog* and half a *mǫrk*.

And the men who are in the fourth degree of kinship on the male side and those who are in the third degree on the female side, counted from brothers and sisters, receive thirteen *penningar* and half a *mǫrk*.

And the man in the fifth degree on the male side and the man in the fourth degree on the female side, they receive not quite seven *penningar* and eight *ertogar*.

And the man in the sixth degree on the male side and the man in the fifth degree on the female side, they receive five *ertogar* each.

And the man in the sixth degree on the female side (receives) six and a half *penningar* and one *eyrir*.

Everyone shall receive as much of the wergild from the one (who is) in the same degree of kinship (to the killer) as the compensation (he has to) pay to one in the same degree of kinship (to the killed man). Whenever compensation is paid to a father it is also paid to his son, except when the killed man's paternal uncle and his sons and their sons (are living), then each of them receives his own compensation, and likewise the killer's paternal uncles and their sons have to pay with him the same amounts as are received by those (who are) in (the same degree of) kinship to the killed man. But as soon as the paternal uncle has passed away his sons receive a single compensation and have to pay in the same way. And whenever daughters outlive the one who should receive or pay the wergild and they (the daughters) have sons, then these sons must pay or receive compensation according to a calculation.

And whoever withholds money he has to pay in wergild or claims larger compensation than he is entitled to and this leads to difficulties,[8] then he is called a violator of a peace pledge.

## 318 How four *merkr* of gold shall be divided among the kinsmen

This is what he shall have who is known as the son of the killed man and receives wergild, if (a compensation of) four *merkr* of gold is imposed for the one who is killed and those four *merkr* include compensation and rings[9] and all money paid as compensation, then the son of the killed man shall receive eight *merkr*, weighed. And the brother of the killed man four *merkr*, weighed. And his father's brother, if he is living, and his sons (receive) seven *penningar* less than three *merkr*. And if a father's brother has passed away but his sons are living, first cousins of the killed man, then they shall have thirteen and a half *penningar* less than fifteen *aurar*, weighed. And if a father's brother is living but has no children, then he receives half an *ertog* less than nine *aurar*.

And if he has daughters but no sons and they are younger than forty when the wergild is paid, then the father's brother receives one *ertog* and five *aurar* on behalf of his daughters' sons. And if he has no children except an illegitimate son, then he (this son) receives that amount, one *ertog* and five *aurar*, which his daughters' sons would (normally) receive.

But if all (these) are living, a daughter's legitimate sons and an illegitimate son and legitimate sons, then the illegitimate son is counted with his brothers in stipulation of the compensation,[10] and in addition to their share in the compensation he receives one *penningr* less than ten *ertogar*. And if they (the daughters) die childless this compensation reverts to the one who receives the wergild.

And if the father of the killed man is living and his son receives the wergild, then he (the father) shall have two *merkr* weighed. But if he is not living, then this compensation reverts to the one who receives the wergild.

8 See note 5.
9 See note 3.
10 See note 4.

And if a father's brother of the same mother is living and a brother of the same mother, then the brother of the same mother receives one *mǫrk* and father's brother of the same mother half a *mǫrk*. And if neither of these can be found, or one of them is wanting, then this compensation reverts to the one who receives the wergild. What these men receive altogether amounts to a total of four *penningar* less than eighteen *merkr*.

And if the man who was killed had a stepson or a stepfather, then the one who receives the wergild has to pay one *mǫrk* to each of them out of the total just given. And if there are such kinsmen by marriage that each is married to the sister of the other, then the one who receives the wergild has to pay them one *mǫrk* out of this compensation. But if their kinship rests on one marriage only, he must pay half a *mǫrk*.

And if the killed man is outlived by both his mother's father and his daughter's son, then they receive twenty *aurar*, (that makes) ten *aurar* to each of them. But if one of them is wanting, or both, then this compensation reverts to the one who receives the wergild. And if the killed man is outlived by both his mother's brother and a sister's son, then each of them receives one *mǫrk*.

And if the killed man is outlived by a son of a paternal uncle's son, and by a son of his father's paternal uncle, then they receive one *ertog* less than fifteen *aurar*, half of it to each of them. But if one of them is wanting, or both, then this compensation reverts to the one who receives the wergild. And if the killed man is outlived by a father's sister and she has sons, then these sons receive six *aurar*. And if the killed man is outlived by a mother's brother and he has sons, then these sons receive one odd *penningr* less than six *aurar*; and the sons of the sisters (of the deceased receive) one *ertog* and five *aurar*. And if the killed man is outlived by a son of his brother's daughter he receives eight *penningar* and one *mǫrk*. And the men who are nearest in kinship to the father's (the killed man's) brothers' sons also receive eight *penningar* and one *mǫrk*.

And if women who are daughters of the brothers of the killed man outlive him and they have sons, then these sons receive half a *penningr* and half a *mǫrk*. But if the women who outlive the killed man are the children of brothers and sisters and they have sons, then these sons receive ten *ertogar*.

And the men who are in the fourth degree of kinship on the male side and those who are in the third degree on the female side, counted from brothers and sisters, receive half a *penningr* and ten *ertogar* each.

And the man in the fifth degree on the male side and the man in the fourth degree on the female side, they receive three and a half *penningar* and six and a half *ertogar* each.

And the man in the sixth degree on the male side and the man in the fifth degree on the female side, they receive four *ertogar* each.

And the man in the sixth degree on the female side (receives) nine *penningar* and two *ertogar*.

Everyone shall receive as much of the wergild from the one (who is) in the same degree of kinship (to the killer) as the compensation (he has to) pay to the one in the same degree of kinship (to the killed man). Whenever compensation is paid to the father it is also paid to the son, except when the killed man's paternal uncle and his sons and their sons (are living), then each of them receives his own compensation, and likewise the killer's paternal uncles and their sons must pay with him such amounts as are received by those (who are) in the same degree of kinship to the killed man. But as soon as the father's brother has passed away his sons receive a single compensation and have to pay in the same way. And whenever daughters outlive the one who should receive or pay the wergild and they (the daughters) have sons, then these sons must pay or receive compensation according to a calculation.

And whoever withholds money he has to pay in wergild or claims larger compensation than he is entitled to and this leads to difficulties,[11] then he is called a violator of a peace pledge.

## 319 How three *merkr* of gold shall be divided

This is what he shall have who is the son of the killed man and receives wergild, if (a compensation of) three *merkr* of gold is imposed for the one who is killed and those three *merkr* include compensation and rings[12] and all money paid as compensation, then the son of the killed man receives six *merkr*, weighed. And the brother of the killed man three *merkr*, weighed. And his father's brother, if he is living, four *ertogar* and two *merkr*, weighed. And if the father's brother is deceased but his sons, first cousins of the killed man, are living, then they receive one *ertog* less than eleven *aurar*. And if a father's brother is living but has no children, then he receives one *ertog* less than seven *aurar*, weighed.

And if he has daughters but no sons, and they are younger than forty when the wergild is paid, then the father's brother receives half a *mǫrk* on behalf of his daughters' sons. And if he has no children except an illegitimate son, then he (this son) receives that half *mǫrk* which his daughters' sons would (normally) receive.

And if all (these) are alive, a daughter's legitimate sons and an illegitimate son and legitimate sons, then the illegitimate son is counted with his brothers in stipulation of the compensation,[13] and in addition to their share in the compensation he receives seven *ertogar*, weighed. And if they (the daughters) die childless, then these seven *ertogar* revert to the one who receives the wergild.

And if the father of the killed man is living and his son receives the wergild, then he (the father) shall have twelve *aurar*, weighed. But if he is not living, then this compensation reverts to the one who receives the wergild.

And if a father's brother of the same mother is living and a brother of the same mother, then the brother of the same mother receives six *aurar* and the father's brother of the same mother three *aurar*. And if neither of these can be found, or one of them is wanting, then this compensation reverts to the one who receives

11 See note 5.
12 See note 3.
13 See note 4.

the wergild. What these men receive altogether amounts to a total of one *eyrir* and thirteen and a half *merkr*.

And if the man who was killed had a stepson or a stepfather, then the one who receives the wergild has to pay each of them six *aurar*, weighed, out of the total just given. And if there are such kinsmen by marriage that each is married to the sister of the other, then the one who receives the wergild must pay them six *aurar*. But if their kinship rests on one marriage only, he must pay three *aurar*.

And if the killed man is outlived by both his mother's father and his daughter's son, then they receive from the wergild fifteen *aurar*, weighed, (that makes) seven and a half *aurar* to each of them. But if one of them is wanting, or both, then this compensation reverts to the one who receives the wergild. And if the killed man is outlived by both his mother's brother and a sister's son, then each of them receives six *aurar*.

Now, if the killed man is outlived by a son of a paternal uncle's son and by a son of his father's paternal uncle, then they receive eleven *aurar*, five and a half *aurar* each. But if one of them is wanting, or both, then this compensation reverts to the one who receives the wergild. And if the killed man is outlived by a father's sister and she has sons, then they receive one *ertog* less than five *aurar*. And if the killed man is outlived by a mother's brother and he has sons, then these sons receive thirteen *ertogar*, and the sons of his sisters (receive) half a *mǫrk*. And if a son of his brother's daughter outlives the killed man, then he receives six and a half *aurar*. And the men who are nearest in kinship to the (killed man's) brothers' sons also receive six and a half *aurar*.

And if women who are daughters of the killed man's brothers outlive him and they have sons, then these sons receive nine and a half *ertogar*. But if the women who outlive the killed man are the children of brothers and sisters and they have sons, then these sons receive two and a half *aurar*.

And the men who are in the fourth degree of kinship on the male side and those who are in the third degree on the female side, counted from brothers and sisters, receive eight *ertogar* each.

And the man in the fifth degree on the male side and the man in the fourth degree on the female side, they receive five *ertogar* each.

And the man in the sixth degree on the male side and in the fifth degree on the female side, they receive one *eyrir* each.

And the man in the sixth degree on the female side (each receives) two *ertogar*.

Everyone shall receive as much of the wergild from the one (who is) in the same degree of kinship (to the killer) as the compensation he has to pay to the one in the same degree of kinship (to the killed man). Whenever compensation is paid to the father it is also paid to the son, except when the killed man's paternal uncle and his sons and their sons (are living), then each of them receives his own compensation, and likewise the killer's paternal uncles and their sons must pay with him such amounts as are received by those (who are) in the same degree of kinship to the killed man. But as soon as the father's brother has passed away his sons receive a single compensation and have to pay in the same way. And whenever daughters outlive the one who should receive or pay the wergild and they (the daughters) have sons, then these sons must pay or receive compensation according to a calculation.

And whoever withholds money he has to pay in wergild or claims larger compensation than he is entitled to and this leads to difficulties,[14] then he is called a violator of a peace pledge.

14 See note 5.

# XV Peace pledge

## 320 H(ere begins the) peace pledge

There were causes of dispute between N. and N., but now cases are concluded and compensation paid with money of full value and delivered into the hands of him who should have it, according to what judges judged, assessors assessed, estimators estimated, investigators investigated . . .[1]

1 Our text ends here. Different versions of the entire formulary can be found in the Icelandic law *Grágás* (ed. 1992, 281, 283, 457–8) and in some Old Icelandic sagas (*Heiðarvíga saga,* Ch. 33, and *Grettis saga,* Ch. 72). Knudsen 1960, 564; Sunde 2007, 306–14, 311, note 25.

# Bibliography

*Ágrip af Nóregskonunga sǫgum* 1984. Ed. Bjarni Einarsson. (*ÍF* 29). Reykjavík: Hið íslenzka fornritafélag.

Andersen, Per Sveås 1972. 'Syssel'. *KLNM* 17, 645–8.

B = Borgartings eldre kristenrett.

Bagge, Sverre 2010. *From Viking Stronghold to Christian Kingdom. State Formation in Norway c. 900–1350*. Copenhagen: Tusculanum.

——— 2011. 'The Ordeal in Norwegian Law and Practice'. In *Liber Amicorum Ditlev Tamm. Law, History and Culture*. Ed. P. Andersen et al., 55–69. Copenhagen: DJØF Publishing.

Bagge, Sverre et al. 1973. *Norsle middelalderdokumenter*. Oslo: Universitetsforlaget.

Bartlett, Robert 1986. *Trial by Fire and Water: The Medieval Judicial Ordeal*. Oxford: Clarendon Press.

Berger, Peter L. 1969. *The Sacred Canopy: Elements of a Sociological Theory of Religion*. New York: Doubleday.

Birkeli, Fridtjov 1995. *Tolv vintrer hadde kristendommen vært i Norge*. Oslo: Verbum.

Bjørkvik, Halvard and Jansson, Sam O. 1972. 'Såld'. *KLNM* 17, 671–3.

Bø, Olav 1961. 'Holmgang'. *KLNM* 6, 653–6.

Bøe, Arne 1964. 'Kristenrettar'. *KLNM* 9, 297–304.

*The* Borgarþing *Law* see Halvorsen and Rindal 2008a.

*Borgfirðinga sǫgur, . . ., Heiðarvíga saga* 1938. Ed. Sigurður Nordal and Guðni Jónsson. (*ÍF* 3). Reykjavík: Hið íslenzka fornritafélag.

Brundage, James 1990. *Law, Sex, and Christian Society in Medieval Europe*. Chicago: Chicago University Press.

*The Christian Theology Reader* 2007. Ed. Alister E. McGrath, 3rd edn. Oxford: Blackwell Publishing (1st edn. 1995).

*Corpus Iuris Canonici I. Decretum magistri Gratiani. II. Decretalium Collectiones* 1879/1959. Ed. Aemilius Friedberg. Leipzig/Graz: Akademische Druck- und Verlagsanstalt.

Corráin, Donnchadh Ó., Breatnach, Liam, and Breen, Aidan 1984. 'The Laws of the Irish'. *Peritia* 3, 382–438.

Crumlin-Pedersen, Ole 1997. *Viking-Age Ships and Shipbuilding in Hedeby/Haithabu and Schleswig*. Ships & Boats of the North, vol. 2. Roskilde/Schleswig: Archäologisches Landesmuseum der Christian-Albrechts-Universität.

——— 2002: *The Skuldelev Ships I. Topography, Archaeology, History, Conservation and Display*. Ships & Boats of the North, vol. 4.1. Roskilde: The Viking Ship Museum in Roskilde & Centre for Maritime Archaeology of the National Museum of Denmark.

*Den ældre Frostathings-Lov* 1846. Ed. Rudolf Keyser and Peter Andreas Munch. (*NGL* I, 119–258). Christiania. (References to section and chapter).

*Den ældre Gulathings-Lov* 1846. Ed. Rudolf Keyser and Peter Andreas Munch. (*NGL* I, 1–118). Christiania.

*Den eldre Gulatingslova* 1994. Ed. Bjørn Eithun, Magnus Rindal, and Tor Ulset. Norrøne tekster, nr. 6. Oslo: Riksarkivet.

*Den eldre Gulatingsloven* 1995. Ed. Finn Hødnebø and Magnus Rindal. Corpus codicum Norvegicorum medii aevi, Quarto series, vol. IX (facs. ed.). Oslo: Selskapet til utgivelse av gamle norske håndskrifter.

*Die Briefe des heiligen Bonifatius und Lullus* 1955. Ed. Michael Tangl, 2nd edn. Berlin: Weidemann (1st edn. 1916).

*Die Gesetze der Angelsachsen* 2007. Ed. Felix Liebermann. Halle: Max Niemeyer, 1906/ Clark, NJ: The Lawbook Exchange.

*DMA* = *Dictionary of the Middle Ages* 1982–9. Ed. Joseph R. Strayer. 13 vols. New York: Scribner.

*DN* = *Diplomatarium Norvegicum* 1849. Christiania/Oslo.

Douglas, Mary 1996/2002. *Purity and Danger: An Analysis of Concepts of Pollution and Taboo*. London: Routledge.

——— 2002. *Leviticus as Literature*. Oxford: Oxford University Press.

E = Eidsivatings eldre kristenrett.

Eckhardt, Karl A. 1927. *Die Lex Baiovariorum: eine textkritische Studie*. Untersuchungen zur deutschen Staats- und Rechtsgeschichte, vol. 138. Breslau: M. & H. Marcus.

*Egils saga Skallagrímssonar* 1933. Ed. Sigurður Nordal. (*ÍF* 2). Reykjavík: Hið íslenzka fornritafélag.

Ehrmann, Arnost Zvi 2007. 'Sotah'. In *Encyclopaedia Judaica*. Ed. by F. Skolnik and M. Berenbaum, 2nd edn., vol. 19, 32–3. Detroit: Macmillan Reference USA in association with the Keter Publishing House.

The *Eiðsivaþing* Law see Halvorsen and Rindal 2008b.

F = *Den ældre Frostathings-Lov.*

*Fagrskinna – Nóregs konunga tal* 1984. Ed. Bjarni Einarsson. (*ÍF* 29). Reykjavík: Hið íslenzka fornritafélag.

Foot, Sarah 2011. *Aethelstan: The First King of England.* New Haven, CT: Yale University Press.

Foote, Peter 1988. 'Scandinavia: Political and Legal Organisation'. *DMA* 10, 698–706.

Freisen, Joseph 1893/1963. *Geschichte des canonischen Eherechts bis zum Verfall der Glossenliteratur*. Paderborn/Aalen: Scientia Verlag.

Frimannslund, Rigmor 1959. 'Festermål. *Norge*'. *KLNM* 4, 233–6.

——— 1975. 'Tyende. *Norge*'. *KLNM* 19, 107–10.

G = *Den eldre Gulatingslova.*

*Gjør døren høy: Kirken i Norge 1000 år* 1995. Ed. Torstein Jørgensen et al. Oslo: Aschehoug.

*Grágás. Lagasafn íslenska þjóðveldisins* 1992. Ed. Gunnar Karlsson, Kristján Sveinsson, and Mörður Árnason. Reykjavík: Mál og menning.

*Grettis saga Ásmundarsonar* 1936. Ed. Guðni Jónsson. (*ÍF* 7). Reykjavík: Hið íslenzka fornritafélag.

*Guta lag. The Law of the Gotlanders* 2015. Ed. and tr. Christine I. Peel. London/New York: Routledge.

Halvorsen, Eyvind Fjeld and Rindal, Magnus 2008a. 'Borgartings eldre kristenrett'. In *De eldste østlandske kristenrettene*. Norrøne tekster, nr. 7. Oslo: Riksarkivet, 2008. (References to version and chapter).

Halvorsen, Eyvind Fjeld and Rindal, Magnus 2008b. 'Eidsivatings eldre kristenrett'. In *De eldste østlandske kristenrettene*. Norrøne tekster, nr. 7. Oslo: Riksarkivet (References to version and chapter).

Hamre, Lars 1971. 'Skøyting'. *KLNM* 16, 155–64.

——— 2003. 'Ein diplomatisk og rettshistorisk analyse av Sættargjerda i Tunsberg'. *Historisk Tidsskrift* 83, 381–431.

Hardinge, Leslie 1972. *The Celtic Church in Britain*. London: S. P. C. K. For the Church Historical Society.

*Heimskringla*. 3 vols. Ed. Bjarni Aðalbjarnarson. (*ÍF* 26–28). Reykjavík: Hið íslenzka fornritafélag, 1941–51.

*Heiðarvíga saga*. Ed. Sigurður Nordal and Guðni Jónsson. (*ÍF* 3). Reykjavík: Hið íslenzka fornritafélag, 1938.

Helle, Knut 2001. *Gulatinget og Gulatingslova*. Leikanger: Skald.

Hertzberg, Ebbe 1895. 'Glossarium'. *NGL* 5, 59–834.

*History of the Archbishops of Hamburg-Bremen: Adam of Bremen* 2002. Tr. Francis J. Tschan. New introduction by Timothy Reuter. New York: Columbia University Press.

Hoch, Klaus 1999. 'Eid. I. Religionswissenschaftlich'. In *Religion in Geschichte und Gegenwart*, vol, 2, cols 1121–2. Tübingen: Mohr Siebeck.

Hødnebø, Finn see *Den eldre Gulatingsloven.*

Huber, Wolfgang 1983. 'Frieden V: Kirchengeschichtlich und ethisch'. In *Theologische Realenzyklopädie*, vol. 11, 618–46. Berlin/New York: W. de Gruyter.

*ÍF* = *Íslenzk fornrit* 1933–. Reykjavík: Hið íslenzka fornritafélag.

*Íslendingabók* 1968. Ed. Jakob Benediktsson. (*ÍF* 1[1]). Reykjavík: Hið íslenzka fornritafélag.

Iversen, Tore 1997. *Trelldommen. Norsk slaveri i middelalderen*. Bergen: Historisk institutt, Universitetet i Bergen. Skrifter 1.

——— 2001. 'Jordeie og jordleie – Eiendomsbegrepet i norske middelalderlover'. *Collegium Medievale* 14, 79–114.

Jacoby, Michael 1986. Germanisches *Recht und Rechtssprache zwischen Mittelalter und Neuzeit unter besonderer Berücksichtigung des skandinavischen Rechts: Gegenthese zu J. Grimm und zu romantischer Auffassung im 20. Jahrhundert. Lexemdistribution und Lexemverhalten in Textsorten und Dialekten innerhalb historischer Sprachstufen*, Band I. New York: P. Lang.

Jakob Benediktsson 1975. 'Ulfljótslǫg'. *KLNM* 19, 274–5.

Jochens, Jenny 1995. *Women in Old Norse Society*. Ithaca, NY: Cornell University Press.

Jón Viðar Sigurðsson et al. 2008. 'Making and Using the Law in the North, c. 900–1350'. In *Making, Using and Resisting the Law in European History*. Ed. G. Lottes et al., 37–60. Pisa: PLUS-Pisa University Press.

Jørgensen, Torstein 2013a. ' "He Grabbed His Axe and Gave Thore a Blow to His Head": Late Medieval Clerical Violence in Norway as Treated According to Canon and Civil Law'. In *Medieval Christianity in the North. New Studies*. Ed. K. Salonen et al., 209–36. Turnhout, Belgium: Brepols.

——— 2013b. 'Insiders and Outsiders: Theological Landscaping'. In *Sacred Sites and Holy Places: Exploring the Sacralization of landscape through Time and Space*. Ed. S. W. Nordeide and S. Brink, 240–2. Turnhout, Belgium: Brepols.

——— 2014. 'Civil and Clerical Homicide in Late Medieval Norway'. In *New Approaches to Early Law in Scandinavia*. Ed. S. Brink and L. Collinson, 67 – 87. Turnhout, Belgium: Brepols.

Jørgensen, Torstein and Saletnich, Gastone 2004. *Synder og pavemakt. Botsbrev fra Den Norske Kirkeprovins og Suderøyene til Pavestolen 1438–1531. Diplomatarium poenitentiariae Norvegicum*. Stavanger: Misjonshøgskolens forlag.

Klinger, Elmar 1987. 'Vows and Oaths'. In *The Encyclopedia of Religion*, vol. 15, 301–5. New York: Macmillan/London: Collier Macmillan.

*KLNM* = *Kulturhistorisk leksikon for nordisk middelalder fra vikingtid til reformasjonstid* 1956–78. Ed. Finn Hødnebø et al., 22 vols. Oslo: Gyldendal norsk forlag.

Knirk, James 2017. 'Kuli-steinen og landsnamnet *Noreg*'. *Namn og nemne. Tidsskrift for norsk namnegransking* 34, 93–8.

Knudsen, Trygve 1960. 'Gulatingsloven'. *KLNM* 5, 559–65.

Kolsrud, Oluf 1958. *Noregs kyrkjesoga: 1: Millomalderen*. Oslo: Aschehoug.

Kværness, Gunhild 1996. *Blote kan ein gjere om det berre skjer i løynd. Kristenrettane i Gulatingslova og Grágás og forholdet mellom dei*. KULTs skriftsserie nr. 65. Oslo: Noregs forskingsråd.

Landau, Peter 1982. 'Eid, V; Historisch'. In *Theologische Realenzyklopädie*, vol. 9, 382–91. Berlin/New York: W. de Gruyter.

Landro, Torgeir 2010. *Kristenrett og kyrkjerett. Borgartingskristenretten i eit komparativt perspektiv*. Avhandling for graden philosophiae doctor (PhD) ved Universitetet i Bergen, Bergen.

Larson, Laurence M. (tr.) 1935. *The Earliest Norwegian Laws, Being the Gulathing Law and the Frostathing Law*. New York: Columba University Press.

*The Laws of the Earliest English Kings* 1922/63. Ed. and tr. Frederick L. Attenborough. New York: Russell & Russell.

*The Laws of the Kings of England from Edmund to Henry I* 1925/2009. Ed. and tr. Agnes J. Robertson. Cambridge: Cambridge University Press.

Lid, Nils 1957. 'Bryde. *Norge*'. *KLNM* 2, 272.

Logan, F. Donald 1984. 'Excommunication'. *DMA* 4, 536–8.

Lynch, Charles H. 1938. *Saint Braulio of Saragossa, Bishop of Saragossa (631–651), His Life and Writings*. Washington, DC: The Catholic University of America.

Lynch, Joseph H. 1998. *Christianizing Kinship – Ritual Sponsorship in Anglo-Saxon England*. Ithaca, NY: Cornell University Press.

Magnús Már Lárusson 1967. 'Månadsnamn. *Island-Norge*'. *KLNM* 12, 130–2.

Matthiessen, Carl C. 1962. 'Husdyrsygdomme'. *KLNM* 7, 124–34.

Meissner, Rudolf (tr.) 1935. *Das Rechtsbuch des Gulathings*. Germanenrechte, Band 6, Norwegisches Recht. Weimar: H. Böhlaus Nachf.

Migne, Jacques-Paul 2006. *Patrologia Graeca et Cetera Graeca Scripta*. Rome: Cooperatorum Veritatis Societas.

Migne, Jacques-Paul 2007. 'Hippolytus, de antichristo'. In *Patrologia Graeca*, vol. 10, 777C–779A. Tr. into English from *The Christian Theology Reader*. Ed. Alister E. McGrath, 3rd edn. Oxford: Blackwell Publishing.

Moilanen, Inka 2011. *Writing the Order: Religious-Political Discourses in Late Anglo-Saxon England*. Avhandling for graden philosophiae doctor (PhD) ved Universitetet i Bergen, Bergen.

Moseng, Ole Georg, Opsahl, Erik, Pettersen, Gunnar I., and Sandmo, Erling 1999. *Norsk historie*, vol. I, 750–1537. Oslo: Tano Aschehoug.

Nedkvitne, Arnved 2011. *Ære, lov og religion i Norge gjennom tusen år*. Oslo: Scandinavian Academic Press/Spartacus Forlag.

*New Catholic Encyclopedia* 2003. Ed. Berard L. Marthaler et al., 2nd edn. 14 vols. Detroit: Gale, in association with the Catholic University of America.

*NGL* = *Norges gamle Love indtil 1387* 1846–95. Ed. Rudolf Keyser and Peter Andreas Munch. 5 vols. Christiania.

Nilsson, Bertil 2001. 'Gudsdomar i Skandinavien under vikingatid och medeltid'. In *Kontinuitäten und Brüche in der Religionsgeschichte. Festschrift für Anders Hultgård zu seinem 65. Geburtstag am 23.12.2001*. Ed. M. Stausberg et al., 503–35. Ergänzungsbände zum Reallexikon der Germanischen Altertumskunde, Band 31. Berlin/New York: W. de Gruyter.

*NK* = *Nordisk kultur* 1931–56. 32 vols. Stockholm: Bonnier.

Nordby, Ole-Albert Rönning 2018. *The Judicial Oath in Medieval Norway. Compurgation, Community and Knowledge in the Thirteenth Century*. Dissertation for the Degree of Philosophiae Doctor. Department of Archaeology, Conservation and History, Oslo.

Noreen, Adolf 1970. *Altnordische Grammatik I. Altisländische und altnorwegische Grammatik (Laut- und Flexionslehre) unter Berücksichtigung des Urnordischen*, 5th edn. Tübingen: Niemeyer.

Olav den helliges saga 1979. 'Finn Hødnebø and Hallvard Magerøy'. In *Norges kongesagaer*. Ed. Snorre Sturluson and Første del Kongesagaer, vol. 1, 207–344. Oslo: Gyldendal Norsk Forlag.

Orrman, Elias 2003. 'Church and Society'. In *Cambridge History of Scandinavia I. Prehistory to 1520*. Ed. K. Helle, 421–62. Cambridge: Cambridge University Press.

Paus, Hans 1751. *Samling af Gamle Norske Love*, vol. I. Copenhagen.

Pernler, Sven-Erik 1984. 'De svenska kyrkobalkarnas inledningsord [The Prefaces of the Swedish Ecclesiastical Codes]'. In *Kyrkohistorisk årsskrift 1984*. Ed. I. Montgomery. Publications of the Swedish Society of Church History, vol. 1:84, 61–99. Uppsala: Almquist & Wiksell.

Plöchl, Willibald M. 1962. *Geschichte des Kirchenrechts. Vol. 2: Das Kirchenrecht der abendländischen Christenheit: 1055 bis 1517*, 2nd edn. Wien: Verlag Herold.

Radding, Charles M. 1989. 'Wergild'. *DMA* 12, 617–18.

*RGA* = *Reallexikon der Germanischen Altertumskunde* 1973–2007 and 2008. Ed. Heinrich Beck et al., 35 vols. Register. 2 vols. Berlin/New York: W. de Gruyter.

Richards, Jeffrey 1992. *Sex, Dissidence and Damnation: Minority Groups in the Middle Ages*. London/New York: Routledge.

Rieber, Ernst 1949. *Die Bedeutung alttestamentlicher Vorstellungen für das Herrscherbild Karls des Grossen und seines Hofkreises*. Dissertation (unpublished manuscript), University of Tübingen, Tübingen.

Riisøy, Anne Irene 2004. *Stat og kirke: rettsutøvelsen i kristenrettssaker mellom Sættargjerden og reformasjonen*. Publikasjoner fra Tingbokprosjektet, 22. Oslo: University of Oslo.

——— 2014. 'Outlawry: From Western Norway to England'. In *New Approaches to Early Law in Scandinavia*. Ed. S. Brink, 101–29. Turnhout, Belgium: Brepols.

——— 2019. 'Ting og konfliktløsning i vikingtidas Norge'. *Collegium Medievale* 32 (2), 11–30.

Rindal, Magnus see *Den eldre Gulatingslova, Den eldre Gulatingsloven.*

Robberstad, Knut 1967. 'Odelsrett. *Noreg*'. *KLNM* 12, 493–9.

——— (tr.) 1981. *Gulatingslovi. Umsett av Knut Robberstad*, 4th edn. Norrøne bokverk, 33. Oslo: Det Norske Samlaget.

Ruthström, Bo 2002. 'Nordic language history and legal history'. In *The Nordic Languages. An International Handbook of the History of the North Germanic Languages*, vol. 1, 344–54. Handbücher zur Sprach- und Kommunikationswissenschaft, 22.1. Berlin/New York: W. de Gruyter.

Sägmüller, Johannes B. 1914. *Lehrbuch des katholischen Kirchenrechts,* vol. 2, 3rd edn. Freiburg i. B.: Herdersche Verlagshandlung.

Salisbury, Joyce E. 1994. *The Beast Within: Animals in the Middle Ages*. London/New York: Routledge.

Salonen, Kirsi 2013. 'Forbidden Marital Strategies: Papal Marriage Dispensations for Scandinavian Couples in the Later Middle Ages'. In *Medieval Christianity in the North. New Studies*. Ed. K. Salonen et al., 181–208. Turnhout, Belgium: Brepols.

Sandvik, Gudmund 1986. 'Sættargjerda i Tunsberg og kongens jurisdiksjon'. In *Samfunn, rett, rettferdighet: festskrift til Torstein Eckhoffs 70-årsdag*. Ed. A. Bratholm et al., 563–85. Oslo: Tano.

Sanmark, Alexandra 2004. *Power and Conversion. A Comparative Study of Christianization in Scandinavia*. Occasional Papers in Archaeology, 34. Uppsala: Department of Archaeology and Ancient History, Uppsala University.

——— 2005. 'Dietary Regulations in Early Christian Norway'. *Viking and Medieval Scandinavia* I, 203–24.

Schmugge, Ludwig et al. 1996. *Die Supplikenregister der päpstlichen Pönitentiarie aus der Zeit Pius 'II: (1458–1464)*. Bibliothek des Deutschen Historischen Instituts in Rom, vol. 84. Tübingen: Niemeyer.

Schneider, Reinhold 1978. 'Karl der Grosse – politisches Sendungsbewusstsein und Mission'. In *Kirchengeschichte als Missionsgeschiche*. Ed. H. Frohnes et al. Erster Halbband: Die Kirche des früheren Mittelalters, vol. II, 227–48. Munich: Chr. Kaiser.

*A Select Library of the Nicene and Post-Nicene Fathers of the Christian Church* 1900. The Seven Ecumenical Councils. Ed. Philip Schaff and Henry Wace. 2. Series, vol. 14. New York: Christian Literature Publishing Co., Canon 52.

Seierstad, Andreas 1959. 'Excommunicatio og interdikt'. *KLNM* 4, 77–83.

Seip, Jens A. 1942. *Sættargjerden i Tunsberg og kirkens jurisdiksjon*. Oslo: Dybwad (komm.).

Seip, Jens A. and Sandvik, Gudmund (ed. and tr.) 1956. *Gammelnorske lovtekster med oversettelse*. Bergen/Oslo: Universitetsforlaget.

Sigurður Líndal 1969. 'Opprinnelsen til de første Islandske Lover'. *Tidsskrift for rettsvitenskap* 82, 467–89.

Skre, Dagfinn 1995. 'Kirken før sognet. Den tidligste kirkeordningen i Norge'. In *Møtet mellom hedendom og kristendom i Norge*. Ed. H.-E. Lidén, 170–233. Oslo: Universitetsforlaget.

Steinnes, Asgaut 1936. 'Mål, vekt og verderekning i Noreg i millomalderen og ei tid etter'. *NK* 30, 84–154.

Steinsland, Gro 2005. *Norrøn religion. Myter, riter, samfunn*. Oslo: Pax.

Steinsland, Gro and Sørensen, Preben Meulengracht 1994. *Menneske og makter i vikingenes verden*. Oslo: Universitetsforlaget.

Stigum, Hilmar 1957. 'Bur'. *KLNM* 2, 366–7.

——— 1958. 'Eldhus'. *KLNM* 3, 555–8.

——— 1962. 'Högsäte. *Norge*'. *KLNM* 7, 292–3.

——— 1969. 'Sal I'. *KLNM* 14, 676–7.

*Stjórn. Tekst etter håndskriftene* 2009. Del I og II. Ed. Reidar Astås. Norrøne tekster, nr. 8. Oslo: Riksarkivet.

Strauch, Dieter 1999. 'Gulaþingsbók'. *RGA* 13, 184–9.

——— 2008. 'Grundzüge des mittelalterlichen skandinavischen Sklavenrechts'. In *Von den Leges Barbarorum bis zum ius barbarum des Nationalsozialismus. Festschrift für Hermannn Nehlsen zum 70. Geburtstag*. Ed. H.-G. Hermann et al., 224–68. Köln: Böhlau Verlag.

——— 2011. *Mittelalterliches nordisches Recht bis 1500. Eine Quellenkunde*. Ergänzungsbände zum Reallexikon der Germanischen Altertumskunde, vol. 73. Berlin/New York: W. de Gruyter.

——— 2013. 'Rechtsbücher und Gesetzbücher im Norden (Laghman – Laghsaga – Lagh – Siðvæniæ)'. *Zeitschrift der Savigny-Stiftung für Rechtsgeschichte* 130, 37–77.

——— 2016. *Mittelalterliches nordisches Recht bis 1500. Eine Quellenkunde*. Ergänzungsbände zum Reallexikon der Germanischen Altertumskunde, vol. 97, 2nd edn. Berlin/Boston: W. de Gruyter.

Sunde, Jørn Øyrehagen 2006. 'Internasjonaliseringa av retten i mellomalderen som forskingsutfordring'. In *Rettstekstar i mellomalderen – Idé og praksis*. Ed. J. Ø. Sunde, 113–34. Rettshistoriske studier nr. 17. Institutt for offentlig retts skriftserie nr. 6/2006. Oslo.

——— 2007. '"De skal vera samde menn." Ei vitskapleg fundering og spekulasjon over den eldste norske prosessen'. In *De lege. Juridiska fakulteten i Uppsala Årsbok 2007. Eftersyn och eftertanke*. Ed. P. Asp, 305–22. Uppsala: Juridiska fakulteten i Uppsala.

——— 2011a. 'Fiende og frende på Gulating i mellomalderen'. In *Frå Gulatinget til Gulatings plass*. Ed. B. Solbakken, 52–69. Bergen: J. Grieg.

——— 2011b. 'Innovative Reception. Reception and Innovation Concerning Fixed Time Periods as a Criterion for the Acquisition and Loss of Rights in the *Gulating* Compilation'. In *Liber Amicorum Ditlev Tamm. Law, History and Culture*. Ed. P. Andersen et al., 217–29. Copenhagen: DJØF Publishing.

——— 2014. 'Daughters of God and Counsellors of the Judges of Men: Changes in the Legal Culture of the Norwegian Realm in the High Middle Ages'. In *New Approaches to Early Law in Scandinavia*. Ed. S. Brink and L. Collinson, 131–83. Turnhout, Belgium: Brepols.

——— 2019. 'Gulatingslova'. *Store norske leksikon*. https://snl.no/Gulatingslova.

Sundmark. Stina F. 2008. *Sjukbesök och dödsberedelse: sockenbudet i svensk medeltida och reformatorisk tradition*. Skellefteå: Artos.

Sundquist, Olof 2016. *An Arena for Higher Powers: Ceremonial Buildings and Religious Strategies for Rulership in Late Iron Age Scandinavia*. Numen Book Series, vol. 150. Leiden: Brill.

*Sverris saga* 2007. Ed. Þorleifur Hauksson (*ÍF* 30). Reykjavík: Hið íslenzka fornritafélag.

Tamm, Ditlev 2002. 'Gulatingsloven og de andre gamle nordiske landskabslove'. *Tidsskrift for rettsvitenskap* 1 (2), 292–308.

Tamm, Ditlev and Vogt, Helle 2005. *How Nordic are the Nordic Medieval Laws?* Medieval Legal History, vol. 1. Copenhagen: University of Copenhagen Press.

Taranger, Absalon 1890. *Den angelsaksiske kirkes indflydelse paa den norske*. Udgivet af Den norske historiske forening. Kristiania: Grøndahl & søns bogtrykkeri.

——— 1926. 'De norske folkelovbøker (før 1263)'. *Tidsskrift for retsvidenskap. Ny Række* V (39. aargang), 183–211.

Tveito, Olav 2004. *Ad fines orbis terrae. En studie i primær trosformidling i nordisk kristningskontekst*. Acta humaniora, 209. Dr. philos. Dissertation, University of Oslo, Unipub, Oslo.

†Vandvik, Eirik 1962. *Magnus Erlingssons privilegiebrev og kongevigsle*. Skrifter utgitt av Det Norske Videnskaps-Akademi i Oslo. II. Hist.-Filos. Klasse. Ny Serie. No. 1. Oslo: Universitetsforlaget.

Vogt, Helle 2010. 'The Function of Kinship in Medieval Nordic Legislation'. In *Medieval Law and its Practice*. Ed. J. Hudson et al., vol. 9. Leiden/Boston: Brill.

von den Steinen, Wolfram 1932. 'Karl der Grosse und die Libri Carolini'. In *Neues Archiv der Gesellschaft für ältere deutsche Geschichtskunde*. Ed. Gesellschaft für ältere deutsche Geschichtskunde, vol. 49, 207–80. Berlin: Weidmann.

Weigand, Rudolf 1994. 'Die Ausdehnung der Ehehindernisse der Verwandschaft'. *Zeitschrift der Savigny-Stiftung für Rechtsgeschichte: Kanonistische Abteilung* 80, 8–17.

Whitaker, Edward C. 1970. *Documents of the baptismal liturgy*. Revised edn. by M. E. Johnson 2003. London: Society for Promoting Christian Knowledge.

Wikman, K. R. V. 1957. 'Bröllop'. *KLNM* 2, 306–17.

Wisløff, Carl F. 1966. *Norsk kirkehistorie I*. Oslo: Lutherstiftelsen.

Wormald, Patrick 1999. *Legal Culture in the Early Medieval West: Law as Text, Image and Experience*. London: Hambledon Press.

Wührer, Karl 1966a. 'Manhelgd'. *KLNM* 11, 316–20.

——— 1966b. 'Mansbot. *Danmark*'. *KLNM* 11, 330–2.

# Glossary

**Agnate** (ON *bauggildismaðr*) A near kinsman on the father's side and in the male line. The agnate received the larger payments in the wergild (q. v.). The circle of agnates included relatives up to and including first cousins. See Robberstad 1981, 343.

**Ale feast** (ON *ǫl, ǫlgerð*) A social gathering so called because ale (ON *ǫl*) was a necessary provision in Old Norwegian festivities. In connection with funerals this feast was generally given on the 7th (most often) or the 30th day after the funeral. Instructions to give ale feasts are mentioned in the king's sagas: the saga about Håkon the Good (in *Heimskringla*), the greater saga about Olav Tryggvason, Odd Snorrason's saga about Olav Tryggvason, and *Ágrip*. See Ch. 115 and Robberstad 1981, 322, 334; Helle 2001, 170, 191.

**Alehouse** (ON *ǫldrhús*) Any locale for social gatherings, such as wedding feasts, funeral feasts, etc. See Robberstad 1981, 350.

**Announcement** (ON *lýsing*) To call certain facts to the attention of assembled men, usually at church, at an ale feast (q. v.), or at the assembly (see Assembly). Such notice had to be given to validate certain acts and to keep alive certain rights, such as the right to redeem odal- land (see Redemption of odal-land).

**Arbitration, court of** (ON *skiladómr*) A panel of twelve men called in by the parties to a suit to hear the contention and, if possible, to pass judgement. The court of arbitration was usually employed in cases that were not entirely clear and could, therefore, not be taken immediately to an assembly. The consequences were left to the negotiation of the parties involved. The *skiladómr* was opposed to the *sættardómr*, which passed judgement on cases in which the circumstances were already clear. See Robberstad 1981, 341, 343; Helle 2001, 91–7, 154; Sunde 2014, 143, 145, 148.

**Arrow assembly** (ON *ǫrvarþing*) An assembly called to deal with a case of killing or serious personal injury. It was summoned by way of sending an arrow as a message stick and took place at the scene of the crime. This assembly required the presence of twenty-seven men in order to be considered valid. The suit was subsequently prosecuted five days later at another assembly (ON *fimtarþing*).

**Assembly** (ON *þing*) A common assembly on a fixed site where regular public meetings were formally held. The participants – only free men – deferred to a common body of rules, customary or prescribed. They met under religious auspices, and an assembly had a special "sanctity" (compensation was increased, for example, for injury suffered at the assembly). See Foote 1988, 700; Helle 2001, 66–83 *et passim*; Introduction, ch. 1.

**Bail** See Surety

**Baptism** (ON *skírn*) The spiritual relationship (*cognatio spiritualis*) that was established by baptism, through godfathers and godmothers. Baptism was regarded as the child's second and spiritual birth, and created a spiritual kinship between the actors involved in the ceremony, with significant consequences: They were forbidden to marry one another in order to prevent sexual relations among spiritual kin, which were regarded as a kind of incest (see Lynch 1998, 17). The concept of spiritual kinship originated in the Eastern Church and was introduced to the western parts of Europe in the early Middle Ages. With some minor variations, all of the Norwegian Christian laws divide the year into several different baptismal terms, with Christmas Eve, Easter Eve, the Feast of St John the Baptist and Michaelmas as the terminus of each period. This arrangement is quite unusual in a European context. In the year 385 pope Siricius prescribed Easter and Pentecost as the only legitimate dates for baptism, with exceptions for emergency situations. Due to the spreading of the Augustinian notion of sin it was later demanded (e.g. in Anglo-Saxon sources) that infants should be baptized as soon as possible. The Norwegian baptismal terms do not correspond to any of these traditions. A reason might be that the baptismal terms follow the *gagnfasta* (see Lent). See also Robberstad 1981, 332, 338; Helle 2001, 184, 190–1.

**Billeting** (ON *gegngerð*) The obligation to provide transport, food, and accommodation for the king and his men when they travelled in the districts. The bishop might also require billeting for himself and thirty men when called upon to consecrate a *fylkis* church, but for fifteen men when he should consecrate a parish church. See Robberstad 1981, 317, 341–2; Helle 2001, 193–200.

**Bishop's representative** (ON *biskups ármaðr, biskups erendreki*) The bishop's local representative, probably a layman, who acted on behalf of the bishop in administrative and judicial affairs. In this function he was also called *erendreki*. The terms *ármaðr* and *erendreki* seem to have been used interchangeably to a certain extent. The present translation uses 'representative' for both. See Iversen 1997, 167–79; Bagge 2010, 197; Strauch 2016, 133.

**Bride-price** (ON *mundr*) What the bridegroom had to give the bride as a counterpart to her portion, at least twelve *aurar*. Cf. Ch. 51. See Robberstad 1981, 346–8; Helle 2001, 138–40.

**Cognate** (ON *nefgildismaðr*) A near kinsman on the female side. In the GuL the circle of cognates extended up to and including first cousins. See Robberstad 1981, 343.

**Compensation** (ON *bót, réttr*) Money, goods or land received as compensation for injuries suffered at the hands of another. The amount due in such cases varied with the rank of the person aggrieved; hence *réttr* in its many gradations came to be used to indicate rank and social position. The gravity of the offence was also considered: some wrongs might demand a double or even a triple compensation; others might be satisfied with half compensation (*halfr réttr*) or even less.

**Co-ownership** (ON *félag*) Common ownership or control of property. The term is used particularly of the union of properties within the family, when the wife's possessions were merged with those of the husband. See Robberstad 1981, 351; Helle 2001, 141–2; Bagge 2010, 220, note 140.

**Cow** (ON *kýr*) The cow was the ultimate standard of value (*kúgildi*, the money value of a cow) A cow normally had the value of two and a half *aurar*.

**Cross payment** (ON *þversǫk*) A part of the wergild payments (q. v.) which was paid by a certain group in the killer's kindred to two other but not exactly correspondent groups in the kindred of the killed man.

**Defaulter** (ON *dómflogi*) A *dómflogi* is literally 'one who flees from the court'. A man might default either by failing to attend the hearing of his case or by violating the accepted rules of court procedure. See Robberstad 1981, 344; Helle 2001, 154.

**Demand, formal, for restitution** (ON *kvaða*) When the merits of a dispute were not known (when the claimant had no legal witnesses to his claim), the claimant proceeded with a *kvaða*, or request that his counterpart (the defendant) should follow a certain procedure in the matter. The defendant must then either comply with the request (e.g. to pay his debt) or agree to have the complaint heard and considered by a court of arbitration. See Hertzberg 1895, 368; Robberstad 1981, 343.

**Door, principal** (ON *karldyrr*) Literally, 'the men's door'. This was the main entrance to a dwelling house and was ordinarily placed in the west end. When there was a door in the east end it was called the women's door.

**Earl** (ON *jarl*) The highest dignitary in the kingdom next to the king.

***Ertog*** See Monetary system

***Eyrir*** See Monetary system

**Family** See Kindred

**Fine** (ON *bót, sekt*) The former term (*bót*) was used for compensation to private persons, while the latter (*sekt*) was used for such as was paid to the public authorities (e.g., king, bishop). See Helle 2001, 35, 82, 94–7, 151, 153–4, 156–7, 199–200; Bagge 2010, 192–4.

**Fire-wolf** (ON *brennuvargr*) One who is outlawed for the crime of arson.

**Five days**, period of The length of a week in early Medieval Norway was five days (a *fimt*) After the introduction of Christianity into the North this had to give way to the new week of seven days; but the change was not complete for a long time. In matters of law and public business the five-day week continued in use. On this and other fixed time periods in the GuL see Sunde 2011b, 223–9. See also Helle 2001, 185–6.

**Foster inheritance** (ON *branderfð*) The foster father's right to inherit from a foster son. The right was not reciprocal. See Robberstad 1981, 359–60.

**Freedman** (ON *frjálsgjafi*,[1] *leysingi, leysingja*) A freed slave whose freedom was limited or imperfect. The *frjálsgjafi* was one whose manumission had been published at a freedom ale (q. v.). The *leysingi* (fem. *leysingja*) was one who had attained a practically free status either by giving his freedom ale or by other means. The freedman was not entirely free from dependence and his disability was inherited in the form of special loyalty commitments (*þyrmslir*). See Robberstad 1981, 348; Iversen 1997, 41–3, 190–1, 199–204, 210–28, 235–40, 281–4; Helle 2001, 125–32; Strauch 2008, 250–3, 2011, 35–47, 2016, 33–7, 233.

**Freedom ale** (ON *frelsisǫl*) An ale feast (q. v.) celebrated to give sanction and publicity to the emancipation of a slave. See also Freedman.

**Freeholder** (ON *hauldr, hǫldr*) Owner of odal-land (q. v.).

***Fylki*** See Introduction, ch. 1

**Grave-goer** (ON *grafgangsmaðr*) A freedman who had come into poverty and was put into an open grave with his family. The one who lived the longest was saved and supported by the former master. See Robberstad 1981, 351; Helle 2001, 133–4.

***Herað*** See Introduction, ch. 1

**High seat** (ON *ǫndvegi*) The most prominent seat in the house, possibly in the north-east corner of the room where it was placed. It was occupied by the head of the family. In certain cases a legal action could be brought against a man only when he was at home and in his high seat. See Stigum 1962; Robberstad 1981, 343, 361.

**Home summons** (ON *heimstefna*) A legal action by which a man is notified to be at home and in his high seat on a set day to hear the plaintiff's claim or demand and to learn what witnesses will be heard, in case witnesses are available. See Robberstad 1981, 342; Helle 2001, 91.

**Hospitality** (ON *drekkulaun*) Literally 'reward for drink'. A gift, usually land, granted by the king to the one who had entertained him. Such land was considered equal to odal-land.

**Householder** (ON *bóndi*) The term *bóndi/búandi* (pl. *bǿndr*) denoted a man fixed to a location (as opposed to *gǫngumaðr*) and usually married. He was a free man, not attached to the service of the king, a bishop, or any other man. In general, the *bóndi* was a farmer and a landowner, and head of a household. But not all farmers were landowners, many were tenants. In W. Norway (the *Gulaþing* law district) there were thus two kinds of free *bǿndr*. See Helle 2001, 117–24; Bagge 2010, 119–20.

**Housekeeper** (ON *deigja*) The highest-ranked bondwoman in a household. She seems to have had a general supervision of the housework. See Lid 1957; Helle 2001, 127.

1 A term not used in the GuL, but the concept must have been known, see Ch. 61.

**Housemaid** (ON *seta*, a word etymologically related to *sitja*) A bondwoman ranking second in a household. It is assumed that her work was principally within the house. See Hertzberg 1895, 549; Lid 1957; Helle 2001, 127.

**Husband's gift** (ON *gagngjald, tilgjǫf*) A gift from the bridegroom to the bride, "donatio propter nuptias". The size of the *gagngjald* was to be in a fixed relation to the size of the *heimanfylgja*. See Hertzberg 1895, 225; Robberstad 1981, 348, 361; Helle 2001, 139.

**Joint drinking** (ON *samburðarǫl*) An ale feast (q. v.) to which several families contributed their brewing. Such a feast was required by law. In the autumn this ceremony took on an explicit religious character in so far as the ale was to be blessed with thanks to Christ and Holy Mary for a good harvest and peace. See Helle 2001, 108, 170, 183.

**Killer's report** (ON *víglýsing*) Announcement given by a killer that he had committed a killing for which he assumed full responsibility. See Helle 2001, 90.

**Kin, kindred** (ON *ætt*) The circle of kinsmen, usually counted on the male side.

**King's representative** (ON *ármaðr, erendreki*) The *ármaðr* was originally the king's steward and manager of a royal estate. Over time he assumed functions as the king's local representative, endowed with the power to act on behalf of the king in administrative and judicial affairs as well. In these latter functions he was also called *erendreki*. The present translation renders *ármaðr* and *erendreki* with 'representative'. See Helle 2001, 149; Bagge 2010, 233; Strauch 2016, 119, 133.

**Kinship** (ON *frændsemi*) Kinship was measured in two ways. In the inherited Norwegian and Icelandic system persons equally distant from a common ancestor, numbered in generations, belonged to the same *kné* (knee): First cousins belonged to the 1st knee, sixth cousins belonged to the 6th knee. According to the canonical system, which was introduced in Norway by bishop Grimkjell, the counting started with brothers and sisters: They were related in the 1st degree, sixth cousins in the 7th degree. The rule in Chapter 24 allows for marriage between sixth cousins, but prohibits marriage between persons more closely related. This corresponds to the rules of the other Norwegian Christian Laws (*Frostuþing, Eiðsivaþing* and *Borgarþing*). We would have expected a wording "sixth knee and seventh degree", but here 'knee' and 'degree' are used synonymously, either erroneously or deliberately, see Hertzberg 1895, 350. See also Robberstad 1981, 334–6; Helle 2001, 182. On the function of kinship in general see Vogt 2010, 9–25 with further references.

**Land on lease** (ON *stefnujǫrð*) Land that had been sold for a term of years and which was subject to redemption at the end of the term. See Robberstad 1981, 385–7; Helle 2001, 118. See also Mortgage.

**Landed man** (ON *lendr maðr*) A local magnate who had been endowed with land from the king and acted as the king's highest representative in his district. He was ranked below an earl, but above a freeholder. He belonged to the group of the king's most important advisers, and was counted among the officers of the king's retinue (the *hirð*). If the son of a landed man was not endowed with land by the king before he was forty years old, he was not counted as a landed man. See Robberstad 1981, 378; Foote 1988, 701; Helle 2001, 149–52, 154–5, 159–60; Bagge 2010, 53, 80, 119, 233.

**Law** (ON *lǫg*) The set of enacted or customary rules recognized as binding for a certain district, as well as this district itself, the law province. See Introduction, ch. 1.

**Legal remedies** (ON *gǫgn*) Proofs, evidence; such advantages as might come to either party in the course of a lawsuit. These might arise from various contingencies, but chiefly from error or neglect on the part of the opposing litigant.

**Legitimization** (ON *ættleiðing*) The act of officially recognizing an illegitimate child and including it in the kindred, thus giving it the right to inherit. See Robberstad 1981, 349; Helle 2001, 15, 127, 138; Bagge 2010, 218.

**Lent** (ON *fasta*) The seven (or nine, see below) weeks before Easter. At the time of the conversion of Scandinavia the actual duration of Lent was not yet fully settled, and the Scandinavian laws witness acquaintance with fasting periods of both six, seven and nine weeks (Taranger 1890, 374) The *gagnfasta* ('preparatory fast') was a period of fasting which especially the clergy (and monastics) were required to observe. They were the three weeks preceding each of the following festivals: the Feast of St John the Baptist, Michaelmas, and Christmas. The two weeks before Lent comprised also a period of preparatory fasting. For the clergy, Lent was, therefore, a nine-week fast. See Robberstad 1981, 331; Helle 2001, 181, 186, 191–2. Both the *Eiðsivaþing* law (E I 20) and the Icelandic *Grágás* (ed. 1992, 31) seem to operate with a general fasting period of seven weeks, whereas the *Borgarþing* law (6.1. and 6.2.) makes a distinction between six and seven weeks of fasting. See Sanmark 2004, 235–42.

**Levy** See Naval levy

**Levy district** (ON *manngerð*) The district which had to equip one man for naval service, usually two or three farms. See Robberstad 1981, 324; Helle 2001, 35, 170–1.

**Monetary system** The central unit of the weight and monetary system was the *mǫrk* (pl. *merkr*). 1 *mǫrk* = 8 *aurar* (pl. of *eyrir*) = 24 *ertogar* (pl. of *ertog*) = 240 *penningar* (pl. of *penningr*). The number of *penningar* per *mǫrk* varied considerably over time and area. In the 11th century the value of 1 *mǫrk* was c. 214 g *brent* (pure) silver, the value of 1 *eyrir* c. 1 ounce. The value of 1 *eyrir* might also be stipulated as 6 ells of wadmal. A distinction was made between a weighed *mǫrk* (*mǫrk vegin*) and a counted *mǫrk* (*mǫrk tǫld*). Although they probably had the same value initially – containing the same percentage of silver (90–95%), the value of the counted *mǫrk* was gradually reduced. In the 12th century 1 weighed *mǫrk* was equivalent to 2 counted *merkr*. Both were units of calculation rather than coins; only *penningar* were used as such. Fines were usually stated in terms of *merkr*, *aurar* or *ertogar*. See Hertzberg 1895, 458–62; Steinnes 1936, 129–30, 152; Robberstad 1981, 306–14; Helle 2001, 157.

**Month's food** (ON *mánaðarmatr*) The amount of food which one man needed for one month when he served in the levy, usually provided as butter (7.7 kg) and meal (24.7 kg). See Helle 2001, 69.

**Mortgage** (ON *máli*) Conveyance of property by debtor to creditor as security for debt. *Máli* was the term for mortgage contract, *málajǫrð* was the term for mortgaged land. See Robberstad 1981, 385–9; Helle 2001, 118. See also Land on lease.

**Moving day** (ON *fardagr*) The day when the tenant's right to remain on the land expired. In the GuL this was a period of nine days after "summer day", i.e. the period April 15th to 23rd. If the tenant could not move all his property within that period he might keep half of the buildings for another nine days. See Helle 2001, 120–2.

**Murder** (ON *morð*) Killing committed in secret or not properly reported. The punishment for murder was more severe than for ordinary manslaying. See Helle 2001, 101–2.

**Mustering assembly** (ON *manntalsþing*) A moot held to number the men available for service in the naval levy, and to prepare the muster lists. It was held each year, probably at some time between May 15th and June 15th. See Robberstad 1981, 394; Helle 2001, 83.

***Mælir*** (pl. *mælar*) A measure of capacity approximately equal in content to one-half bushel. The *mælir* varied in size, in the GuL it was probably 16.2 litres. See Robberstad 1981, 322, 349; Helle 2001, 69.

***Mǫrk*** See Monetary system

**Naval levy** (ON *leiðangr*) The military service connected to the system of naval defence, and the dues and taxes that the subjects owed to this service. When mobilized, the soldiers were obliged to stand at the king's disposal, usually for two months, in order to protect the country, esp. the coastal areas, against attacks from enemies. See Robberstad 1981, 389–93; Helle 2001, 32–4, 158–75; Bagge 2010, 72–80 and passim.

**Nones** (ON *nón*) The ninth hour of the day, approximately three o' clock in the afternoon. The major saints' days and other prominent holy days normally began at *nón* on the preceding day. See Robberstad 1981, 328.

**Nookling** (ON *hornungr*) The illegitimate son of a free man by a free-born mistress (*friðla*) See Helle 2001, 134, 138.

**Oar bench** (ON *halfrými, hamla*) The place of a rower on a ship. The *sess* is the thwart. The size of a ship is indicated by the number of thwarts (benches); thus a twenty-bencher (*tvítugsessa*) would have seats for twenty pairs of oarsmen. The *hamla* was a grummet, a loop or strap (usually of osier) which held the oar in place; the word was also used to point out that part of the ship where the rower sat, this place was also called *halfrými* (half room). See Robberstad 1981, 353, 396–7; Helle 2001, 163, 165–7, 175.

**Oath** (ON *eiðr*) An oath was sworn to confirm loyalty and obedience; and it was a frequent way of proving one's innocence when faced with an accusation of crime. In this latter case it was often taken with some form of compurgation, with two others (a three-man oath, ON *lýrittareiðr*), five others (a six-man oath, ON *séttareiðr*), or eleven others (a twelve-man oath, ON *tylftareiðr*). It was sworn on a missal or a gospel-book in or in front of the church. See Robberstad 1981, 331, 363; Helle 2001, 103–4; Bagge 2010, 189, 212–14; Nordby 2018, 54–68, 93–151, 155–8, 200–2.

**Oath day** (ON *sǿrr dagr*) Any day on which oath taking was permitted. See Chapter 135.

**Odal-land** (ON *óðalsjǫrð*) Freehold tenure; inherited land that has been passed on from father to son in direct line of descent for at least six generations. See Robberstad 1981, 385; Helle 2001, 117–20, 138.

**Odal, odal-right** (ON *óðal*) The right to inherit odal-land and the right of pre-emption of such land, in order to keep the property within the family. On odal-right in general, see Robberstad 1967; Helle 2001, 117–20; Iversen 2001, 91–2; Bagge 2010, 189, 212; Vogt 2010, 209–15, 223–4.

**Outlawry** (ON *útlegð*) Outlawry was a common form of punishment in the Middle Ages. In Norway it was of two kinds: (1) common outlawry, which meant the same as expatriation and from which the outlaw could be released by making certain payments (so-called *skógarkaup*) to the king – in which case he was allowed to stay in the country (usually in the woods) – and to the family of the aggrieved party; (2) permanent or irredeemable outlawry, from which there was no escape. One who was sent into permanent outlawry was an *úbótamaðr* (q. v.) or a *níðingr* (villain), an outlaw from whom, or for whom, no fine could be received. The outlaw was usually denied Christian burial. See Iversen 1997, 57–8; Helle 2001, 99–101, 153; Riisøy 2014, 111.

**Overseer** (ON *bryti*) The man who distributed work between the slaves. He was the foreman among the slaves. See Lid 1957.

***Penningr*** See Monetary system

**Personal Rights** (ON *mannhelgi, réttr*) The rights that every free person enjoyed as a member of the social body, particularly the right to be compensated for wrongs and injuries to oneself or to one's kindred. To be deprived of "right" was equivalent to exile. See Wührer 1966a; Helle 2001, 94–5, 117, 150–1.

**Plaintiff** (ON *sǿkjandi*) One who brought legal action against another.

**Private church** (ON *hǿgendiskirkja*, lit. 'church of comfort') An individual man was allowed to build a private church when the journey to another church was considered to be (too) long and strenuous. The private churches were gradually included in the parish organization, were used by other people in the surrounding areas and even obtained the right to receive tithes. In this way they formed the basis of a new parish organization which from the second half of the twelfth century onwards partly replaced the one of the regional laws. See Robberstad 1981, 326; Skre 1995, 198; Helle 2001, 201–4; Bagge 2010, 232.

**Quarter** (ON *fjórðungr*) See Introduction, ch.1

**Redemption of odal-land** (ON *óðalsbrigði*) While it was possible to convey odal-land (q. v.) with odal-right (q. v.) to a buyer in another kindred, ordinary sales were conditional and would allow redemption. But an odal man who wished to keep his right active would have to publish, at the assembly or in some other place where men came together, and some time before the close of the twenty-year period, the fact that he had the odal-right to some specified farm or to a part of it. See Helle 2001, 90, 92, 101, 118–19, 126.

**Robbery** (ON *rán*) There was a clear distinction between robbery and theft. The thief operates in secret or under the cover of night, whereas the robber (*ránsmaðr*) commits his depredations by daylight and often uses violent methods, which were, however, regarded as less reprehensible than those of a sneak thief. Both material property and immaterial rights could be robbed. *Rán* entailed compensation for the one who had suffered the robbery and the payment of a *ránsbaugr* to the king. See Helle 2001, 94.

**Runaway** (ON *flannfluga, fuðflogi*) In the context of matters related to marriage a runaway was a person who refused to enter into marriage after betrothal. If a man did this he was a *fuðflogi,* if a woman refused she was a *flannfluga.* Since marriage was regarded as a contract between two families, breach of promise of marriage was tantamount to a breach of contract and had to be prosecuted. The aggrieved party (i.e. the family of the fiancée or the family of the fiancé, as the case might be) was entitled to compensation. See Frimannslund 1959, 235 and Wikman 1957, 309.

***Sáld*** (ON *sáld*) A measure of grain, varying in size, probably ranging from 64.8 to 97.2 litres. See Bjørkvik and Jansson 1972, 672; Robberstad 1981, 349; Helle 2001, 69.

**Scrubling** (ON *hrísungr*) An illegitimate son of a free man by a free woman, but begotten in the woods. See Helle 2001, 134, 138.

**Seventh-day ale** (ON *sjaund*) An ale feast (q. v.) given by the heir of one deceased on the seventh day after the death. It might also be given on the thirtieth (see Thirtieth morning) At this feast the heir seated himself in the high seat, entered formally into his inheritance and heard all the claims against the estate. See Helle 2001, 191.

**Sheriff** (ON *sýslumaðr*) He was the king's official and conducted the king's business within a *fylki.* He was among the highest-ranking officials and was responsible for collecting royal incomes, overseeing legal proceedings and nominating judges. The *sýslumaðr* was also involved in organizing military operations and overseeing trade. He had armed men under his command, probably at least twenty, and received large parts, maybe as much as two thirds, of the fines. See Helle 2001, 152, 154–6; Bagge 2010, 102, 130, 201, 221, 236–7, 287.

**Slave** (ON *þræll*) A bondman or bondwoman, an unfree person enjoying no legal rights. They might be bought or sold on a par with cattle. If they had children, these were born into slavery. In the case of a *þéborinn* child the father was most often a bondman, while one that was called *þýborinn* was the child of a bondwoman by a free man and was acknowledged by the father as his child. See Iversen 1997; Helle 2001, 125–8.

**Summer** (ON *sumar*) The summer was the period April 14th–October 13th.

**Surety** (ON *tak*) Money, or its equivalent, delivered to a plaintiff to make sure that his opponent in a lawsuit would proceed home to receive summons (*brautartak*), that he would be present when the suit came to a hearing, and that he would comply with the decision of the assembly or the court (*lagatak*). The amount of the surety that might be demanded would roughly correspond to the amount involved in the action. If surety was not forthcoming the defendant's own person might be seized and held as surety. See Robberstad 1981, 357–8.

**Tenant** (ON *leiguliði*) One who pays rent for land. Land was rarely leased for long terms; contracts for one year were apparently quite common. During the later centuries of the Middle Ages there was a continuous concentration of landed properties in the hands of the king, the church, and the local magnates. See Helle 2001, 120–5; Bagge 2010, 113, 116–17.

**Thirtieth morning** (ON *þrítugsmorgunn*) An ale feast (q. v.) given by the heir of the deceased on the thirtieth morning after the death. See also Seventh-day ale.

**Trial by ordeal** (ON *guðs skírslir*) This special form of trial implied, i.a., carrying hot iron or walking on such with bare feet. If the person's skin was unhurt afterwards, he or she was considered free of guilt. See Robberstad 1981, 337–8; Helle 2001, 72, 104–5, Nilsson 2001, 506, 516–20; Bagge 2010, 189–90, 213; Bagge 2011; Sunde 2014, 159–60.

***Úbótamaðr, údáðamaðr.*** A criminal who had committed a crime which could not be compensated for, e.g. murder. He could not be pardoned by the king. See Robberstad 1981, 340, 357; Helle 2001, 88, 95, 100, 102; Vogt 2010, 127–8. See also Outlawry.

**Ultimate court of law** (ON *lǫgrétta*) The highest judicial authority in the law district, probably identical with the whole body of delegates to the assembly. See Hertzberg 1895, 423–4; Helle 2001, 71–2; Bagge 2010, 200–1.

**Villain** See Outlawry

**Wadmal** (ON *vaðmál*) The standard homespun woollen cloth. It was also used as a standard of value; an *eyrir* was sometimes reckoned as the equivalent of six (usually) or ten ells of wadmal. See Robberstad 1981, 307–8, 311, 369.

**Warship district** (ON *skipreiða*) A coastal district (within the *fylki*) which had to provide a warship fully equipped with crew and food for a period of two months. See Robberstad 1981, 318–20, 390–2, 394, 399–401; Helle 2001, 35, 77–8, 163–5, 168, 171, 174–5; Bagge 2010, 75.

**Well-born** (ON *ættborinn*) Born of a family whose freedom was not qualified by any form of dependency. Usually a man or a woman from a householder's kindred. See Robberstad 1981, 351.

**Wergild** (ON *bót*, *bøtr*) The sum of money that a killer owed to the kin of the victim to compensate them for the homicide. This compensation was to be paid by members of the killer's family to corresponding members of the family of the killed person. Outside the circle of the closest relatives (i.e. those up to and including first cousins, the so-called 'ring men' mentioned in Chapters 218–22) the GuL distinguishes three circles, i.e. groups of receivers, based on different degrees of relationship to the victim (the killed person). Each group of receivers was called an *uppnám*. To each *uppnám* there was a corresponding group of payers within the family of the killer, based on different degrees of relationship to the latter. See Hertzberg 1895, 751; Robberstad 1981, 380. The amount to be paid was differentiated between the values of the lives of individuals of various social classes. The GuL contains different systems of assessing the wergild. A detailed account of the relationship between these and a survey of wergild in other Teutonic countries are given by Robberstad 1981, 370–5. See also Radding 1989, 617; Helle 2001, 14, 110, 117, 144; Vogt 2010, 121, 133, 143–51.

**Winter** (ON *vetr*) The winter was the period October 14th–April 13th.

# Index of names, places and titles

# Index

For Product Safety Concerns and Information please contact our EU representative GPSR@taylorandfrancis.com
Taylor & Francis Verlag GmbH, Kaufingerstraße 24, 80331 München, Germany

www.ingramcontent.com/pod-product-compliance
Ingram Content Group UK Ltd.
Pitfield, Milton Keynes, MK11 3LW, UK
UKHW020148200926
475702UK00016B/2615
*9780367681470*